EXPANDING THE PRACTICE OF
SEX THERAPY

Look beyond behavioral treatments, pharmaceutical interventions, and performance goals to a more comprehensive picture of what your clients want and need when they enter sex therapy. Gina Ogden is a master therapist, supervisor, researcher, teacher, and author with four decades of helping clients and training health professionals. Her ISIS Wheel of Sexual Experience is an innovative template that recognizes the full range of sexual issues: physical, emotional, mental, and spiritual. *Expanding the Practice of Sex Therapy* offers you new language to discuss sexual issues and creative ways to engage clients in their own therapeutic process—whether or not you are trained as a sex therapist. The text is organized in four practice-oriented sections that introduce the ISIS Wheel, show you how you can use it with individuals, couples, and groups, and encourage you to explore it on your own.

Gina Ogden, PhD, LMFT, conducts ISIS retreats and training in the United States and Mexico. She lives in Cambridge, Massachusetts, where she supervises sexuality professionals, leads teleseminars, and continues to write about sexuality and spirituality (www.GinaOgden.com).

OTHER BOOKS BY GINA OGDEN

The Return of Desire
The Heart and Soul of Sex
Women Who Love Sex
Food for Body and Soul
Sexual Recovery
Safe Encounters (co-authored with Beverly Whipple)
When a Family Needs Therapy (co-authored with Anne Zevin)

ADVANCE PRAISE

Expanding the Practice of Sex Therapy presents a dynamic, innovative approach to helping our clients. This elegant, perceptive, and profound treatment model will furnish counselors and therapists with unique skills to help any relationship. A must read!
—**Michele Sugg, MSW, LCSW, CST**, President, American Association of Sexuality Educators, Counselors and Therapists (AASECT); Sex Therapy Advisor, Alexander Foundation for Women's Health

This book is the essential reference for future generations craving a new way to serve their clients. Gina Ogden's ISIS model reflects a new paradigm for how to address sexual issues and resolve them through integration of the whole human being. Her contribution to the field of sex therapy will last far beyond the quest for a new pill or the diagnostic search for treatment of pathologies. The cure instead is finding the sexual self, moving through a matrix of discovery in collaboration with the sex therapist or coach, and reaching peace with one's sexual story.
—**Patti Britton, PhD, MPH**, Author of *The Art of Sex Coaching*; Past President, AASECT; Co-Founder, SexCoachU; Board-Certified Clinical Sexologist; Master Sex Coach; Adjunct Professor, The Chicago School of Professional Psychology and the Institute for Advanced Study of Human Sexuality

Expanding the Practice of Sex Therapy incorporates the holistic integrative ISIS approach that has helped so many clients to feel better and more accepting of themselves as sensual and sexual beings. Gina incorporates sexual science and brain research into her approach. As a scientist, I respect Gina's ISIS approach and her contributions to sexual health.
—**Beverly Whipple, PhD, RN, FAAN**, Co-author of *The G Spot*; Professor Emerita, Rutgers University; Past Vice-President and Secretary General/Treasurer, World Association for Sexual Health (WAS): Past President, Society for the Scientific Study of Sexuality (SSSS); Past President, AASECT; Past Director, International Society for the Study of Women's Sexual Health (ISSWSH)

Dr. Gina Ogden has created a completely new way of listening to sexuality concerns. Therapists who learn to use her ISIS Wheel quickly see how interventions—usually suggested by the patients or clients themselves—become crystal clear and are much more effective than those we might suggest from an outside perspective. This book, grounded in ten years of research and more than forty years of experience, is as important to the field of sex therapy as was *The Kinsey Report* or either of Masters and Johnson's early volumes.
—**Ginger Manley, MSN**, Psychiatric Mental Health Clinical Nurse Specialist-BC; AASECT Certified Sex Therapist and Supervisor; Associate in Psychiatry, Vanderbilt University School of Medicine; Clinical Professor of Nursing, Vanderbilt University School of Nursing

Every therapist should read *Expanding the Practice of Sex Therapy*. Gina Ogden's unique style combined with her ISIS research brings incredible, real-life clinical experience and data into the work to make her message dynamic, innovative, exciting, and practical. Sex therapy has until now been bogged down with old models of health care, pharmaceutical myths, and misinformation about relationships and couples dynamics. Gina is at the top of her field and knows what trained, certified sexuality therapists and couples therapists everywhere need.

—**Tammy Nelson, PhD, LPC**, Author of *Getting the Sex You Want* and *The New Monogamy: Redefining Your Relationship After Infidelity* (in press); Board Certified Sexologist; AASECT Certified Sex Therapist; Licensed Alcohol and Drug Counselor and Certified Imago Relationship Therapist

There is a critical need for marriage and family therapists and counselors to be able to effectively address questions and issues around sexuality with their clients. Dr. Gina Ogden provides a user-friendly, readable, and practical text that will assist therapists "in the room," who are striving to provide research-based information and interventions to their clients. A sex therapist, supervisor, and researcher herself, Dr. Ogden takes both novice and experienced therapists, using numerous case illustrations, through the process of understanding and using a model that will enhance clinical practice.

—**Marvarene Oliver, EdD**, LMFT, LPC, Associate Professor of Counseling, Texas A&M University-Corpus Christi; Clinical Fellow and Approved Supervisor of the American Association for Marriage and Family Therapy (AAMFT); Executive Editor of the *Journal of Professional Counseling: Practice, Theory, and Research*

Gina Ogden is a major spokesperson for the diversity in female sexuality and the importance of spirituality in sexual desire. *Expanding the Practice of Sex Therapy* is her latest and best integration of the ISIS model of sex therapy and is highly recommended for clinicians.

—**Barry McCarthy, PhD**, Workshop Presenter; Professor; Author of *Sexual Awareness* (5th Edition), *Enduring Desire*, *Discovering Your Couple Sexual Style*, *Men's Sexual Health*, and *Rekindling Desire*

From one of the foremost leaders of integrative sex therapy, this tour-de-force of elegant theory, accessible writing, and sound clinical practice is a "must-read" for anyone working with individuals or couples who wants to serve them best. Dr. Ogden's sound, comprehensive, and de-pathologizing approach to the complexity of human sexual experience will surely prove to be a welcome addition to the book shelves of novice and seasoned professionals alike.

—**Evelyn Resh, MPH, CNM**, Author of *Women, Sex, Power, and Pleasure* and *The Secret Lives of Teen Girls*

This book is a rare combination of clinical skill and the art of caring—engaging, accessible, humorous, and informative.

—**Ruth Neustifter, PhD**, Assistant Professor, Couple and Family Therapy, University of Guelph, Ontario, Canada

Ogden's book is filled with whole-hearted wisdom and creativity. The case illustrations provide insight and inspiration. Clinical gems sparkle throughout!

—**Peggy J. Kleinplatz, PhD**, Professor, Faculty of Medicine, University of Ottawa, Canada

Who better to advance a model of expanding the practice of sex therapy than Gina Ogden, one of the world's leading experts in sex therapy? Informed by four decades of practice, as well as her groundbreaking research, Dr. Ogden steers today's sex therapist away from traditional therapeutic models that focus on deficiency and dysfunction, and toward visualizing and carrying out a new model that integrates the physical, emotional, mental, and spiritual aspects of sexual health. *Expanding the Practice of Sex Therapy* is one of those MUST-HAVE resources that should find its way onto the required reading lists of sex therapists in training, and of practicing sex therapists looking to stay current in the field.

—**Bill Taverner, MA, CSE**, Editor-in-Chief of *American Journal of Sexuality Education*

EXPANDING THE PRACTICE OF SEX THERAPY

An Integrative Model for Exploring
Desire and Intimacy

Gina Ogden

Routledge
Taylor & Francis Group

NEW YORK AND LONDON

A portion of the author's proceeds will be donated to organizations promoting women's health.

The author and Routledge/Taylor & Francis thank Shambhala Publications for permission to adapt the template and descriptions of the ISIS Wheel from Gina Ogden's books *The Heart and Soul of Sex*, and *The Return of Desire*.

First published 2013
by Routledge
711 Third Avenue, New York, NY 10017

Simultaneously published in the UK
by Routledge
27 Church Road, Hove, East Sussex BN3 2FA

Routledge is an imprint of the Taylor & Francis Group, an informa business

© 2013 Gina Ogden

Library of Congress Cataloging in Publication Data
Ogden, Gina.
Expanding the practice of sex therapy: an integrative model for exploring desire and intimacy / Gina Ogden.
pages cm
Includes bibliographical references and index.
1. Sex therapy. 2. Intimacy (Psychology) I. Title.
RC557.O33 2013
616.85′8306—dc23
2012045215

ISBN: 978-0-415-82954-0 (hbk)
ISBN: 978-0-415-82955-7 (pbk)
ISBN: 978-0-203-38267-7 (ebk)

Typeset in Perpetua
by Book Now Ltd, London

TO THE ISIS NETWORK
AND ALL ITS MEMBERS, PAST,
PRESENT, AND FUTURE

DISCLAIMER

This book and the information contained herein has been prepared with diligence and is based on the author's own research, therapeutic model, and experiences. However, we do not make any guarantees about the completeness and effectiveness of the information and disclaim all implied warranties. The content of this book may not be suitable for your situation, and it should not be considered a substitute for the care of a doctor or skilled sex therapist.

Confidentiality has been maintained in case examples throughout this book by altering names and other identifiers.

CONTENTS

INTRODUCTION

Engage Your Clients and Expand Your Practice

It is widely recognized by sex therapists that addressing sexual performance alone is not always enough to help our clients. This book expands the field of sex therapy beyond frequencies of intercourse, orgasm, and other activities we can count and measure. It looks beyond behavioral treatments and pharmaceutical interventions to invite you and your clients to explore sexual health rather than focus on what is wrong. It offers dynamic language you can use to open discussion with your clients even if you are not specifically trained as a sex therapist. It suggests multiple ways you can engage individuals and couples in their own process of growth so you do not find yourself working harder than your clients.

At the heart of this "expanding" practice is the ISIS Wheel of Sexual Experience, a template that serves as an organizing principle for exploring a full range of sexual issues: physical, emotional, mental, and spiritual. This is a profoundly simple concept that you can use immediately in your sessions. Yet its implications are complex and nuanced because the ISIS framework offers your clients compelling access to a vast arena of sexual potential, healing, health, and pleasure.

What Is in This Book and How Will It Benefit You?

This book represents four decades of my practice as a sex therapist and supervisor, researcher, teacher, and author. It also represents countless hours of consultation with colleagues who have worked with me to develop crucial nuances of this integrative model for exploring desire and intimacy.

Part I introduces the ISIS Wheel and the scientific research and clinical experience on which it is based. The acronym "ISIS" is derived from "Integrating Sexuality and Spirituality," an independently conducted nationwide survey with 3,810 respondents, aged 18 to 86, who come from every state in the US. This opening section demonstrates that the responses therapists

1

elicit from clients are often shaped by the questions we ask. When we shift our focus from sexual pathology and dysfunction to a more comprehensive picture of what clients want and need, our clients often feel recognized in a way that frees them to engage creatively in their own therapeutic process.

Part I helps you find new ways to frame the questions that will engage your clients and also grow your practice—whether you are already practicing sex therapy or whether you are an individual or couples therapist looking for ways to initiate conversations with your clients about the sexual issues that affect their lives.

Part II offers a graphic, practical guide to the ISIS quadrants—physical, emotional, mental, and spiritual—along with activities and exercises to help both therapists and clients explore each one. Here, you will learn ways to map the varieties of sexual experience and to convey a spirit of curiosity and adventure to your clients. You will discover fresh ways to listen to what your clients tell you—and *how* they tell you: their verbs, their breathing and body language, the parts of the story they leave out. Along with guidance for helping your clients explore their stories, you will be encouraged to investigate both the ways in which their stories may affect you and the ways you practice therapy.

Part III offers a guide to clinical practice, including the four core dynamics of ISIS practice: creating and holding space, directing movement, ritualizing ordinary activities, and concretizing abstract concepts. Each of these core dynamics is clearly described and contrasted with cognitive behavioral and medical approaches to sex therapy. You will find details of how you can use the ISIS Wheel in a variety of clinical settings—in sessions with individuals and couples, in group seminars, and in personal growth intensives. You will be invited to incorporate into ISIS practice all of the skills you have already acquired during your own practice of psychotherapy, family therapy, Gestalt, sensorimotor work, meditation, energy healing, recovery groups, and more—bringing into play a rich tapestry of therapeutic possibilities beyond traditional sex therapy.

Part IV focuses on ISIS training for professionals, along with caveats for therapists who use the ISIS model. The final chapter, "Exploring ISIS for Yourself," addresses some of the unique challenges that face therapists and sex therapists—from ego involvement and countertransference to confronting our personal demons as they are triggered by issues our clients bring us. For some practitioners, it is a radical notion that we can help ourselves as well as our clients.

This book is not intended to be the last word on ISIS practice. Once you have read it, look for follow-ups. One of these is *The ISIS Workbook*, a clinical guide to facilitate your work with clients. Another is *Sex Therapy Meets Shamanism*, which offers strategies for expanding your practice drawn from the spiritual bases of the ISIS approach. Still further, the ISIS Network is alive and growing, with practitioners from various corners of the globe. It is my hope that future practitioners will expand ISIS practice still more, and you can look for their work as well. Better still, perhaps you will contribute to it.

Gina Ogden
Cambridge, Massachusetts
October, 2012

Part I

THE RESEARCH

When your research is published, it will change the way we think about sex in this country.

Oprah Winfrey to Gina Ogden
on the Oprah Winfrey Show, May 11, 2000

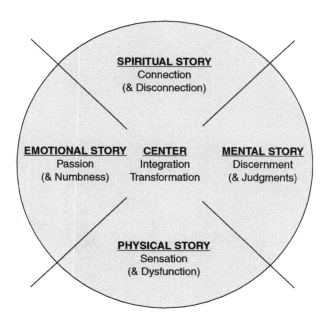

1

"INTEGRATING SEXUALITY AND SPIRITUALITY"

A Nationwide Survey

In the mid-1990s, I became an accidental sex researcher. By accidental, I mean that my path to research suddenly veered off the usual academic route so that I could investigate the kinds of questions my clients were asking in therapy sessions. Thus began a ten-year adventure into sex research that vastly expanded the way I now understand both sex and the profession of sex therapy.

By that time in history, the women's movement had given us powerful ways to say "No" to unwanted sex. But "No" does not tell the whole story of sexual experience. I knew a next step was required. We needed to develop safe ways to say "Yes" to the kinds of sex that nourish and empower us. We needed new and believable role models. We needed to hear from ordinary women who had discovered their own unique paths to pleasure, orgasm, and ecstasy. I knew all of this from listening to clients, for some two decades by this point. To help broaden the conversation about sex, I had already recrafted my dissertation research on just such ordinary and pleasure-loving women into a book for general readership. It was published in 1994 and is still in print in a third edition. Its title is *Women Who Love Sex*.

It was on the road while promoting this book that my notions of sex and sex therapy took a dramatic turn. For one thing, I experienced first-hand just how entrenched, twirly, and scary the national conversation about women and sexual pleasure can be. I heard the women whose stories were in my book being called sluts, whores, and bimbos by people who had never read beyond the title. On TV shows in San Francisco and Los Angeles, interviewers joked about wanting the names of these women who love sex—so they could enter them in their little black books. In San Antonio, Texas, I was thrown off a rock radio station for promoting "a secret feminist agenda." On talk radio across the Bible Belt, I was told I was a witch and should burn at the stake.

The good news is that for a number of months I had a national stage to talk about what women want. And aside from the jokers, naysayers, and witch hunters there was heartwarming support from all parts of the country. A frequent comment was: "These women in your book are talking about sex—but they're also talking about *spirituality*. Why don't you write a book about that?"

Spirituality—What Does That Have to Do With Sex?

The naming of a spiritual dimension as crucial to women's sexual pleasure struck a resonant chord that continued to vibrate. It also raised questions and concerns. Sexuality and spirituality are seemingly irreconcilable concepts in most of mainstream American culture. Perhaps they are especially irreconcilable in current sex research and therapy, where sexual norms are based on what can be counted and measured in random controlled trials and evidence-based treatments. Clearly, there was no place for spirituality here. Yet, from my decades of talking with clients, colleagues, and friends, I knew that beyond the realm of numbers and frequencies there exists a vast uncharted dimension of human sexuality, a landscape of sexual feelings, connections, and meanings—a sense of expanded consciousness of the kind that transformational psychiatrist Carl Jung famously called the "irrational facts of experience."

To explore some of these "irrational facts" of human sexuality, I began asking new questions, such as:

"Does sex always mean intercourse to you?" (To introduce the idea that sexual desire and satisfaction may center on dimensions other than intercourse.)

"Does sexual satisfaction always involve orgasm?" (To challenge the orgasm standard dictated by sexual science and most sex therapy modalities.)

"Do you ever experience a spiritual component in your sexual relationships?" (To begin probing the range of how people describe their spiritual dimensions of sexual experience.)

This and the questions that follow were an attempt to begin to name and expand on the kinds of experiences I was hearing from clients, colleagues, and friends:

"How have your spiritual beliefs enhanced (or limited) your enjoyment of sexual pleasure?"

"Does sex ever involve a sense of mystical union?"

"In a moment of sexual ecstasy, have you ever experienced God or universal energy?"

"In a moment of spiritual ecstasy, have you ever felt a surge of sexual energy?"

Because I could find no survey research focusing on sexuality and spirituality, I decided to step into the role of researcher in a much bigger way—to conduct a study that would reach well beyond my personal reach. I named the study "Integrating Sexuality and Spirituality" (ISIS).

The ISIS Study: Asking New Questions

Some 700 sex surveys have been conducted in the US since the 1930s. Results of these surveys almost always portray women as sexually deficient or dysfunctional, certainly as less interested and experienced than men. These survey data were so different from what I was hearing from clients, colleagues, and friends, I came to the conclusion that these surveys were systematically short-changing women by asking the wrong questions—all about intercourse, an activity less likely to appeal to women than to men.

The prototypical question that underlies most of these sex surveys defines sex as intercourse: "How many times have you had intercourse in the last week/month/year?" Other questions investigated other activities that are also generally less appealing to women than to men, such as anal penetration, voyeurism, forcing and being forced, and a standard of sexual normality that includes a goal of orgasm.

Because these surveys focused on performance issues, I realized that they were fundamentally biased, even when they scrupulously followed the rules of scientific objectivity. In focusing on details that could be counted and measured, these surveys omitted all emotional and relational issues. From my vantage point as a therapist and a woman, emotional and relational issues are an essential component of women's experience of sex. The omission of these factors constituted a conceptual, and crucial, research flaw.

Ultimately, I came to understand that quantitative, performance-based research was short-changing all of us. Sexual experience involves far more than performance for men as well as women. Or, more specifically rephrased: the feelings and meanings involved in sexual performance impact the sexual experience of all human beings. Feelings and meanings are prime contributors to sexual pleasure and healing, as well as to dysfunctional dynamics that keep our clients locked into a kind of cultural missionary position—in and out of the bedroom.

The ISIS study is biased as well, but the bias is different. It was designed to address what was left out of the quantitative surveys. Its two central research questions were: How does sex feel? and What does sex mean in your life? These questions embodied numerous issues that clients had brought into my practice of sex therapy over more than two decades, none of these issues measurable by numbers.

Questions about sexual feelings reached into areas of emotions, heart-to-heart connection, and body intelligence as well as physical sensations in response to touch.

Questions about sexual meanings reached into the area of spiritual exploration: thoughts, ideas, longings, a sense of belonging and connectedness—again, Jung's "irrational facts of experience."

The ISIS survey included no questions about intercourse, orgasm, or other forms of sexual performance already covered in earlier sex surveys. Nor did it include questions about pharmaceutical interventions. In fact, the ISIS questionnaire predated Viagra, which hit the US market in March, 1998—and which arguably changed some time-honored performance values of sex in the US and beyond.

A copy of the questionnaire is on my website (www.ginaogden.com).

The ISIS Survey: Logistics and Methodology

The ISIS survey was an independent project that snowballed into the first, and so far only, national survey to investigate the feelings and meanings of sexual experience. It took more than a decade to research, pilot, implement, and report. Analyzing the results plunged me back into academia from 1999 to 2004 with visiting scholarships at the Radcliffe Institute, the Wellesley Centers for Research on Women, and Harvard Divinity School's Center for the Study of World Religions. Exploring implications of the results plunged me into the mind-altering practice of ceremonial shamanism—which has brightly colored my experience of how we use and communicate sexual energy. Along the way, my subject of sexuality and spirituality led to invitations to write, to speak, to contribute to *Our Bodies, Ourselves* and to the Surgeon General's guidelines for healthy sex, even to an invitation to appear on the Oprah Winfrey Show. Somewhere, I still have a clip from May 7, 2000, of Oprah saying to me: "When your research is published it will change the way we think about sex in this country."

ISIS methods and outcomes have since appeared in a peer-reviewed paper, three book chapters, and two trade books, plus countless web entries and radio interviews—thankfully no more media hosts that tried to throw me under the bus. Because so much is already out there about the survey, I will be brief here.

Suffice it to say that the survey sample was not representative, in the sense that academics require. Scientifically generalizable samples begin with placing a grid over a map of the US and picking respondents randomly out of salient phone books—or the electronic equivalent of this technique for randomizing. The purpose is to produce a non-biased sample of respondents, as distinct from a so-called convenience sample who opt to participate. My belief is that this exercise in randomness is fine as long as the attitudes being surveyed belong to something relatively neutral, like laundry soap. But just about everybody has a deeply ingrained opinion on sexual issues, so there is no such thing as a truly random sample.

That said, the ISIS sample was a convenience sample of highly engaged respondents. It was also larger and far more diverse than most sex surveys. There were 3,810 respondents aged 18 to 86 (82 percent women, 18 percent men, fewer than 1 percent transgender). They came from every state in the US, and they embraced a range of sexual orientations, religious faiths, races, ethnicities, economic strata, and political attitudes. Of these respondents 1,465 wrote unsolicited letters about their lives. These are vivid narratives of spiritual (and unspiritual) sex, spontaneously written by people all over the country: red states, blue states, small towns, big cities—everywhere. Because these narratives address more than intercourse and orgasm, they challenge the performance definitions of sex addressed in quantitative surveys.

It should also be noted that all the ISIS data were collected via paper questionnaires between late 1997 and early 1999, just before the whole world went digital (remember paper and pen as a form of communication?). The downside of this was the inconvenience—my house was strewn with shopping bags full of surveys from the post office (remember snail mail?). The upside was that I enjoyed at least some sense of personal connection with each of the respondents—if only to open their envelopes and commune with their hand-written responses.

There were three phases of collection. I began by handing out questionnaires to audiences to whom I was speaking in late 1997. This accounted for 1,098 responses. Next, *New Age Journal* (a spirituality based magazine that morphed into *Body and Soul* and most recently into *Whole Living*) published the survey in its 1998 January–February issue. This accounted for another 1,285 responses. Finally, *New Woman* (a large-circulation women's magazine until its demise in 2008) published the survey in its 1998 July issue. This accounted for another 1,427 responses: 3,810 responses in all.

The ISIS Findings

The data analysis revealed numerous fascinating insights, including how connecting sex and spirit may have promoted factors that enhanced respondents' overall health and how the process of recovery from sexual abuse and/or substance addiction may have promoted respondents' integrating sexuality and spirituality. These insights applied to the 684 men who responded as well as to the 3,110 women, 11 trans people, and five respondents who did not identify their gender.

One of the most telling insights concerns the language used by ISIS respondents. Specifically it concerns the word counts of the elements of greatest focus in all of mainstream sex research—that is: intercourse, orgasm, and the genitals. Since the ISIS respondents largely overlooked these mainstream elements, the survey offers a graphic example of how asking new questions may alter the definitions of sex. At the very least, it illustrates that our research answers are shaped by the questions we ask. When offered questions only about intercourse, orgasm and genitals, no wonder so many women are considered to have dysfunction and low desire. The word counts for these elements in the 1,465 letters written by ISIS respondents are as follows:

- intercourse: 108 mentions—only 6 percent of some 1,800 sexual activities specified;
- orgasm: 247 mentions—compare with 4,412 mentions of emotional and spiritual outcomes, such as ecstasy, energy, love, connection, freedom, acceptance, and safety;
- the genitals: 23 mentions.

Moving on from details, the three major findings from the ISIS survey are given below.

"Sexual Experience Is Multidimensional . . . "

The overall major finding from this ISIS sample of respondents was that sexual experience included much more than intercourse and more than only physical sensations. Respondents reported overwhelmingly that, for them, sexual experience was multidimensional, involving body, mind, heart, and spirit. This finding may seem overly simple, but its significance is profound because this is the first sex survey to report multidimensional experience.

This finding on multidimensionality is consistent with what my clients, colleagues, and friends have reported ever since the mid-1970s, when it first occurred to me to open up discussion about sexual issues. It has also proved to be consistent with what contemporary brain research says about sexual response, in reports that began to be published about the same time as I was gathering the ISIS findings. The clearest brain-research parallels to the ISIS findings stem from the laboratory work of my colleagues Beverly Whipple and Barry Komisaruk, whose fMRI studies regarding women and orgasm show that sexual response activates multiple centers of the brain, not only the centers of physical gratification. Their research became part of their co-authored book *The Science of Orgasm* and is detailed in chapter 11 of *The Heart and Soul of Sex*. Beverly Whipple and I went on to present these parallels together between 2006 and 2009 in a series of keynotes at sexuality conferences in the US and Europe.

Many more examples of sexual multidimensionality follow throughout this book.

"Sexual Satisfaction Is Embedded in Relationship . . . "

ISIS respondents also overwhelmingly reported that erotic satisfaction was embedded in relationship with a partner or partners, and most importantly with themselves—not only as masturbation but also as a sense of extraordinary awareness, self-esteem, and connection. This finding, too, was consistent with what my clients and colleagues were saying and underscored Jung's notion that experience is filled with "irrational facts." Clearly, it departed from the increasing trend toward medicalizing sexual satisfaction: focusing on physical orgasm with the objective of labeling dysfunction that could be treated by behavioral adjustments and/or pharmaceutical interventions.

When sex and spirit connect, the measure of sexual satisfaction is far beyond physical orgasm. Many respondents used the term "ecstasy" to describe sexual satisfaction. For some, ecstasy meant love and nurturing with an empathic partner or a soul-mate. For others, it meant the creation and nurturing of new life—conception, childbirth, and breastfeeding a baby, occurrences that literally embody the spirit of sexual union. For still others, ecstasy meant physical sensation so intense that the body could not contain it without merging with imagination, memory, love, hope, and other non-physical energies. The overall experience of satisfaction was expressed as ability to expand the senses of self, love, creativity, altruism, and even religious experience. "I have experienced sex as a gateway to the soul," wrote one woman. "More oneness with All and more power to open doors to create what I choose."

In these ISIS narratives, not all sexual relationships are positive. Some respondents reported that social or religious pressures could shrink them to relative nothingness. "Man, Catholicism sure does screw up one's 'pleasure thoughts,'" stated one of the letters, reflecting the guilt, shame, fear, and sexual paralysis that can be imbued by fundamentalist religious practices.

Yet, taken together, these narratives suggest a relational perspective of integrating sexuality and spirituality that can serve to supplement the present orgasm standard for assessing sexual satisfaction. This challenges the present sexual definitions that limit, and often control, women, men, and the rest of us. More importantly, a relational perspective broadens the concept of sexual satisfaction to fit our clients' experiences, rather than having our clients feel they have to fit their experiences into already prescribed definitions.

"Sexual Satisfaction Increases with Age . . . "

Perhaps most remarkable were the findings on sex and age. For ISIS respondents, sexual satisfaction did not automatically plunge progressively "down hill" with age, as is invariably reported in other surveys. Respondents in their fifties, sixties, and seventies wrote of deeply felt experiences at a stage of life when, according to conventional wisdom, they ought to be Viagra-dependent if not sexually dormant. For these respondents, sexual satisfaction increased with every decade. They reported experiencing more sexual pleasure, vitality, eye-contact, sharing, and ecstasy than the 20- and 30-year-olds. One of my favorite responses was from a Vermont couple who stated their age as "74 years young" and their occupation as "sexually active." An overwhelming message from this sample is that growing older can be a time of aligning body and soul rather than defining one's self by medical conditions and sex-negative attitudes.

To make sense of this unusual finding, I mined the narrative data from some 536 respondents who were aged 50 and over. Reading through details of their life stories revealed three general secrets to sexual satisfaction increasing over the life-spans of these respondents—and none of these secrets had to do with pharmaceutical interventions for better performance.

Secret number one was that many of these respondents had discovered freedoms that came with outliving both their own expectations of sexual performance and those of the culture. Specifically, these respondents had found ways to move beyond the negative and conflicting messages of their youth—messages such as "good girls don't," "real men score," and "sex is dirty." When you think of this phrase coupled with the belief in virginity until marriage, it translates into a truly mind-twirling notion: "sex is dirty . . . save it for the one you love." Many respondents said they had outgrown messages like these, no longer believed them, and above all no longer believed that women did not enjoy sexual pleasure.

Secret number two was that many of these respondents had come to terms with past sex negativity. Specifically, they had found ways to move beyond the - sexual disappointments and even abuses of their early lives. Missing was the sense of bitterness, sarcasm, and denial so often associated with mid- and late-life comments about sex. Rather, as these respondents factored spirituality into their sexual equations, they reported that they reflected on what they had learned as survivors of negativity—and eventually as lovers, and lovers of sex.

Secret number three reflects a learning curve, illustrating that relationships can ripen over time, and that some women and men grow more proficient with years of practice. Specifically, many of these respondents had acquired the experience and wisdom to appreciate the erotic richness in their present relationships. Those in long-term partnerships were able to revel in the years of emotional and physical sharing that deepened their sense of erotic connection, even as their focus on genital performance was lessening. Those whose sex lives were characterized by a series of relationships were able to relax into the enjoyment of what they had in the present, instead of seeking perfection that might be discovered in yet another relationship just around the corner.

Potential for Change

These ISIS responses transformed the way I approach the practice of sex therapy. I took permission from the flood of affirmation that crucial aspects of sexual experience reside in emotional and spiritual realms. I was moved to ask new questions. I began to explore multiple states of consciousness. Perhaps most importantly, I began to listen differently.

As I broadened my own perspectives, I began to recognize the limitations in the sex research and therapy I had been trained to practice. I understood even more emphatically that performance models of sex address only one aspect of human sexual experience and omit nuances that play crucial parts in the whole sweep of sexual experience. Finally, I understood that an expanded model of sex therapy was needed. This expanded model would challenge the sexological flat-endians and shed light on a sexual landscape that is fully rounded and fully fluid. It would incorporate the spirit of the ISIS findings. It would encourage movement of body, mind, heart, and spirit. It would engage therapists in nuance and wonder as well as diagnosis and treatment. It would invite clients to collaborate vigorously with therapists in the experience of therapy.

But where would I find this model? Like an explorer setting off for new horizons, I girded for the journey.

2

THE ISIS WHEEL OF SEXUAL EXPERIENCE

As soon as I began to understand the full scope of sexual experience revealed in the ISIS study, I began to search for a container that could be expansive enough and also non-judgmental enough to hold all of these dimensions: physical, emotional, mental, and spiritual. No such model existed in sexology. The Masters and Johnson sexual response cycle (1966) is based on male ejaculatory response. Helen Singer Kaplan's model of desire and desire disorders (1979) is focused on physiological phenomena. Rosemary Basson's model of female sexual intimacy (2001) ties physical arousal to emotions but bypasses mental and spiritual dimensions. Even more narrowly focused are the pharmaceutical protocols, introduced increasingly since 1998 with the advent of Viagra.

The Medicine Wheel: Template for Awareness and Transformation

In searching for a coherent way to organize and teach the sprawling lessons of the ISIS material, my attention finally moved away from sexological models and focused on a core template of my spiritual practice: the Medicine Wheel. The Medicine Wheel is an ancient template for personal awareness and transformation. It appears in many cultures to represent the unending circle of life, on all levels, from the most ordinary to the most magical: past, present, and future. It brings together spiritual and earthly realms through paths that embody physical, emotional, mental, and spiritual experience—and it brings them together for the purpose of information and healing.

In a bolt of insight, I understood that this was the template comprehensive enough to serve as a frame for the ISIS stories that so overflowed the limits of sexological models. I adapted the basic template of the Medicine Wheel into a model I call the ISIS Wheel of Sexual Experience.

The ISIS Wheel: Key to the Sexual Mysteries

As I began to use this template as a teaching model, I found that the contents of the ISIS Wheel need not be limited to stories from the survey. The ISIS Wheel could include stories from anyone and anywhere. It could include stories from clients and also from ourselves, the therapists and healers. Plus, I discovered that it could serve as a container for all the aspects of our sexual stories. It could hold the performance aspects of sex. It could encompass intangible aspects that promote pleasure and intimacy, desire and function, orgasm and ecstasy. It could also encompass aspects that promote constriction and defensiveness, fear, pain, numbness, violence, abuse, and dysfunction. I realized it might encompass whatever issues clients bring into our offices.

The more I worked with this ISIS Wheel, the more I found it to be expansive, flexible, and relevant. I realized that it could hold the totality of our sexual stories—taking in a wide spectrum of behaviors, partner preferences, gender variance, and cultural messages, along with hot-button issues such as affairs, pornography, compulsivity, drugs, orientation, kink, abuse, and any other concerns clients might present, including the nuances of relationship interactions.

As I worked still further with the Wheel, I found that hidden dynamics of sex and intimacy began to emerge in a clarifying way, as if the Wheel itself held some kind of key to the sexual mysteries. I realized that it could serve as a primary organizing principle for helping us help our clients explore the totality of their sexual stories—past, present, and future.

It is imperative to state at the outset that the ISIS Wheel is not a prescriptive or predictive model such as Masters and Johnson's Cycle of Sexual Response or Basson's model of female sexual interaction. Rather, it is simply, and profoundly, a generic template for sexual awareness. As indicated by the lines leading beyond the perimeter of the Wheel, figure on p. 18, this diagram indicates that sexual experience connects with the rest of life rather than being separated out into its own orbit, as it is in other sexological models. The function of the Wheel is to help us guide our clients in exploring crucial nuances of their sexual stories and how these affect their lives.

Using the ISIS Wheel to Map Sexual Experience—Past, Present, and Future

I developed the ISIS Wheel to illustrate the ways in which sexual experience involves far more than simply the aspects of sex that can be counted and measured. The ISIS Wheel includes mental, physical, emotional, and spiritual aspects that are always present in our sexuality, whether we are aware of them or not, and whether or not we are actively engaging in sexual activity. By

17

THE ISIS WHEEL OF SEXUAL EXPERIENCE
An Organizing Principle for Exploring Our Sexual Stories—Past, Present, and Future

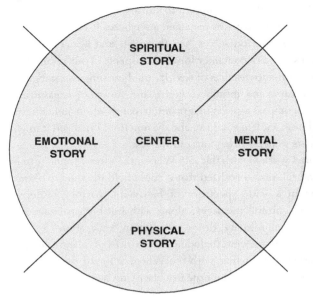

showing all the aspects at once, the Wheel invites clients and clinicians to consider the whole picture, not only one piece of it. In a therapy setting, that piece is most often defined by pathology, such as the dysfunction, the argumentative relationship, the childhood abuse. Interactions like these tend to become frozen in time. The Wheel can help clients explore those places where their stories are stuck.

As I have worked with the template of the Wheel I have found that using it invites explorations in time, so that seeming divisions between past and present become fluid, with all their implied connections to the future. To help unstick clients, I often place the template of the Wheel on the floor and ask clients to tell their stories from each quadrant. Moving one's story around the Wheel can become an adventure in quantum leaps of time-shifting, so that, for instance, a 32-year-old woman's aversion to sex morphs into her inability to protect her three-year-old self from her older brother's torturous ways:

> Standing in the emotional quadrant, I felt time collapse—and could rage with the energy of my three-year-old, then move to the physical and mental quadrants and feel how much power I have now. Actually

standing in the quadrants I could experience these things—much more powerful than sitting in a chair and just talking about them.

In further working with this template, I have found that it also invites movement between the perimeter and the center. At the perimeter of the Wheel, the sexual stories are tentative—a glance, a fleeting question, a peck on the cheek. At the center, where the energies of body, mind, heart, and spirit all meet and merge, something else occurs—a concentration of erotic energy I call the "ISIS connection." On a good day, the ISIS connection is a transformative experience of ecstasy and mystical revelation. When the story is irreconcilably negative, the ISIS connection is one of hopelessness and despair. Either way, here is where sexual experience enters territory that science has yet to chart fully. Because this connection cannot be counted and measured, it is also beyond the domain of evidence-based therapies.

The ISIS Wheel can be used to map a wide range of sexual responses. Our stories can start anywhere, and it is possible for clients and therapists to see all of the paths and hold them all in awareness even if they are focusing on only one quadrant. Anyone who has worked the Wheel knows that the ISIS paths do not always follow the strict and even boundaries shown in the figure on p. 18. As one client says, "I started out in the physical place looking for what drives my fear of sex, but this place got smaller and smaller until I ended up straddling the spiritual and mental places that encompassed my family background of repression."

As clients experience their sexual journeys in the contexts of their whole lives, the paths are likely to twist, turn, detour, bump, even come to dead ends. Following these paths of their stories can sometimes feel like slogging through a wilderness, because sexual experience is not always positive, and even positive experiences may restimulate past pain instead of pleasure. The good news is that some of our painful experiences may ultimately lead to positive outcomes. The client above adds this:

> Being a recovering Mormon, I dug up plenty of signature moments when I felt the whole weight of the church coming down directly onto my poor little sexual organ. But getting out from under means I have moved through years of shame. I feel really light for the first time ever—light because I don't have all that pressing on me, and light because I feel bright, illuminated. I think I finally understand the phrase "the joy of sex."

When other complexities of our sexual relationships are considered, with factors such as age, social class, ethnicity, race, gender, gender identity, and sexual orientation, it becomes apparent that these factors range across all the quadrants of the Wheel and that they may color our sexual responses in some unpredictable hues. Two of my close colleagues focus on class issues in their therapy and report that their clients have responses much like the "recovering Mormon" above. They point out that it can feel like walking out of the mists and into daylight for clients when they finally understand the social roots of what have been labeled their personal sexual problems and dysfunctions.

The template of the ISIS Wheel looks simple. Yet working with it may be both wide-ranging and deep. I can say this with the conviction of one who has journeyed the Wheel with over a thousand clients and trained dozens of practitioners who have now worked it with countless of their clients. It is exhilarating to see the movement in my trainees and to hear stories of their clients spontaneously moving from negative responses to positive ones.

The ISIS Wheel as an Arena for Change

When I introduce the ISIS Wheel to clients and trainees, I present it as an arena for awareness and change that invites clients to tell their stories from each quadrant, as a kind of multidimensional sex history-taking. In practical terms, I have also found the Wheel to be a vehicle that allows clients to reveal a large amount of complex information in a short time.

There is a deep purpose to all of this. When clients can identify for themselves the locus of their discontents—and also their pleasures—they are in a position of choice to initiate their own new directions rather than depending on a partner or therapist to point the way. Such new directions might involve attitude shifts, such as taking responsibility for their own feelings as distinct from reactive responses like shame, blame, partner-pleasing, and even violence against themselves and others. They might include proactive actions, such as exploring new sensual outlets or finally leaving a relationship that no longer nurtures them.

One woman stands out for me in this regard. Maria is a survivor of ritual abuse. She came to an ISIS weekend in chronic depression and on the edge of suicide. It became immediately apparent as she brought her story to the Wheel that the abuses she had suffered by the age of eight had taken away much more than her sexual innocence. They had co-opted her spirit as well. Maria was nearing 40, and beneath her chronic depression and fear she also confided that she was longing to "take off and fly"—both sexually and spiritually. But she had no clue where, or how, to begin. It was the safety of the ISIS Wheel that finally allowed her to reach into her past and experience how sex and spirit had been disconnected for her.

Maria's story told of ritual abuse by a father and uncles who were pillars of the community—therefore there was an extra strong injunction about her ever telling. Maria could retrieve only flashes of cognitive memory: being in a circle of men, being passed from one to the other, candles, fire, touching, terror.

20

Relating details from each quadrant took enormous courage for her, especially from the quadrants of body and spirit, because joining them came so close to the rituals with which she had been brutalized—and sworn to secrecy.

As Maria explored her story around the Wheel, she said her world expanded almost instantly beyond despair. She still feels cautious about sex with men, and may always do so. But she is no longer a prisoner of fear and depression. She is able to talk about her life—past, present, and future. When we last spoke, she said identifying her story on the Wheel had given her a sense of safety and control and had felt like a "launching pad for hope."

How ISIS Can Expand Sex Therapy

As illustrated by Maria's story, introducing clients to the ISIS Wheel has the effect of asking fresh questions. Often these are questions about feelings and meanings—to which there are no right or wrong answers, and certainly no answers that can be proven by evidence-based methods favored by many health professionals. Entering into the Wheel tends to arouse curiosity and engage clients in their own therapy. The process expands sex histories regarding sensations, feelings, meanings, messages, desires, self-esteem, decision-making, relationships, and whatever other issues clients may bring in. Clients seeking to expand (or limit) their sexual identities (e.g., to heterosexual, gay, lesbian, bisexual, or transgender) can explore multiple aspects of gender and orientation along with their motivations to change. Many more possibilities will unfold in the following chapters.

Therapist–Client Collaboration

Central to the ISIS Wheel concept is that clients' interpretation of events is the most meaningful factor in positive change. The therapist's role is crucial, of course, but it is not definitive, as it is in therapeutic models based on diagnosis and treatment of pathology. In ISIS work, the therapist's role becomes that of witness, guide, expander of stories, and sometimes stage director rather than uncontested "expert." The relationship between therapist and client is necessarily collaborative, which is a strong factor in the healing process, as revealed in recent studies on the placebo effect that challenge the dominator model of doctor–patient relationships.

Exploring Dysfunction

Descriptions of the ISIS Wheel have so far dismissed a focus on pathology. But clients do come into our offices with conditions of pain and performance dysfunctions that distress them and wreak havoc with their relationships. These must be taken seriously. And it is important for clinicians to understand the difference between pathologizing clients and their complaints and taking clients' complaints seriously. By "pathologizing" I mean, for instance, pre-judging clients' levels of desire and satisfaction according to academic standards of normality. By taking clients seriously, I mean listening creatively, without holding them to an impossible standard of performance. I mean helping clients enlarge their perspectives, so that they are in a position of choice, with a sense of power and ability to exercise that choice for themselves.

For clients presenting with DSM-categorizable sexual dysfunctions, using the ISIS Wheel can maximize therapeutic options. As with Maria, the abuse survivor above, the process allows clients to explore for themselves how their symptoms of physical dysfunction may be linked to emotional, mental, or spiritual issues. For instance, exploring each quadrant to investigate issues such as erectile problems, orgasmic blocks, or vaginismus offers both client and clinician a visible way to consider the implications of these dysfunctions beyond medical models that prescribe limited courses of treatment. Exploring multiple dimensions of these issues invites clients to factor in past, present, and future, family history, race, class, economics, cultural narratives, collective memory, and myth, along with physical symptoms and pharmaceutical interventions.

Exploring Desire

For partners with discrepancies of desire, using the Wheel can function as a safe place for each partner to speak—and listen to each other. Telling their stories of desire from each quadrant offers a potentially informing narrative about the past, the present, and possibly even the future. It allows each partner the space to weave both memories and possibilities into their perceptions of the here and now. Couples who wholeheartedly enter the Wheel often emerge with broader ways of understanding their levels of sexual desire.

I am thinking of a lesbian couple who recently presented with desire discrepancies. Ranee had been diagnosed with breast cancer three years earlier. Although her cancer was caught early and treated without surgery, the trauma for the couple was deep and took a toll on their sexual desire. The chronic drop in desire was not from the cancer survivor, who had long been ready to reconnect sexually. It was from her partner, Carole. This couple had not been fully sexual since the cancer diagnosis. Their visit to another sex therapist had been unsuccessful: "We were told to try non-demand touching and a bunch of lubes and vibes, and they didn't work."

The question that brought these women into ISIS therapy was: "What's wrong with us? Are we suffering from Lesbian Bed Death?" This is a slang phrase for a condition where women partners become essentially asexual on a permanent basis. I pointed out that there were no diagnostic criteria for this term, so we could not call it a bona fide sexual dysfunction. Instead, I suggested that we could seek out answers to their question together, beginning with each speaking about her sexual desire from each quadrant of the ISIS Wheel.

Carole spoke from the physical and emotional quadrants of her terror that she might hurt Ranee, and that Ranee might die and leave her. Ranee spoke from all four quadrants of how much it meant to her to stop being treated like an invalid so that she could renew the life-restoring activities of giving and receiving sexual, sensual pleasure.

Once Carole and Ranee had shared this information in the safety of the Wheel, their story shifted dramatically. Their assessment of Lesbian Bed Death morphed into mutual interest in each of them speaking up about what she wanted and into listening to each other—a focus on life rather than "bed death" or death itself. In the end, this couple discovered they could reinvent their sexual approach to each other and put their "bed-death" diagnosis to rest. Their new path to sexual engagement began with humor and reassurance rather than seduction with a genital focus—as they had been conditioned to imagine that sexual interaction required. What they called their "sex rehab program" started with breathing together instead of the lubrications and vibrators prescribed by their former therapist. With these and other changes, Carole's fears diffused. Ranee began to initiate, and Carole began to open up and receive. On one level the change was that simple. On other levels, it was life changing.

In the following chapters of this book we will look at many more examples of how exploring the quadrants can open up life-changing choice points for clients to explore on their own.

A Growth Arena for Therapists as Well as Clients

As I use the template of the Wheel in supervising and training therapists, unexpected byproducts of ISIS work keep surfacing. The overwhelming response is that introducing the ISIS template broadens the therapeutic focus beyond specific sexual behaviors (such as intercourse or orgasm or using lubes and vibes) to include a nuanced exploration of the feelings, meanings, and motivations that impact desire and a spectrum of sexual behaviors.

It continually astonishes me that such a simple shift in perspective can wield such a powerful impact. Why should broadening the field make such a difference for therapists? I believe its power lies in the liberation clinicians feel when freed from the constricting nature of the training to which most of us are subject as we prepare for our degrees and licenses to practice. The ISIS Wheel acts as a kind of generator for therapists who are hungry for healing modalities beyond performance-oriented and evidence-based approaches to sexual dysfunction.

A refrain I hear from many is that their training centered on cognitive-behavioral therapy (CBT). This is an approach to clients' issues that focuses on evidence-based practices to treat dysfunctions and that seeks problem-oriented solutions in a goal-directed manner. This approach is effective for many of the sexual problems clients bring in to our offices, and very importantly it meets crucial criteria for insurance panels. But CBT does not allow for exploring a full range of sexual complexity. Nor does it address some of the subtle issues regarding clients' individual and relational concerns. These limitations have left many clients with important needs unaddressed—and have left some of my therapist colleagues feeling frustrated because they are unable to help clients move beyond focus on their symptoms.

Expanding the practice of sex therapy through the ISIS approach is not for the timid, however. Just as exploring the Wheel of feelings and meanings may unearth layers of emotions for the client, it may also bring up unresolved issues for the therapist. Even a most basic exploration of the Wheel can trigger an "Aha!" response that can plunge a therapist into a morass of personal issues that may be unexplored or perhaps intentionally ignored. Responsibility for our own feelings is a theme that permeates the rest of this book; the issue of countertransference and how therapists can explore ISIS for ourselves is specifically addressed in chapter 10.

Concretizing the Boundaries of Therapeutic Interaction

The subject of countertransference brings me to Serena, a conventionally trained marriage and family counselor who coordinates the sexual health department of a residential clinic in the Midwestern US. When she asked me to supervise her work with the ISIS approach she was in her mid-forties, and she had begun actively searching for answers to some of her unresolved life dilemmas as well as seeking to expand her practice of sex therapy. She said she was looking "beyond her comfort level"—exploring her spirituality, revamping her therapeutic belief systems, rediscovering her connections with nature, and reviewing her personal edges in relationships. This was a great deal to tackle all at once, and she found herself both excited and confused. Moreover, Serena felt some of her clients paralleling her own issues: "Put it this way," she said. "They're certainly looking for more than the mechanics and performance aspects of sex, and so am I."

In some cases, Serena's parallels with her clients went deep. As we helped her guide these clients through the labyrinthine boundary issues raised by their work on the ISIS Wheel, Serena found that she was gaining insights into her own boundary issues, which included sexual violation by almost every male member of her family of origin. Serena has used the Wheel herself to gather enough courage and insight to delve into the pain of her abusive and conflict-ridden childhood. "I've had years of therapy about this," she points out, "but it always stopped short of the spiritual piece. And it never connected sexuality and spirituality."

What helped Serena with both her clients' and her own issues was to make them concrete so that they emerged from the shadows of abstraction and into plain view. I suggested she choose objects to represent both her past pain and the spiritual approach she was seeking. Concretizing in this way made these abstract concepts real, invoked new images, and put her experiences literally into her own hands so that she could move them to different quadrants at will, instead of allowing herself to be swung this way and that.

Concretizing is an ISIS strategy I will discuss at length in chapter 9 and beyond. Suffice it to say here that choosing to work with concrete objects around issues such as boundaries and spirituality helped Serena expand her practice of sex therapy. Exploring all the ways she was able to choose and control the objects with which she worked offered her clues as to how she could begin to exercise choice and control over areas of her life that had been beyond her powers. Through these personal explorations on the Wheel, she developed insights and skills she could pass on to her clients.

Developing the Ability to Bilocate

Jorge, another sex-therapy supervisee, also came to ISIS work as a licensed therapist, specializing in adolescents and adults who presented with substance abuse problems. These problems often involved sexual issues, whether or not these were openly acknowledged. Jorge admitted to me that he possessed a great fear of working with couples in therapy and understood that this was because he had never been able to address fully the traumas of his own childhood. He was self-aware enough to point out that couples with whom he worked became, in his eyes, his own toxic parents. As he witnessed each client couple's distress in his office he felt as if he were plunged back in time, where he was a skinny eight-year-old trying to mediate his parents' violent battles. On one occasion he had witnessed his father smash a beer bottle on the kitchen counter and wave the jagged edge at his mother's throat.

Jorge described how he would feel alternately intimidated and enraged by some of the couples he saw in therapy. To maintain some degree of equilibrium over his roller-coaster emotions he would act ultra-rational, overbearing, and didactic—telling his client couples what to do and in some cases (I feared) where to get off. Jorge recognized that he was doing these couples no good by projecting his old unresolved feelings on them, but he had no idea how to change. By the time he began ISIS training he had stopped working with couples altogether. This was a protective measure. But he recognized that his refusal to work with couples was limiting his effectiveness as both a general therapist and a potential sex therapist.

Because Jorge's clinical skills were being so influenced by his personal story, our supervision needed to factor in the intersection of professional and personal before it could move forward. I explained to Jorge that he could use himself as his own laboratory to help him understand his own reactions and responses. I further explained that this was not crossing some kind of clinical boundary. Studying one's self is a time-honored approach of scientists in many disciplines.

The ISIS Wheel proved to be an arena where Jorge could explore his dilemmas. Telling his story in all of the quadrants of the Wheel took him beyond a merely intellectual understanding of his issues. Telling his story in the emotional quadrant, for instance, allowed him to connect his past helplessness with his present power—actually to feel both of these energies and to experience the swirling tides and currents as they came together. In the spiritual quadrant, he was able to extract some positive meaning from all the violence he had witnessed as a child—the comfort he received from a beloved aunt. In the mental quadrant, he had an opportunity to verbalize definitively and out loud that he was not to blame for his family's craziness and violence; that he was powerless to "cure" the family situation; and that if any surviving members of his family wanted to change they would have to do it themselves. In short, these explorations and insights allowed Jorge to gain a broader perspective on his early life, so that eventually he was able to view his violent childhood without either terror or judgment.

Most importantly for expanding his own practice of sex therapy, working with the ISIS Wheel enabled Jorge to see his clients as separate from either his family members or himself. As he contemplated his relationships with his clients, he could place himself in each quadrant of the Wheel with great clarity. He saw (and experienced) himself as he was then—as that scared eight-year-old boy. And he saw (and experienced) himself as he is now—as a powerful 50-year-old man with highly developed conflict-resolution skills and a desire to heal. He was able to take himself repeatedly around each quadrant—as a man, as a boy, and as a therapist—speaking from his own body, heart, mind, and spirit. At one point he took the role of both little boy and powerful therapist, seeing his clients' inner children reflected in his own inner child. In this exercise, Jorge was learning the art of bilocation—the ability to step back and forth from one persona to another and to move fluidly among past, present, and future.

The next section will explore the quadrants of the ISIS Wheel.

Part II

THE ISIS WHEEL

A Guide to the Quadrants

Sex isn't everything. But it is a part of everything.
                                            ISIS Respondent

3

MAPPING THE VARIETIES OF SEXUAL EXPERIENCE

Exploring the quadrants of sexual experience is a journey of curiosity and adventure for both clients and therapists. Every story is different. Listen to what your clients tell you. And *how* they tell you. Notice the verbs. Notice the breathing and the body language. Notice parts of the story they leave out. Notice your own feelings as they tell their stories.

You may not have to use the information to form a diagnosis or a treatment plan. Often it is enough simply to witness it as part of that client's story. Other times it can be transformative to ask some simple questions: "What quadrant are you in?" "What quadrant would you like to be in?" Notice if there is a lead quadrant—one to which a client typically goes or one which a client avoids or views as a source of discomfort or distaste.

Clearly there is confluence among all the quadrants, because body, mind, heart, and spirit are connected. But one of the benefits of working with the Wheel is that you can encourage clients to make distinctions between each quadrant, as if they are pieces of the vast and intricate fabric of their lives. Such distinctions can help clients (and therapists) clear confusion and be guided to places and issues that hold the most charge and juice.

Offering clues to help clients make those distinctions is the purpose of this section. The point is not to replace sex therapy that works well but to propose an adjunct for whole-person healing—and perhaps some cultural healing as well. The point also is to expand our understanding of sexual experience.

As we go further into the ISIS Wheel, we find ourselves in the land of vast differences between the kinds of sexual experiences our clients want to nurture and enhance and the kinds of sexual experiences they want to move away from or get rid of entirely. And sometimes we find ourselves in the land of paradoxes—where that which some clients may crave is also what they most despise, and where that which makes them weak and defensive also has the

THE ISIS WHEEL OF SEXUAL EXPERIENCE
An Organizing Principle for Exploring our Sexual Stories

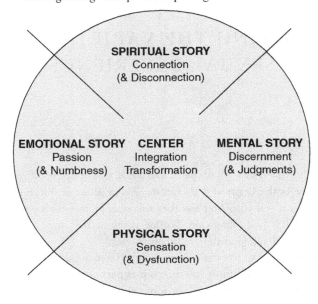

potential to make them strong and open. The lesson for us as therapists is to help clients open up new insights and solutions through collaborative inquiry rather than through judgments and diagnoses.

The figure above is the same basic diagram you saw on p. 18, with the added dichotomies that are addressed in this chapter and those that follow. Note, too, that the size and shape of the quadrants may vary, depending on the circumstance. For instance, if the presenting issue is primarily physical—focusing on the sexual awkwardness caused by menopausal symptoms, for instance—the client's physical story takes the most space, so that her ISIS Wheel might look like that on the first figure on p. 31.

When the same client begins to explore her menopausal symptoms on the Wheel, the focus may morph into an emotional conflict—perhaps shame at her inability to perform sexually, or fear of losing control, or fear of losing her mate. Or it might plunge into an unresolved incident from childhood. Her emotional story may assume priority, and her ISIS Wheel might then look more like that in the second figure on p. 31. Or perhaps this client's issue morphs into a matter of self-judgment, centering on societal messages about how a woman *should* be able to "put out" sexually. Her ISIS Wheel might

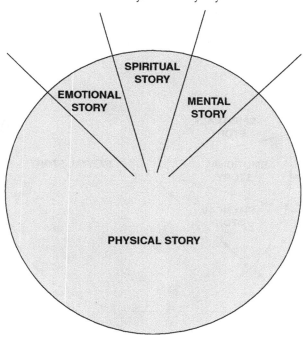

THE ISIS WHEEL
When the Story Is Primarily Physical

SPIRITUAL
STORY

EMOTIONAL
STORY

MENTAL
STORY

PHYSICAL STORY

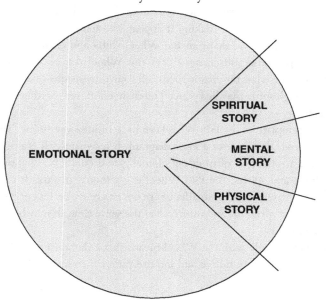

THE ISIS WHEEL
When the Story Is Primarily Emotional

SPIRITUAL
STORY

EMOTIONAL STORY

MENTAL
STORY

PHYSICAL
STORY

THE ISIS WHEEL
When the Story Is Primarily Mental

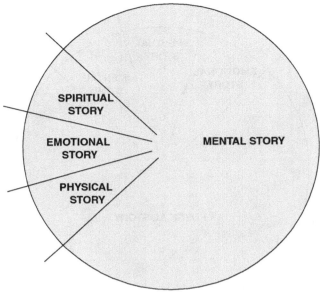

appear to have a huge mental story, so that it appears more like that in the figure above.

Or perhaps meaning and connection become the central issues: "This sexual problem gets between me and my partner . . . we just don't seem to be on the same wavelength anymore." Then this client's ISIS Wheel would have an enlarged spiritual quadrant, making it appear like that in the figure on p. 33. You get the picture. The shape of the Wheel shifts and changes as the major focus of therapy shifts and changes. Yet the Wheel retains its integrity as a whole. No matter what the major focus, all four dimensions of experience are present, although some may be reduced or changed in size—either temporarily or permanently.

The basic template of the ISIS Wheel can have infinite variations. The important lesson here is that it is not a static diagram. It is dynamic. It is a reflection of the moment, a reflection of multiple elements and conflicts. Like our bodies, hearts, minds, and spirits, the ISIS Wheel is constantly in flux. It may change shape. It may grow bigger or smaller as it contains more or less energy. It may be located in past, present, and future all at the same time. It may be off balance or evenly centered.

Working effectively with the Wheel means that a therapist must be flexible, too. Our ISIS lesson is to notice and inquire rather than leap to judgments and

THE ISIS WHEEL
When the Story Is Primarily Spiritual

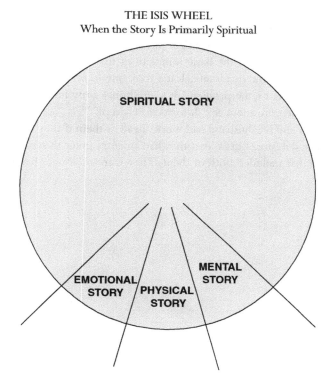

diagnoses. This can be a stretch for therapists who are trained to focus on pathology and to interpret symptoms. But, when we make the shift, we are better able to lead our clients to discover for themselves what their issues are, what their blocks are, and how to balance these in their lives.

By exploring each quadrant of the Wheel, a layered story will emerge, one with many perspectives. The story may connect body, mind, heart, and spirit. It may connect past, present, and future. Most importantly for many clients, expanding the sexual story in this way interrupts the sexual story they may have been telling themselves for years—stories with self-defining, self-limiting, foregone conclusions such as: "I'm a person who doesn't come to orgasm because I was molested by my stepfather when I was eight" or "I'm someone who can only have an erection when I masturbate to pornography." This is not to deny the power of the stories our clients bring to us, only to suggest that exploring these stories will likely lead to more nuanced understanding—and hopefully toward what the clients want to experience more of in their lives.

Occasionally the first sight of the template of the Wheel can create an instant opening or recognition—as in the story of Katja, a menopausal woman who presented with low sexual desire. A nurse-practitioner colleague had been unsuccessfully treating her with testosterone over a period of many months. Having decided to look for other than physical causes for Katja's low desire, she handed her a copy of the basic template of the ISIS Wheel, intending to begin by explaining the quadrants. Katja took one look, burst into tears, and said, "That's it! That's the problem! It's emotional—my husband and I are at each other all the time about sex. It turns me right off."

True, Katja and her husband had work ahead of them if they were going to reset her sexual desire. But at least they had an entry point that was more than physical and that included both of them. They were no longer barking up the wrong tree.

4

THE PHYSICAL QUADRANT
Exploring Sexual Sensation and Dysfunction

The Body Intelligent

The physical quadrant of the ISIS Wheel involves a full range of sensory experience: smell, taste, touch, sight, and hearing. It includes genital stimulation, intercourse, and orgasm. It also includes all-over sensation—fingers, toes, neck, earlobes, that oh-so sensitive skin on the inside of the thighs, and on and on. Extragenital touch is sometimes called "outercourse" to distinguish it from intercourse and genital stimulation. At its most optimal, the physical ISIS experience is characterized by positive body image and by heightened senses: brighter colors, increased sensitivity to touch, taste, smell, and hearing, along with positive body image and exquisite awareness of how all parts of the body connect to all the senses—and to the thoughts, emotions, and experience of life-force energy.

The physical quadrant also encompasses issues such as pain, disease, disability, distorted body image, and sexual dysfunction, including the dysfunctions that are listed in the DSM, such as anorgasmia, vaginismus, erectile dysfunction, and premature, delayed, and retrograde ejaculation.

The physical quadrant is where clients typically describe their issues with sexual performance—by which I mean the difficulties they experience with intercourse, orgasm, ejaculation, and the like. It is a primary container for negative body issues and also body memories—even beyond the scientific parameters of the physical aspects of sex.

Exploring the physical quadrant of the ISIS Wheel may bring up a deeper physiological aspect of sexual dysfunction which I find is rarely addressed by medical practitioners or sex therapists—that is, the disrupted adrenal function and increased cortisol levels as a response to old trauma, post-traumatic stress disorder (PTSD), or current stress, including fear, anger, or depression regarding sexual interaction. If you suspect that adrenal depression may be part of a client's picture, it is important that you collaborate with an appropriate medical colleague as you help the client address the physical, relational, and emotional issues.

A special note on the physical aspects of desire disorders—by way of an alert about pathologizing clients or trying to "fix" them by automatically suggesting testosterone or other hormones. When clients say, "I don't like sex," or "My partner doesn't want sex," it is crucial to ask them to clarify exactly what they mean by "sex." If it is intercourse these clients do not desire, it may be break-through information for them to hear from you that intercourse is not the only sexual activity on the planet. Further, you can let them know that intercourse is not the sexual activity that gives most pleasure to all human beings, especially women, who may long for other kinds of physical and emotional contact. A desire problem may lie mainly in the definition of desire. This is because our sexual norms are so focused on intercourse. For instance, sex surveys quantify behaviors, laboratory studies target genitals and goals, pharmaceutical compa-nies pathologize natural life developments such as difficulties with intercourse as a negative effect of aging—and on and on.

Often, what clients think of as a generalized desire disorder may be simply a lack of desire for a certain sexual activity or a particular partner. Or clients may desire emotional, spiritual, and even intellectual stimulation as well as physi-cal. When you check out assumptions and offer some education, you may expand your clients' frame of reference for sexual experience and thereby bypass the notion of dysfunction—and its prescribed treatments.

What Science Says About the Physical Aspects of Sex

Sexual science has exhaustively covered the physical aspects of sex, especially the act of heterosexual intercourse. Over the last century, more than 700 sex surveys attempted to quantify the activity of intercourse, recording data about when, how often, and with how many partners. The issues left unasked in these surveys are those that include feelings and meanings.

The first great quantifier of sexual activity was Alfred Kinsey and his team of interviewers, whose two surveys focused on male sexual behavior (1948) and female sexual behavior (1953). Both of these Kinsey reports investigated numerous sexual outlets, among them marital intercourse, extra-marital inter-course, intercourse with animals, masturbation, and same-sex behaviors. Both also included the revolutionary 0–6 "Kinsey Scale" of sexual orientation, which posited that most human beings fall somewhere in the range between 1 and 5—that is, if you count in our wishes and fantasies along with our active beha-viors, relatively few of us are exclusively heterosexual or homosexual.

As a side note: when it seems relevant to mention Kinsey's work to clients, I often refer them to the 2004 movie *Kinsey* in order to humanize the statistical nature of his research. Kinsey was a noted taxonomer before he was a sex researcher. He was the world's foremost collector of gall wasps and recorded detailed measurements on some half million of these minuscule beings. His studies of human sexuality reflect his taxonomer's mindset.

The physical aspects of sex have been minutely studied in the laboratory as well, most notably by researchers William Masters and Virginia Johnson, whose 1966 study of human sexual response pioneered the contemporary field of sex therapy. The Masters and Johnson Sexual Response Cycle focuses on the goals of intercourse and orgasm, diagramming a four-phased sequence of physiologic inevitability: arousal, plateau, orgasm, and resolution. This still stands as the gold standard for human sexual response, although it has been challenged by researchers, therapists, and sociologists as being too linear, stereotypical, and dogmatic. This cycle is clearly in contrast with the multidimensional approach offered by the template of the ISIS Wheel.

Finally, pharmaceutical companies have played a major role in sexual science, especially since March, 1998, with the introduction of Viagra—"the little blue pill that changed sex in America," as it is called by Meika Loe in *The Rise of Viagra*. The pharmaceutical industry has been criticized and chastised for financing and conducting its own clinical trials, most recently during its attempts to create a "pink Viagra" that would serve as an antidote to what the industry was hyping as an epidemic of low sexual desire in women. Thanks to efforts of the New View Campaign, a watchdog organization to monitor such activities, the FDA withheld approval for the products Intrinsa and, most recently, Flibanserin, both aimed at increasing women's sexual desire but with disturbing side effects. To check on current activities of the New View, see their website (www.newviewcampaign.org).

The relevant issue for clinicians in all this information is that there is a wide range of research on the physical aspects of sexual experience—medical, alternative, socio-political, academic, activist, and popular. When clients are exploring this literature, it may be important to help them understand that most of what they read will be narrowly focused and biased. Practically none of this literature relates to the larger picture of sexual experience or even sex therapy—that is, the emotional, mental, and spiritual aspects that inform sexual interest, desire, arousal, orgasm, and satisfaction. Interestingly, the field of integrative medicine omits sexual issues from its protocol. At this writing, I am working with a fellow of integrative medicine to create an intake and treatment protocol based on the ISIS approach. Stay tuned.

The ISIS approach addresses sexual experience as physical experience—and much more, too. Moreover, it demonstrates that focusing only on physical symptoms is not the most optimal, or even objective, route to relieving sexual problems or to helping clients move toward more satisfying sexual experiences or relationships. Expanding the practice of sex therapy often means helping clients look beyond what medical and sexual science say about the physical aspects of sex to explore more integrative approaches, and to find creative ways to help clients tune into their own internal messages about desire, sensation, and satisfaction.

What Our Culture Says About the Physical Aspects of Sex

American culture is obsessed with the physical aspects of sex, from gender differences and locker-room exploits to jokes about the effects of aging. Spam messages assault our computers, urging us to "bigger," "better," "longer-lasting" organs of penetration. Other media flood us with stereotypes about male "hunks" and female "hotties," offering us models that are way beyond possible for most human bodies and delivering the message that looking like a hunk or a hottie is what is really sexy—even if it takes reconstructive surgery to get there. Educator Jean Kilbourne has been eloquent since the 1970s in showing how advertising images distort women's bodies, depersonalize sex, and emphasize gender stereotypes; her prizewinning film *Killing us Softly* is now in its fourth update. Kilbourne's work takes into account that sexual images of men are distorted as well.

Expanding the practice of sex therapy invariably means helping clients look beyond what our culture says about the physical aspects of sex. Moreover, it includes finding innovative ways to encourage clients to stop, look, and listen to their own bodies for feedback about what feels good, what feels bad, and what direction they want to go for pleasure and satisfaction.

Skills Training for Body Awareness

There are countless awareness exercises that can encourage clients to heighten their sexual and sensual awareness as well as to alleviate what they perceive as negative physical symptoms. I love the bodywork approach of my colleague Suzanne Scurlock-Durana, who conducts powerful workshops and training all over the globe. In her book *Full Body Presence*, she addresses sexuality via the intelligence of the whole body, not just the genitals. "Listen, your body is speaking to you," she says, inviting her readers to expand their awareness of who they are and who they might become—body, mind, heart, and spirit—a view entirely consistent with the ISIS approach.

Exercises I regularly use for body awareness involve breathing, movement bathing, floating, and choosing and using a vibrator. They also involve practicing Kegel exercises for vaginal health. These exercises are all spelled out in *The Return of Desire* in ways that emphasize the complexity and subtlety of sexual health and therapy. Another resource for Kegels and other exercises to appeal to the intelligent body is A Woman's Touch, a sexuality boutique and resource center in Madison, Wisconsin (see www.a-womans-touch.com).

Even though the ISIS focus is on the whole picture of sexual interaction, I want to be clear that it is not always necessary or even appropriate to extend a complex treatment of sexual issues to each of your clients. For some clients who present with issues of performance, a narrower focus may be called for. In these cases, behavioral sex therapy and/or pharmaceutical intervention are what provide the most help. Of utmost importance is that you listen closely to your clients and that you maintain a sense of therapeutic flexibility and balance.

I encourage you to read the literature and also to be aware of the ads for products—and wary of their commercialization. It is important that therapists be familiar with interventions such as the role of sex toys for pleasure, hormones to balance women's mood and desire, the efficacy of Viagra, Cialis, and other pharmaceutical enhancements for men, and also the sensate focus exercises developed by Masters and Johnson for couples who need basic awareness about sexual touch. And it is important to understand that pelvic floor issues, such as vaginismus and vestibular pain, may require referral to a clinician with special expertise in physical therapy and sexual body work, along with a license to touch their patients. A controversial approach to vaginismus involves Botox injections, with dilators inserted under anesthesia by a physician. This is a process that offers success in some otherwise unyielding cases, but it should be considered only when other options fail to provide relief.

My point here is that it is impossible to be an expert in all aspects of sexuality. Therefore, it is imperative to keep an up-to-date list of approaches and referrals you trust. Read, attend trainings and workshops, talk with colleagues. I have found an invaluable resource for such referrals in the listserv of the American Association of Sexuality Educators, Counselors, and Therapists (AASECT), a certifying organization whose members come from all over the world.

Back to what you can do in your office as a sex therapist. When clients explore deeply the physical quadrant of their sexual issues, therapists have an opportunity to offer a variety of exercises. These can be used for assessment and diagnostic purposes as well as for healing. Two exercises that are specific to ISIS work are below. I call them "Down-There Dialogues" and "Exploring the Extragenital Matrix." You can tailor either of these exercises to help your clients connect their physical experience of sexual pleasure with the emotional, mental, and spiritual aspects of sex.

Down-There Dialogues: Activating the "Vagina Fairies"

There are some clients for whom a vulva conversation, a penis conversation, or a penis and vulva conversation can be extraordinarily moving and useful, whether or not these clients are involved in intercourse or other performance-directed sexual activity. At the very least, these exercises are attention-getting, so they encourage clients to think creatively and, hopefully, to initiate their own paths to healing.

Such conversations remind us that our genitals are connected to our minds, hearts, and spirits, whether or not we are consciously aware of specific connections. They may also remind us that all too often our genitals become a stand-in for our entire sexual selves—our sense of masculinity or femininity, our sense of ourselves as sexual beings and lovers. Too often a penis or vulva becomes a negative stand-in for the whole person. How often have you heard someone called a "prick" or a "cunt?" In short, our genitals may take on the roles of potent characters in our life's drama, and understanding can dawn big-time when we acknowledge this dynamic and play it through. Even if women have had Botox injections to relieve painful symptoms of vaginismus, it is necessary for them to expand their awareness of their own bodies in order to incorporate the treatment successfully.

A note on terms: I use the term "vulva" because it is all-inclusive. It includes the wonderful vagina and all its inner and outer surroundings. It also includes the wonderful clitoris—which is the body's only (repeat, *only*) organ whose sole purpose is pleasure. For a grand tour of the entire clitoral system, read Rebecca Chalker's *The Clitoral Truth*. I use the word "dialogue" in honor of Eve Ensler and her wonderful play *Vagina Monologues*, which has found a world stage and has helped women all over the globe, especially survivors of sexual abuse.

How to Talk with Your Body

The classic way to set up this kind of internal conversation is the one made famous by Fritz Perls, father of Gestalt therapy. Place two chairs opposite each other and invite clients to talk with different parts of themselves—some clinicians refer to these parts as "inner characters." You might begin with the part that feels turned off and the part that feels turned on. You can explain that this is simply about externalizing the Yes–No dialogue these inner characters are carrying on all the time, but too often beneath the level of their conscious awareness.

Make sure that your client identifies exactly who is speaking from each chair. An introductory statement might begin: "I am Sandra's vulva. I am old and dry. I feel very tired. I'm tired of being used. I'm tired of being called dirty names. I'm turning off and turning in."

Notice the client's body language, breathing, emotional affect, and language.

A statement from Sandra's other chair might begin: "I am Sandra's hot, juicy, sacred prostitute. I've been living in Sandra's DNA for thousands of years and I'm here to seduce you into mind-blowing sex that will take you into erotic worlds you can't even imagine . . ."

Clients may also benefit from having similar conversations with figures in their emotional and relational history whose influence may have invaded their vulvas, or perhaps inspired their vulvas. These figures might include parents, mentors, ancestors, or religious teachers, along with partners, ex-partners, fantasy lovers—whoever. So, if the conversation needs to involve more than two chairs, you can set up more and invite clients to talk with all the parts of their genital selves they can identify. This kind of conversation is used effectively in psychosynthesis and Internal Family Systems (IFS). For an articulate look at how you can explore an entire inner cast of characters, read *Negotiating the Inner Peace Treaty* by Chelsea Wakefield, a Jungian therapist and ISIS colleague.

What can be most telling in a vulva conversation such as this is not only the characters who show up, but also the transition from one chair to another. When you ask clients to notice how they move between feeling turned on and turned off, be ready for answers that may surprise you—and surprise your clients. A woman in a recent ISIS group identified what she called her "vagina fairies." She discovered she could use her breathing to activate them. She brought away from this conversation a sense of sexual confidence and power that she had never felt before.

Exploring the "Extragenital Matrix"

The Extragenital Matrix is a checklist and touch grid that clients can consult to raise their awareness (and their partners' awareness) about where and how they enjoy touching and being touched beyond what one client calls "the homing sites" of penis and vulva—those powerful and quirky characters you may have just been dialoguing with above. Creating the matrix was inspired by a research respondent who once admitted to me: "I don't know where on my body I'm not orgasmic. I think I need to be mapped."

Over the years I have introduced the Extragenital Matrix to clients for whom it seems important to affirm that sex is more than just penis—vagina intercourse. This is a radical notion for clients who are locked into the notion that intercourse is "real" sex and that everything else is relatively meaningless, or simply an appetizer to the main meal.

The Extragenital Matrix is an especially valuable concept for clients who are unable to perform intercourse because of age or disability, for clients who cannot enjoy intercourse because of vaginismus, pain, or painful memories that are restimulated, and for clients who are lesbian, gay, or transgender, for whom penis—vagina intercourse is not on their sexual radar. It is also valuable for any clients who want to expand their repertoires for more pleasure and power.

A few lines of this Extragenital Matrix are shown in the next page (the entire matrix is available on my website). You will see that this is set up like a

EXTRAGENITAL MATRIX

AREAS OF BODY AND KINDS OF STIMULATION

	Hand stroke	Hand pinch	Hand slap	Lips suck	Lips blow cold	Lips blow warm	Tongue lick	Tongue flutter	Teeth	Hair	Feet	Genitals	Other	Toys
Hair														
Face														
Eyes														
Nose														
Lips														
Tongue														
Ears														
Lobes														
Neck														
Throat														
Shoulder														
Breasts														
Nipples														
Armpits														
Upper arms														
Behind elbows														
Lower arms														
Wrists														
Hands														

definitive chart that lists parts of the body along with activities such as stroking, blowing, and more. Please understand that the items on this matrix are not meant to be carved in stone. They are only suggestions. I urge you to invite your clients to make this Extragenital Matrix their own. They can take suggestions from it; they can also add to it and subtract from it as they draw from their own sexual experience and consciousness.

When I introduce the Extragenital Matrix to clients, I usually go over the terms with them first and find out how they might want to begin exploring them. Then I suggest they take the matrix home and explore their own responses—with their partners if they have them.

- To personalize the Extragenital Matrix, invite your clients to use their own terms or to create their own touch grid, starting from scratch (so to speak). Using the Extragenital Matrix may expand the sexual language for clients. It is an especially effective way to help long-term couples update their turn-offs and turn-ons.
- Or offer your clients a box of colored markers and ask them to draw an outline of their bodies—to mark what kinds of stimulation feel especially good or bad. They can use red for STOP, green for GO, and yellow for PROCEED WITH CAUTION. This exercise can evoke deep levels of stories the body tells and is another effective activity for couples.
- Or draw from the classic Masters and Johnson exercise that involves non-demand touching, where partners touch each other everywhere except the genitals and report on what feels good or bad. Make sure to remind your clients to discuss the emotional feelings connected with their physical sensations, along with any old messages that might come up regarding where and how touch "should" or "shouldn't" occur.

Any of these options offers clients something of their own creation that they can set beside sexual messages from the culture, or their partners, to discover new sensual and erotic horizons. As follow-up, I routinely help clients broaden their sexual awareness by connecting their experience of touch to the emotional, mental, and spiritual paths that inform each experience with passion and meaning.

The chapters that follow open up routes to all these paths.

5

THE EMOTIONAL QUADRANT
Exploring Sexual Passion and Fear

The Way of the Heart

The emotional quadrant of the ISIS Wheel incorporates a full range of the feelings associated with sexual experience, such as longing, love, caring, and passion—whatever touches the heart. This quadrant is characterized by the comment made by countless ISIS respondents (men as well as women): "We don't just have sex, we make love." Please note that the spirit of the phrase "make love" does not refer to old moral injunctions about having to be in love in order to have sex. Rather, it is an acknowledgment that the physical experience of sex is intrinsically connected to emotional experience.

In its most positive sense, the emotional ISIS experience is characterized by open-heartedness and heightened feelings. It includes trust, the willingness to let go of control. It includes empathy, the capacity to feel what others feel. It also includes compassion, a complex concept famously described by the Dalai Lama as the ability to love yourself and others no matter how conflicted your feelings may be. (When His Holiness was asked: "How do you feel about the Chinese, who invaded your country?" he answered: "I feel the Chinese want to be happy too.") When trust, empathy, and compassion are part of sexual intimacy, it means that the well-being of your partner is essential to your own. As one client put it, toward the end of her therapy: "Narcissists need not apply."

All of this said, the emotional quadrant is also the container of the so-called dark feelings: anger, fear, angst, disgust, and any emotions that are the fallout from sexual experiences that are disappointing, controlling, scary, painful, violent, abusive, or just plain boring.

Many clients present with problems that are emotionally mired in a past that needs to be fully revealed before it can be fully healed. For some clients, this past is characterized by deep wounds, such as the trauma of rape or repeated abuse. For others, emotional problems arise because of disrupted attachment and bonding somewhere in their histories. For still others, emotional problems that affect sex are a result of misinformation or lack of information about essential facts of sexual development, or about what it means to be an adult sexual being in an ongoing relationship with another adult sexual being. Although a fact gap can be relatively easy to fill, the emotional fallout from years of living in an informational void can be complex and devastating, and it can lead to a lifetime of missed sexual cues and errant sexual choices.

The emotional quadrant is where clients bring into therapy sessions whatever lies heavy on their hearts. Their sexual explorations here often center on some aspect of desire or loss of desire. These aspects of desire may vary. For some clients, the aspects center on how to intensify sexual intimacy with their partners. For others, they center on how to defuse negative feelings about their partners and/or themselves or how to unhook themselves from searing emotions that keep their hearts guarded and even hardened. Emotional issues may call on therapists to help clients fill in missing information, encourage clearer communication with partners, or explore with clients when and how to end a relationship with the least amount of trauma to themselves, their children, and other family and friends.

What Science Says About the Emotional Aspects of Sex

Sexual science has largely ignored the emotional aspects of sex, perhaps because these aspects are intangible and cannot be counted and measured in the way that physical aspects can. This thought is not original to me. In his 1948 volume on male sexual behavior, Kinsey, the great taxonomer of sex, broached the need for hard science as the reason his team was seeking to investigate only the behavioral aspects of sexual experience, not the emotional aspects.

Enter brain research! Helen Fisher (*Why We Love*) and various of her colleagues have helped put the psychoneurobiology of sex on the map. With brain imaging, even the most literal minded can see that multiple areas of the brain light up when laboratory subjects are asked to remember their feelings of sex, love, romance, or rejection. That said, it is important to understand that brain research is just one piece of the diagnostic puzzle; it does not tell the whole story of sexual experience. As a witty colleague pointed out, the whole brain may light up when you think about an orgasm—but it can also light up when you think about a ham sandwich. Food fantasies aside, brain studies are now showing graphically what many of us already know instinctively: that sexual experience affects us emotionally as well as physically. Fisher's studies routinely report that love is an aphrodisiac and that rejection is a turn-off.

Beginning in the late 1980s, a model of female sexual response that ties emotional intimacy to physical satisfaction has been developed by Rosemary Basson, a psychiatrist from British Columbia. Bassson's premise is based on a radical notion as to her understanding about what women want. According to Basson, desire is not the prime mover of lovemaking (or sex-making). The prime mover is emotional intimacy along with physical connection, and desire may follow these rather than precede them. This is a revolutionary concept, especially for peri-menopausal and menopausal women, who may wait in vain for desire to move them to initiate sexual action, but who may well experience desire once they are aroused. Further, Basson's model of female sexual response is circular, which distinguishes it from Masters and Johnson's linear genital model. This has provided an important distinction for many therapists and their clients because it admits complexity.

Beyond Basson's model and the implications drawn from brain studies, there is relatively little in sexual science to authenticate the significant role played by the emotions—both as they interact with the physiology of sexual stimulation and arousal and as they initiate sexual desire and result from sexual desire. Expanding the practice of sex therapy means helping therapists and clients look beyond physiological measures and generalized theory to acknowledge and explore how the emotional aspects of sexual experience inform the total sexual experience of sexual pleasure—and distress—for each individual client and situation.

What Our Culture Says About the Emotional Aspects of Sex

Our culture offers unrealistic models for the emotions of sexual experience and relationship. These models have changed through the centuries, but they universally depict stereotypes rather than accurate portrayals of sexual complexity. For instance, today's media images tend to show stock responses for performance anxiety along with the excitement generated by sexual conquest and the bliss of romantic love—especially as these focus on a goal of marital bliss. The media also depict the devastating falling apart of excitement, conquest, and bliss. Usually there is a Mars–Venus component to the emotional story, showing that women speak one language (love, longing, and need) and that men speak another (lust, conquest, and invincibility). All bets are off on how the sexual emotions are depicted if the relationship is between two women, two men, a couple that is gender fluid, or a polyamorous group with exotic tastes.

Throughout recorded history, the emotions of sex have fueled art, fiction, poetry, and music. This has made for fabulous art and entertainment and has inspired subtle, soaring, and searing performances over the ages. But pictures, stories, poems, and songs do not necessarily offer a practical template for clients exploring sexual relationships in the twenty-first century. This is especially true when you acknowledge that our present generation of human beings is expected to live longer than any previous generation—meaning that previous ideas about sex and aging are already, well, so "yesterday." So we are inventing new approaches to sex therapy along with new approaches to our lives. Expanding the practice of sex therapy means helping clients look beyond what our culture says about the emotions of sex to discover what is deep in their own hearts and in the hearts of their partners.

Skills Training for Opening the Heart

When clients begin to use the ISIS Wheel to explore their emotions, because sexual performance has been so culturally separated from the emotions, they may have difficulty articulating what issues are before them. Often (but not always) this separation is divided along gender lines, because men and women are socialized so differently. Women often reveal that they are supposed to feel loving and needy but never angry; men often reveal that they are supposed to feel horny but never tender or needy; and on and on. The kinds of issues that arise in therapy may involve skills training for therapists in a number of related areas that help clients open their hearts to their partners—and to themselves. This may include coaching clients to access and express their feelings—through words, eye contact, heart contact, and that indefinable something called "presence."

Sharing Deep Feelings

On the "A" list for exploring the emotional quadrant is the skill of sharing feelings. In the ISIS survey, what most respondents said made sex most satisfying was exactly this emotional skill: the ability to acknowledge their own feelings, communicate these feelings to their partners, and receive feedback in a way that enhanced pleasure, and possibly growth and change as well.

Teaching clients to connect with, share, and witness deep feelings may involve introducing affirmations and appreciations and helping them find the courage to speak from the heart. Teaching about feelings may also include the important notion of appreciating each other's differences—in physical ability, in desire for sex, in whatever seems to act as a barrier between them and sexual satisfaction. Appreciating differences is a concept introduced by Fritz Perls in the 1950s. A basic premise of such appreciation of differences is that true emotional contact incorporates understanding that differences can be a turn *on* as well as a turn *off*. More recently, New York couples therapist Esther Perel raises the question: "Can we be satisfied with what we already have?" She posits that it is often our differences that are most attractive and arousing. Her book *Mating in Captivity* suggests scores of ways to foster what she calls erotic intelligence—even when one's partner is having an affair.

Asking for What You Want

Closely related to the skill of sharing feelings is the skill of asking for what you want—whether it is more sex, less sex, or a different kind of sexual expression. I call this an acquired skill, because it is so often easier said than done. There are very often gender differences at play here, because men and women are socialized so differently about what it is OK to want and how they are expected to ask—and to respond. But I have found that, when all is said and done, the broad strokes of what most human beings want are remarkably similar, at least in long-term intimacy. Among these are acceptance and love, a sense of positive self-image, nurturing, power—and pleasure instead of pain.

For women who have been conditioned to believe that they are second-class citizens, it is difficult to come right out and say "I want . . ." Women who expect to be unheard may resort to age-old wiles of seduction and withholding. Women who need to stay in control of their relationships may feel far too vulnerable to let their partners know what really turns them on, lest this information be used to breach their sexual defenses in moments of passion.

For men who have been conditioned to believe that being a great lover means being self-centered and demanding in and out of the bedroom, the suggestion that they let down their guard may feel literally life-threatening. These men are conditioned to protect and paternalize "the little woman" and to defend their own egos, sometimes to the death of their sex lives. They may need support in overriding what I call the "tenderness taboo," the admission that they want love and affection too; that their hearts need affirmation too; - that they, too, would find it a relief not to be in charge at all times. I always praise the courage of macho-conditioned men for daring to explore the vast and scary new territory of emotions.

When therapists are working with heterosexual couples, it helps to go slow in this area of asking for what you want. Partners may see themselves and each other only in their old culturally prescribed roles. It can take time for them to recognize and trust the new images they find. The operational words here are patience and practice.

Setting Communication Guidelines

Another emotional skill that is essential for clients to learn is how to set their own ground rules for sexual communication. You can start by suggesting that they use "I" statements instead of ascribing their feelings to their partners or others, whether this is blame for their painful feelings or responsibility for their good feelings. "I feel (sad/mad/glad/scared)." "I hear you say." "I want." "I need."

Essential emotional guidelines also involve the intention to listen to one another. There is no pat formula for teaching empathic and compassionate listening. Underlying effective, satisfying listening are honesty and respect—for one's partner and also for one's self.

What you can teach is that listening is not a one-way street. Both partners need equal opportunity to speak. It is not respectful or informative to talk all the time. Neither is it respectful or informative to clam up and not talk at all. And it is important to find a positive way to frame this thought so you are not perceived as coming on like a punitive parent or school marm. As therapists, we can create protected space for a less talkative partner, explaining that both sides of a story need to be expressed if a couple is to be helped appropriately. Given such space, a long-held story may emerge that the silent partner needs to tell and that the other partner needs to hear and honor.

Most important of all, we can model empathic communication by the way we speak and listen, so that we are teaching by our own example.

If we want to intensify our teaching of sexual communication skills to couples, Imago techniques can be helpful. See especially the work of Tammy Nelson, who is both an Imago therapist and a sex therapist and the author of *Getting the Sex You Want*. She and I have collaborated on training teleseminars since 2008.

Finally, I have sometimes found it valuable to introduce the concept of a "safe word" that couples can use if they feel their conversations about sex are spiraling out of control. This should be a word each partner chooses for himself or herself and communicates, with agreement, to the other partner. It is best to pick a word that is not used often and one that does not carry any emotional resonance for either partner. For this reason, words such as "Stop!" or "Enough!" do not necessarily work. A safe word I have used in my own life is "pickle." It is guaranteed to stop conversation and allow a time to regroup.

Ad for a Lover

This is a fun and potentially trenchant exercise that adapts itself easily to individuals, couples, and groups. It can be used as a major focus or as a thought-provoking aside to help expand the frame of emotional reference. One major benefit of this exercise is to help clients identify what they truly want in a sexual relationship—in their hearts and also their bodies, minds, and spirits.

What do clients wish for? "Sensitivity!" "Someone who loves me!" "Dances like a dream!" "Wants kids!" "Doesn't want kids!" and on and on. The more time you allow for this exercise to develop, the deeper your clients will delve into their true desires.

With individuals or couples, you can open up a conversation in the session or assign the writing of a "personal ad" as homework to discuss in the next session. In groups, I may invite each person to create an ad for a lover.

The instruction is simple. Write an ad for the perfect lover—for *you*—a lover who will fill your desires of body, mind, heart, and spirit. Allow 45 minutes for participants to compose their ads. Then I may ask group members to read their ads. Or I may collect the ads, shuffle them, and pass them around to be read aloud anonymously—and responded to after all are read.

In a large group, rather than asking members to write individual ads, I may ask them to call out the qualities popcorn style as I write them on a blackboard or flip chart, so that we can all see the collective overview of desirable (and undesirable) qualities. There may be a long list, which may range from sexy and seductive to insensitive and even abusive acts.

Each of these approaches has its advantages in terms of providing ideas, feedback, and inspiration for participants. Be open for surprises. In one group, when I asked for wished-for qualities in a lover, a woman called out, "A recent pedicure!"

A potentially deeper benefit of this exercise comes at the end. When clients have articulated all of their wishes, I ask them to take the list they have created and apply it to themselves. When they are asked to own the qualities they want and the qualities they reject, there is a clear distinction between the notion of longing for someone outside ourselves who is sensitive, gentle, exciting, creative, and understanding, etc., to the realization that "I am a lover who is capable of embodying all of these qualities I so desire." There may also be a recognition of some insensitivity, withholding, and even cruelty on the part of the client. Both positive and negative qualities will be open for exploration.

Recent pedicure aside perhaps, creating this ad can be a surprising and powerful exercise. The work here is about owning one's projections—and finally understanding the most important aspect of the law of attraction: that the energy one puts out tends to attract similar energy. Love attracts love; rage attracts rage; gloom attracts gloom. This can be a breakthrough notion for some clients, especially those who put themselves down, or who consistently look for affirmation and pleasure to come from outside themselves rather than from within.

I often conclude this exercise with my favorite line from one of Christiane Northrup's talks to empower clients: "The greatest predictor of great sex is a new partner. *So become that new partner!*"

Letter to a Sexual Abuser

For many clients, the dark emotions must be acknowledged and honored before sexual or sensual pleasure can fully flower. There are clients who will greatly benefit from the catharsis of writing a letter to their abuser or abusers, especially a letter they never actually send. Sometimes the perpetrator is an individual, such as a relative or ex-spouse. Sometimes it is society at large.

More than one of my clients has written such a letter to the Catholic Church or the American Medical Association.

You can suggest a letter to an abuser as a free-form exercise, to be written in or out of the therapy office, or you can use the idea in your office with a client speaking the letter to you rather than writing it. It can also be an effective group exercise if this is an issue that concerns all of the clients in your group.

Because writing (or speaking) a letter about one's abusive past can stimulate a tsunami of feelings, I require initial ground rules for this exercise in order to help keep clients from being engulfed in flashbacks or a backlash of trauma. My belief is that emotional growth comes ultimately from strength, not weakness, so I preface the assignment with a few minutes of self-affirmation and grounding for clients before they begin the exercise.

I invite clients to be aware of their breathing and to connect deeply with positive qualities, such as safety, self-esteem, nurturing, power, and pleasure. For clients who are unable to access their own positive qualities, it is important to work with them until they are able to find ways to connect with a positive sense of self. A next step is to give clients specific guidelines for creating their letter. These include a place to begin, a place to end, and plenty of freedom in the middle to say whatever they need to say. It is important for you to tailor these guidelines for each client's specific issues.

I ask clients to complete the following sentences—using however many words they want to write or speak. Since it is understood that this letter is not to be sent, you can emphasize that there are no possible consequences or repercussions to consider beyond the clients' own feelings.

> *Dear* . . . (name the abuser)
>
> *Here's what I learned from you* (e.g., "Women are worthless"/"I am a piece of trash . . . ").
>
> *Here's what I did with what I learned* (e.g., "I put myself down for years"/"I married another abuser"/"I damaged my children . . . ").
>
> *Here's what I plan to do with it in the future* (e.g., "Take myself seriously"/"Love myself"/"Make amends to my children . . . ").
>
> *And furthermore* (whatever else needs to be said . . .).
>
> *Signed* . . . (your name).

If you assign this letter as homework, you can ask individuals or couples to read their letters in the next session, if that feels appropriate. In a group, you can ask participants to read their letters in the group, calling for the kinds of feedback from group members that affirm and empower.

A participant's letter may well trigger fear and anger in another group member. It is crucial to address the emotions of the triggered participant and at the same time to help everyone in the group understand that the true trigger is not the present letter or letter writer, but past events that are returning unbidden. With this kind of understanding, there can be full group support and sharing.

The impact of all these exercises on sex therapy is that they encourage clients to open up emotional and relational issues that affect the locus of desire and dysfunction. The exercises also offer specific ways to invite clients to dig deeply into their own stories and resources. Moreover, the exercises may present opportunities to foster relational understanding and to set boundaries when warranted.

6

THE MENTAL QUADRANT

Exploring Sexual Discernment and Judgments

Activating and Trusting the Analytic Self

The mental quadrant of the ISIS Wheel is where clients express their thoughts and beliefs about their sexual experiences. It includes imagination, intuition, memory, dreams, and fantasies. It includes intentions, wishes, anticipations, and expectations. In its most positive aspects, the mental ISIS experience is characterized by illumination, an open mind, increased understanding, and expanded beliefs about sexual possibilities—at any age, whether or not your clients have partners. Embedded in the mental aspects of sexual experience are some basic questions about sexual identity, orientation, and expression that may determine the course of therapy—as well as the course of a client's life.

But sexual choices are not always easy. One of the singular characteristics of our culture is that its messages sow doubt about our sexuality. Doubt about pleasure. Doubt about our bodies. Doubt about what we feel and what we know. These doubts lodge in our minds to affect our feelings, choices, and actions. So the mental quadrant becomes the container of judgment, guilt and shame—underscored by beliefs and messages instilled in us by a society, a religious practice, or a community moral code that fears sex and its consequences.

A caveat here: You may need to explain (or validate) to clients that, given the incidence of rape, incest, and other monstrous sexual aggressions over the course of human history, sometimes sex is absolutely to be feared. But you can temper this caveat by pointing out that most often the monster is the violence and not the sex. And, very often, it is the negative messages about sex that create that monster.

The truth is that the fear of sexual pleasure is free-floating in much of American culture. This is not surprising when you consider that the United States was pioneered by Puritans. The 1950s definition of Puritanism by the satirist H. L. Mencken—"the haunting fear that someone, somewhere may be happy"—has long resonated with me.

Fear of pleasure is not confined to the US, however. Wilhelm Reich, the father of bioenergetic therapy, was a resident of fascist Germany before he moved to America. He coined a term for this free-floating dread. He named it pleasure anxiety, and he pointed out that, for some people who grow up with repression and sexism, the fear of pleasure may be stronger than fear of pain, illness, or even death.

The task of the sex therapist is to understand how best to help clients who have been brainwashed to believe that they do not deserve pleasure—or, conversely, that they have the right to dominate others sexually regardless of what others may want.

When clients enter therapy, a question that lurks in the minds of many is: "Am I normal?" Another question is: "How much sex is too much? . . . or not enough?" The implication is: "What's wrong with me?" Some clients present with a long list of what they know to be wrong and need to get over, or have the therapist fix for them.

The mental quadrant is where clients can explore those judgments about what sex *should* be like and the self-judgments about where they fall short. When clients can connect their negative and confining judgments to the whole picture that involves their hearts, bodies, and spirits, they are in a much more powerful position to define sex for themselves—what sex means, what pleasure means, what partnership means. With this information, they are also more flexible, able to move from their critical judging minds to their discerning minds and, ultimately, to the minds that illuminate.

What Science Says About How We "Should" Experience Sex

"How many times have you had intercourse in the last week? . . . month? . . . year?" As mentioned in chapter 1, some 700 quantitative sex surveys in the last century have posed these very questions or questions that are similar. Results of these surveys have influenced most of the hypotheses explored by laboratory science. Results of laboratory science have driven the direction of pharmaceutical products from Viagra and its spin-offs to the search for a "pink" Viagra that would incite wild desire for intercourse in previously turned-off women. The outcome of the scientific focus on quantitative inquiry is that the national conversation about sex is limited to performance—that is, penis–vagina intercourse. There is little scientific vocabulary for how sexual experience actually feels and what it means in our lives.

This scenario is, I believe, an unfolding of an interesting paradox in sexology that began as science's attempt to move beyond the moral interpretations of sex so prevalent in the nineteenth and early twentieth centuries. If we can just quantify sexual behavior, the argument went, then we can begin to define sex beyond the moral "shoulds" and "oughts" of organized religion. Yet, in its attempt to move sexual behavior out of the realm of moral judgments, science has created constrictions of its own. It has narrowed the parameters of sexual experience to only those which can be counted and measured.

All of this said, expanding the practice of sex therapy means helping clients look beyond what sex surveys and laboratory reports dictate about what is normal sexual behavior. To open clients' minds to expanded ways of conceptualizing and imagining sexual experience, the sex therapist may need to take on some of the skills of the psychotherapist, the family therapist, and, in certain instances, perhaps the addictions counselor or even the priest or priestess. ISIS practitioners also conduct many forms of therapy, which are outlined in chapter 15.

What Our Culture Says About How We "Should" Experience Sex

Because our national conversation dictates that sex means intercourse, that creates the strong message that the only "normal" or "natural" expression of erotic feelings and impulses is sex between a man and a woman. Anything beyond heterosexual attraction and bonding comes under headings that range from "alternative" to "deviant" to "sick" to "illegal."

Much of the cultural conversation that defines sex so narrowly stems from Judeo-Christian religious definitions, which are characterized by commandments that begin, "Thou shalt *not* . . . ." Where rules and prohibitions apply, I find that religious constructs often belong in the mental rather than the spiritual quadrant. It is vitally important, however, not to make assumptions about how religion affects sexuality for clients and to determine with each client exactly where religion fits for them on the ISIS Wheel.

Closely attached to the notion of sexual *shoulds* is the Mars–Venus double standard that delivers the perennial messages "Good girls don't" and "Real men score"—the gender discrepancy that locks many of us into a kind of cultural missionary position, man on top—as outlined in chapter 1.

From various quarters, I hear the belief that there is no double standard anymore—now that women have the vote and a few members in Congress and the Supreme Court. But my experience says that the double standard is still alive wherever sexual mores and customs are concerned and that it may affect our clients, sometimes profoundly. When women bring into therapy their issues regarding dysfunctional intercourse and low desire, both often boil down to the phrase "There's something wrong with *me*." This sense of personal disenfranchisement goes way beyond sex therapy. The deep-seated conviction that women are intrinsically defective echoes cultural beliefs over the centuries. Simone de Beauvoir named it "the second sex," which was the title of her groundbreaking 1949 study of inequality and otherness.

The latest edition of the Boston Women's Health Collective's *Our Bodies, Ourselves* (OBOS) cites increasing immediacy in the need to define sexual experience as a women's story as well as a story told by men and by the scientific models based on male experience. In my recent conversation with social worker Joan Ditzion, one of the OBOS founders, she states:

> There is a major transition going on in our culture with regard to sexual power balances between men and women. We need to help shape it and change the underlying sexism in our culture, balance the positive with the problematic realities without giving in to gender bias, and embrace the diversity and complexity of our lives.

Even beyond the male–female double standard about sex, all of us grow up with the cultural message that sex is dirty and erotic pleasure is downright bad—whether we are young, old, or somewhere in between. The truth is that our culture is still a training ground for every man, woman, and child to grow up believing "I'm not normal." When we are young and our hormones are leading us to sexual experimentation, we are told: "Just say No!"—especially if we are women. Then, when we hit 50, 60, or 70 we get the message that there is something wrong with us if we are not craving hot sex. We are urged to buy hormones, creams, and pills to get back on track (see the science section of the physical quadrant).

A more poignant and dangerous permutation of this "I'm not normal" thinking is self-blame. I hear this especially from women: "The reason he doesn't love me is that I'm too . . . (fat/thin, big/small, turned-off/turned-on . . . "). "If only I were more (or less) . . . , he wouldn't hit me/he wouldn't cheat on me/he wouldn't beat me, abandon me, kill me."

Expanding the practice of sex therapy means helping clients look beyond what our culture says about how sex *should* be experienced, so they can begin to make these decisions for themselves.

Skills Training for Opening the Mind

Thought creates form. For some clients, it is here in the mental quadrant that the process of healing begins. There are many ways to help clients let go of negative judgments about what sex *should* be like and expand their beliefs about themselves as sexual beings. One route to expanding the mind is reading, and I refer you to the books in the bibliography and to the burgeoning resources available on the Internet. Films and DVDs are another way to help clients open their minds. As you run an Internet search on what is available, you will find a range from romantic stories to hard porn. All of these genres have aficionados and detractors. Rather than pass judgment on the genres, I encourage most clients to explore these for themselves and come to their own assessments.

I do offer a caveat about watching Internet porn, however. For some clients, getting sucked into porn sites can become obsessive, even addictive, to the point of interfering with their intimate relationships, their lives, and their jobs. There are reasons for this. First, porn is designed to excite the imagination with unrealistic examples of what sex can offer. Second, watching porn is easy. It offers maximum stimulation without requiring any relational participation from the viewer. Wendy and Larry Maltz offer thoughtful suggestions about the complexities of this subject in *The Porn Trap*.

Take a Creative Sex History—With Feeling

On a more personal level, I encourage you to encourage your clients to explore their own sex histories—alone, or with you as a guide.

A sex history consists of much more than the usual count-and-measure questions such as: "How many times have you had intercourse in the last week/month/year?" Below are some deeper questions to ask your clients to ask themselves—and to answer for themselves in an honest way, both factually and with feeling. This exercise is not so much about your clients being able to answer these questions correctly. It is more about expanding their sense of what questions to ask themselves and gaining clear directions as to how they might explore these questions during their lives.

Begin by inviting your client to take a self-history. Questions might include some basics.

What is sex? Does it always mean penis–vagina intercourse? Or are there some other ways to express my erotic feelings and longings? What about masturbation? Oral–genital stimulation? Anal stimulation? All-over massage? Making eye-contact across a crowded room? Does sex always have to include orgasm? Is there anything *more* than orgasm? Does sex have to go downhill once I reach 50? 60? 70? Or beyond? Is there such a thing as Lesbian Bed Death? What about Lesbian Bed *Life*? What is sexual beyond the bedroom?

When, how, and with whom does sex feel right to me? This is a question that literally haunts some clients who come into sex therapy. Perhaps the haunting is due to rigidity of religious backgrounds or to strict social upbringing. Perhaps it is culturally induced, by such time-honored traditions as compulsory monogamy or arranged marriage. The truth is that some clients long for sexual expressions that go far beyond the scenario of "girl marries boy, and they live happily or unhappily until death do them part." For a percentage of clients, satisfying their sexual longings may mean engaging in affairs outside of the commitment of marriage. For others it may mean "kink" behaviors such as bondage or sado-masochism (S/M) within or outside of their committed relationship. Or it may mean "poly" relationships (as in "polyamory"—that is, having more than one intimate relationship at once).

Exploring these options in any depth is beyond the scope of this book, but a Google search will reveal thousands of websites to help you further your journey.

Am I male? Am I female? Am I something else? And what does that mean? This is a question that is becoming more and more relevant as we learn more and more about the broad variety of intersexed conditions—check out the Intersex Society of North America (www.isna.org). An estimated one in every 2,000 infants comes into the world with genitalia ambiguous enough to make it diffi-cult for them to be classified as definitively male or female. Historically, there has been routine intervention to "correct" surgically any sexual ambiguities at birth. This intervention has proven to create enormous disruption for the child and eventual adult. Recently, medical thinking is to leave infants' genitals alone, allowing the child to determine his or her own experience of gender during the process of maturing.

Am I transgender? An estimated one in 30,000 to 100,000 of Americans has a sense of having been born into the wrong body—a condition labeled gender dysphoria. The number of these who actually transition from male to female (MtF) or female to male (FtM) is notoriously difficult to track. This is partly because gender reassignment surgeries vary greatly in procedure. Further, many trans persons do not pursue surgery at all and rely only on hormones to help them transition. Others use no drugs or surgery. For more information, see www.surgeryencyclopedia.com/Pa-St/Sex-Reassignment-Surgery.html.

What is my sexual orientation? Am I heterosexual? Lesbian? Gay? Bisexual? Queer? Research shows that many human beings are gender fluid over their lifetimes— meaning that they may change their sexual orientation rather than remain com-mittedly heterosexual or homosexual. The term "queer" generally means that one's sexual attitudes and possibly behaviors are far from the cultural main-stream—what I call "living curly in a straight culture." Queer is a variable term, however. For instance, queer in New York City's Greenwich Village may mani-fest very differently from queer in Peachtree City, Georgia. Again, the data are primarily speculative here, depending on who is asking the questions and tabu-lating the numbers. To help your clients pursue this question, check out Lisa Diamond's *Gender Fluidity*, along with the website www.avert.org/gay-people.htm.

Activate the Sexual Imagination

There is no one right way to activate anyone's sexual imagination, and it is important to note that sometimes negative information as well as positive information needs to emerge. Here are a few suggestions to get your clients started. Invite your clients to:

- Write down all the names they can think of for: *women who love sex, men who love sex, young people who love sex,* and *older people who love sex.* Which ISIS quadrant do they associate with each of the names they write? Where did their attitudes about each of these names come from?
- List their thoughts about: *sex before marriage, affairs, divorce.* Which ISIS quadrant do they associate with their thoughts about premarital sex, marriage, and fidelity? Where did their attitudes about these originate? Have their attitudes changed over time?
- Remember a sexual fantasy or dream or memory that turns them on. Explore this from each ISIS quadrant.
- Tell their sexual story to a partner or a friend—and listen to their partner's or friend's sexual story; use the ISIS template to help you help them organize their stories.

All of these subjects—and more—have been the focus of countless books, films, journal articles, and blogs. Here is not the place to go into details. My point is that, as clients expand their minds to explore new sexual horizons, it is in the mental quadrant that much of the work about expanding these horizons may be initiated, or even completed. At its most connected, experience in the mental quadrant can illuminate and expand. It is gratifying to see, as a therapist, that even a small opening in a client's entrenched beliefs about sexuality can allow a flood of light to pour in.

7

THE SPIRITUAL QUADRANT

Exploring Sexual Connection and Disconnection

Making Meaning from Chaos

In American culture, the concepts of sex and spirit are split. For some of our clients there is no connecting the two. That said, it is important to define terms before we begin discussing the spiritual quadrant of the ISIS Wheel.

In popular culture, sex is physical. It is dirty. We do it in the dark. Our conversation involves jokes and bragging about conquests. By contrast, spirituality is pure. It is moral and irreproachable. We do it on hallowed ground; no joking allowed.

The term spirituality is often conflated with religion. For some clients, exploring the spiritual quadrant of the ISIS Wheel does include religious experience, but for most clients it includes something other than religion, at least once they understand their spirituality in the context of the entire Wheel. In truth, the concept of spirituality may mean many things to many people. For this reason, it is important to make no assumptions about how clients define it and how it affects their sexual experience. I routinely ask clients what spirituality means to them, and I accept their definitions. Sometimes I encourage them to expand on these definitions if I feel it might help them explore their own issues more effectively. For our purposes here, I take the following definitions and descriptions of spiritual experience from ISIS survey respondents as well as from common usage.

Spirituality means a sense of direct, personal connection with the Divine (however one defines Divine) as distinct from a mediated connection of the Divine through organized religion, with its cultural traditions and rules. In terms of sexuality, the spiritual quadrant involves an intimate sense of connection with one's self, one's partner, and/or a power beyond one's self—whatever clients may chose to name that: God, Goddess, Higher Power, Tree, Wolf, and so on. In its most positive sense, the spiritual ISIS experience is characterized by ecstasy, increased energy, heightened meaning, and a sense of enduring satisfaction.

The spiritual quadrant is also the path of disconnection and control. It is here that clients will be examining and re-evaluating a variety of "irrational facts" about their sexual responses and relationships. These may range from religious and cultural messages to aspects of abuse and trauma that have wounded their spirits as well as their bodies, minds, and emotions.

What are indications that it would be useful for clients to explore the spiritual quadrant? When clients present with a sense of disconnection, isolation, depression, dissociation, and/or not knowing why they do the things they do, I make a special effort to guide them to explore the spiritual quadrant. I also urge clients to explore the spiritual quadrant when they present with a problematic need to dominate a partner, or to be subservient to a partner, or to keep themselves or their relationship inflexibly controlled. All of these issues have their roots in connection and meaning.

In addition, I have found it useful to help clients explore the spiritual quadrant to seek a new level of what they may already have explored in the emotional and mental quadrants, such as fear, rage, judgments, blame, and self-blame—also ecstatic union. It is in the spiritual quadrant that they may discover unique routes to understanding and forgiveness that relate both to others and to themselves.

Helping clients delve deeply into these kinds of issues of sexual connection and meaning lies beyond the scope of cognitive behavioral sex therapy. Expanding the practice of sex therapy into the spiritual quadrant may involve every one of the skills a therapist has acquired in psychotherapy, sex therapy, energy healing, and spiritual counseling.

What Science Says About Sex and Spirituality

Sexual science has a great deal to say about religion as a repressive factor in sexual expression. But it has little to say about spirituality—as it is impossible to measure spiritual experience by most of the evidence-based methods that require quantitative data. An exception is the evidence-based method of brain imaging. Komisaruk, Beyer-Flores, and Whipple (*The Science of Orgasm*) demonstrate that the temporal lobe (the locus of spiritual connection) lights up on genital stimulation. Still to be explored by brain researchers, however, are the spiritual implications of sexual relationship.

Even though spiritual experience lies beyond the paradigm of evidence-based research, my clinical experience regards it as essential if sexual growth and change is to involve more than physical performance—a view affirmed by depth psychologist Jenny Wade, for one, whose book *Transcendent Sex* enumerates a fascinating spectrum of what can happen when "lovemaking opens the veil."

Telling layers of their stories in each quadrant of the ISIS Wheel encourages clients to explore how their spiritual beliefs and practices impact their sexual beliefs and practices. The client's journey around the Wheel intrinsically connects physical, emotional, mental, and relational experience by offering the large picture—the connections and meanings of sex. In that sense, expanding the practice of sex therapy means helping clients to create their own science in the pure sense of the word: knowledge.

What Our Culture Says About Sex and Spirituality

Much of the cultural divisions between sex and spirituality are dictated by religion. Most of the major world religions teach that sexuality and spirituality are in some way separate. Each religious doctrine has its own way of expressing this separateness, but there is a general sense of a dualistic cosmology in which both spiritual and sexual experience are controlled by rules and roles, proscriptions and prescriptions. Spirituality means morally pure, a path to heaven, to Nirvana, to the Shekina. On the other hand, sexual experience is earthbound—literally defined by dirt—animal, brutish.

Negative implications of the religious control of sexuality are hinted at by the remark of an ISIS respondent struggling with her rigidly religious upbringing: "Man, Catholicism sure can screw up one's pleasure thoughts."

The flip side of this dualistic view was expressed by a generous handful of ISIS respondents from a range of denominations who observed that their religious training was actually helpful to their sexual experience. They reported that the faith and love instilled by their religious education helped them to hang in with difficult relationships until they could find a positive path. An example of how this counter-intuitive idea functions comes from a Methodist minister colleague, who speaks of her religious experience offering her "rules that work." She sees the various articles of faith as providing parameters within which she can explore her partnership more deeply. Similarly, Peggy Kleinplatz and David Ribner, who are scholars and colleagues, are both eloquent in describing the role of religion in promoting spiritual dimensions of sexual relationship.

Tantra and Other Eastern Approaches

A discussion of sexuality, spirituality, and religion must include Tantra, a sexual practice with a religious base in ancient Hindu and Buddhist texts. The major teaching of Tantra is that sex is a path to the Divine. I invite you to investigate the vast literature on Tantric sexuality, which ranges from erudite tracts to contemporary couples workshops that teach techniques such as eye-gazing, chakra balance, worship of the genitals, and ways to extend orgasm—all without a goal of intercourse or injunctions about procreation or monogamous commitment. Closely related to Tantric practices are other Eastern approaches to sexual energy, such as the Chinese Tao. Their practices and approaches clearly fit into the ISIS Wheel and are reflected in suggestions throughout this book.

If we take a steep dive back into human history, we find that the very earliest religious rites provide other exceptions to the religious negation of sexual expression. Here we find that sexual celebration and ceremony were part and parcel of religious ritual (true, by the way, of some pagan and indigenous religious rites today). We find religions in which both sex and spirit are routinely embodied in deities, such as Shakti and Shiva, the Divine Couple of India, Oshun, the Yoruban goddess of love, and of course Isis, the Egyptian goddess known as Initiator into the Sexual Mysteries, who has lent her name to the ISIS template for expanding the practice of sex therapy. In some of the ancient and indigenous practices, we also find a body–mind–heart–spirit continuum, which includes the medicine wheel on which the ISIS model is based.

The Language of Sex and Spirit

One way therapists may find religion influencing clients' experience of the spiritual quadrant is through language—or sometimes through the lack of language. Many clients have only religious terms to describe their spiritual experiences: "worship," "prayer," and "sacrifice," for example. While some clients find that terms such as these also match their sexual experiences, this is not so for all clients. Many are at a loss for words to describe their spiritual experiences, let alone their experiences of sex and spirit. Some say this is because their experience runs too deep for words.

True though this may be, I see an additional dynamic at play here: the collective arrogance of those religions that effectively excommunicate all personal connection with spirit. This can produce lasting conflict about spirituality. I have often found clients to be as anxious about divulging the depths of their personal spiritual longings and experience as they are about divulging their sexual longings and experience.

In addition, clients may be offended by certain kinds of spiritual language just as they may be with certain kinds of sexual language. For example, many ISIS respondents referred to their experiences of sexual–spiritual connection in New Age terms such as "life-force energy," "oneness with self, partner, and nature," "inner visions," "communication with divine forces," and "experiencing one's self as part of all that is sacred." A client who is firmly ensconced in the mental quadrant of linear thought will likely have problems with this language and find it unclear or meaningless, easy to dismiss as "woo-woo." This becomes a problem, for instance, when a New-Age-speaking wife tries to tell her linear husband what might excite her in bed. This couple may need a skilled therapist to help open his mind, or help her translate her longing for spiritual connection into more grounded and linear terms—perhaps "excitement" instead of "life-force energy," or "inspiration" instead of "communication with divine forces."

As always, ISIS work is about helping clients find their own way, in their own terms. In the spiritual quadrant, the work is sometimes about helping clients develop new terms to convey their own meanings—likewise for therapists. Familiarity with the subject of spiritual and sexual energy can offer valuable insights when it comes to your clients' journeys in the spiritual quadrant of the ISIS Wheel.

Ultraconservative Belief Systems

A possible complexity in exploring the spiritual quadrant may arise with clients who possess ultraconservative religious beliefs about sex. Hundreds of conservative, fundamentalist, and evangelical respondents in the ISIS survey spoke movingly about ecstatic sexual experiences within the acceptable bonds of marriage. Interestingly, however, others spoke of heightened pleasure from behaviors that were considered sinful by their church—such as sex before marriage, affairs, and same-sex relationships. Again, the ISIS approach is about putting aside assumptions and encouraging clients to discover what is important and useful in their own stories, even if these clients maintain that certain behaviors are intrinsically sinful.

Even a cursory understanding of the complex historical and cultural shifts involved in the connections between sexuality and spirituality has affirmed my notion that expanding the practice of sex therapy means looking beyond cultural dualism to explore the connections of sexual experience and life experience. This means listening with great care and sensitivity, however your clients interpret the scientific and religious "truths" about the spiritual aspects of sex.

Skills Training For Opening Spiritual Awareness in Sexual Relationships

For ISIS respondents and many others, erotic satisfaction may involve oneness with self and partner, and also a power greater than both, whether that is called God, Goddess, Higher Power, or whatever. This sense of oneness differs from a co-dependent kind of merging, where power comes from the outside—and which invariably leaves one or both partners feeling powerless. The kind of oneness that leads to connection and meaning is characterized by spiritual awareness. Experiencing this for the first time may feel scary for clients. This is where the ISIS template can be helpful, offering clients a visual and cognitive frame for their experience. A woman who experienced a week with the ISIS Wheel at Esalen Institute writes:

> The grounded physical interaction with the Wheel we shared concretized the work for me in a very profound way. What we shared as a group embraced all the dimensions and bodies. This is big! To say that I'm grateful is not near strong enough for the impact and permanent changes that occurred.

Sometimes this fluid and ecstatic sense of oneness occurs spontaneously. It is possible to open oneself to this state quite consciously, however. Consider the exercises below.

Meditation: Opening Your Heart and Mind to Sacred Pleasure

Meditation and guided imagery can help clients experience connections between sexual energy and spiritual energy. One of my supervisees mentioned that she often began therapy sessions by playing for her clients a short meditation by Jack Canfield. I affirmed to her that it can be beneficial to help clients bring their full energy into the therapy room by starting a session with meditation. But I also reminded her that it is important to remember that no one approach fits all. While Jack Canfield may be just the ticket for some clients, what works for others may be music, a grounding exercise, a yoga stretch, or some other meditative form.

I encourage you to create your own meditation and guided visualizations and to tailor them directly to your clients. Further, you can create personalized meditations with your clients in language that will speak directly to them, because you will be using their own words and images. You can focus on full body presence, gratitude, beauty, light, and/or whatever your clients need to expand the connections between sexuality and spirituality. You can begin by suggesting they explore body, mind, heart, and spirit—essentially guiding them to journey around the ISIS Wheel to learn whatever is right for them from each quadrant at this moment.

Energy Balancing

Basic to the understanding of spiritual awareness in sexual relationships is the notion of energy—the invisible, but often palpable, force that moves us, inspires us, attracts us, repels us, turns us on sexually, and also turns us off. Before helping clients balance the flow of sexual energy in their relationships, it is first essential to assist each individual to be aware of his or her energy flow.

One way to help clients understand the concept of energy is through the chakra system, an ancient spiritual approach that charts the energy centers in our body and also the energy fields that radiate beyond our physical bodies. The study of chakras is complex and interwoven with spiritual practices, but you do not have to be a chakra adept to use some basic concepts to help your clients.

Combining even a simple explanation of chakras with the ISIS Wheel can help couples show each other where their energies are focused. There are at least seven energy centers in the human system; some say there are many more. In the simplest form, you can ask clients to explore the following energies in each quadrant of the ISIS Wheel.

The first chakra (base of the spine) and the energies of "I am."
The second chakra (the sexual organs) and the energies of "I feel."
The third chakra (the solar plexus) and the energies of "I want."
The fourth chakra (the heart) and the energies of "I love."
The fifth chakra (the throat) and the energies of "I communicate."
The sixth chakra (the third eye) and the energies of "I see."
The seventh chakra (the crown of the head) and the energies of "I know."

Ask clients to stand in each quadrant of the Wheel and speak about each of the seven energies outlined above. Or ask them to speak of each of the seven energies and move on the Wheel to where they experience the energies of love, communication, etc. If you are working with a couple, you can use the guide to help each partner sense his or her own energies, then be able to play with them to meet the energies of the other. To emphasize the concept of play, I sometimes describe this as a game of hide and seek: "If you wanted this energy to be found, how would you express it? If you wanted it to remain hidden how would you express that? If you wanted your energies to play with each other, what would you have to do?"

To deepen this exercise, ask your clients to communicate the answers through body movement only, without talking. Allowing the body's intelligence to come forth in this way can produce profound spiritual insights.

Energy balancing is especially relevant when couples present with discrepancies of sexual desire they are not able to change just by talking about their likes and dislikes. A presenting problem for many couples is that one partner wants much more (or less) sexual interaction than the other. For the sake of illustration, imagine that one partner is beaming out a wide spectrum of heart energy, the center for love and compassion—which manifests in the emotional and spiritual quadrants. And imagine that the other partner's energies are focused squarely in the sexual organs, the center for physical feeling and gratification— which manifest in the physical quadrant. The fact that energy is concentrated in different places may result in such common complaints as: "My partner just isn't interested in sex" or "My partner just wants to use me as a sex toy."

But what is actually occurring may not be a discrepancy of sexual desire. Rather, it may be a discrepancy in each partner's lead system and a discrepancy in communication. In this instance, both partners may be desiring sexual connection, but they may be manifesting their desire with different energy coming from different places. Helping them understand and feel and communicate and play with the energies in themselves and their partners can seem like a magical intervention. If you want to look further into the intricacies of chakra energies, a user-friendly guide is Anodea Judith's *Wheels of Life*.

Tantric Techniques

To open clients to the spiritual aspects of sexual experience, it can be helpful to suggest some techniques that are usually associated with Tantra. This is not the place to go into the intricacies of Tantra, other than to refer you to books by Margo Anand and Kenneth Ray Stubbs and the plethora of information on the Internet, and to urge all sex therapists to be aware of Tantric techniques and of the many courses offered on Tantra and other energetic approaches to sexual energy. The following techniques, which are drawn from Tantra, can help couples open both sexual and spiritual energies to each other.

- *Breathing together* One way I describe breathing for sexual and spiritual awareness is to experience the inward breath as *inspiration*—a taking in of these energies, and the outward breath as *expiration*—a letting go of that which is no longer needed or wanted. This is a personal energy exchange—a cleansing and taking on that can occur naturally thousands of times a day. When a couple breathes together with the intention of inspiration and letting go, I call that *con-spiracy*—a coming together in a deep, sacred, and often sexual way.

  A simple way to help partners attune their sexual energy is by suggesting that they hold each other—naked or clothed—and breathe in unison until they feel that they are both inhaling and exhaling with one breath . . . in perfect conspiracy. This creates a way for partners to connect without words, with no goal of sexual performance or notion that one partner wants something the other cannot or will not deliver. You can suggest they try this attunement in your office at first if they seem to need your encouragement and guidance—and of course they will be clothed if they do a practice run in your office.
- *Eye-gazing* This is another way of attuning energies without words, especially if it is practiced after partners have synchronized their breathing.

Looking deeply into each other's eyes can move partners to find new depths of their sexual and spiritual energies. When suggesting eye-gazing to clients, it may be useful to acknowledge that such intensity can bring up anxiety. The point is for each partner to keep returning to center—focusing on their breathing, and closing their eyes if necessary, until they feel ready to open again to gazing. When couples can move beyond the anxiety, they can sometimes see deeply into their own and each other's depths.

- *Yab Yum* Another classic Tantric position is "Yab Yum." Ask the couple to sit face to face, torsos connected—hearts, and genitals touching—with arms around each other and one partner's thighs over those of the other. Yab Yum can be a balancing challenge for newbies or for partners who are not slim and agile or who have other physical challenges. Suggest that they shore themselves up with pillows and try different permutations of the position that feel most comfortable and doable. If partners keep their sense of humor, positioning themselves into Yab Yum can feel like childhood play, which can add its own frisson of excitement.

- *Spoon position—keeping it simple* This is my version of Tantra Lite—a connecting exercise for partners who are not drawn to esoteric practices. Suggest that partners breathe together, lying down in "spoon position"—with one partner's chest and belly against the other partner's back and buttocks, knees bent and legs connected at thighs and all the way down to the toes. This is a lovely practice for partners to do in bed before going to sleep, attuning themselves to enter dreamtime together. It is also a delicious way for partners to wake together in the morning, to begin the day connected in both spirit and body.

To coordinate any of these practices with the ISIS Wheel, ask clients to explore their reactions and responses in terms of body, heart, mind, and spirit. It may be particularly useful for partners to move around the Wheel to show each other their responses. In this way, couples can expand their capacity for understanding themselves and each other, and also expand their vocabulary for sexual and spiritual communication as they begin to attune both to their own energy and to that of their partner.

8

THE CENTER

Exploring Sexual Integration and Transformation

The Shadow and the Light

The center of the ISIS Wheel is where body, mind, heart, and spirit merge. Clearly, the experience of the center cannot be described through evidence-based methods because it is not a quantitative entity. The experience of integration and transformation is subjective, a process for each client to define for herself or himself. And the experience may differ from person to person and from time to time.

Some clients describe a state of ecstatic oneness. Others describe an extraordinary sense of knowing and ability to commune with a partner. Others describe a kind of high-definition Oz—a vividly colored landscape in which a partner may or may not factor. Others express the kind of shape-shifting Jenny Wade describes in *Transcendent Sex*, where the veil between the worlds literally dissolves into a vortex of timelessness, light, and lightness of being. Many say that their experience is that there is no past and no future here, only a greatly expanded now. Still others describe it as a place of clarity and vision, of vastness, of unconditional love. In *The Heart and Soul of Sex*, I have written in detail about the center of the ISIS Wheel, with descriptions from both clients and survey respondents.

The experience of the center is way beyond physical orgasm. It is where we open to ultimate connections with ourselves, our partners, and the universe. At its most positive, the center of the ISIS Wheel is a place of magic, beauty, love, altruism, and bliss. It is filled with understanding and purpose and may include spontaneous healing of physical, psychic, or relational distress. This is also a place of divinity, where some people experience direct connection with the cosmos. I have come to call the center the place of "O God!"—because this is the phrase we cry out in bedrooms across the land at the moment of sexual ecstasy.

There is another aspect of the "O God!" experience. Carl Jung called it the shadow side—the experience of pain and repression of pain, of the feared and the unexplored. It is when sex falls apart. Call it *"Oh GOD! . . . "* Therapists recognize this voice when clients come in expressing the agony of despair, the terror of sexual violence and abuse, the burden of shame, guilt, loneliness, isolation—and dysfunction. This shadow side can be a place of dissociation as well as of association. When physical, emotional, mental, and spiritual experience meet in shadow, the combination can blow our circuits, especially if there is unresolved density and negativity. One client named it "the valley of the shadow of death."

With some clients, I have found that it is only when they can walk deep enough into this valley of their shadows that they can find their way to the full experience of pleasure. Sometimes they can literally reframe pain into pleasure: "It was only when I could dive into my anger at my stepfather that I could move past my numbness and come through to a place of discovering my body again, and also my soul," remarked a client who had struggled with low libido. Throughout this book we will look at ways to use the ISIS template to help guide our clients through the dark valleys of their own lives.

On a less dire note, the shadow aspect of the center is where desire discrepancies may emerge full blown. One partner may be having transformational experiences that the other partner has no idea about, does not understand, cannot share in, and may actually be disturbed by. Here, it is important to validate the experience of both partners. One of the valuable uses of the Wheel is to help desire-discrepant couples find ways to acknowledge each other and communicate effectively with each other. Numerous examples of these ways are spelled out in chapters 10 and 12.

What Science Says About the Merging of Body, Mind, Heart, and Spirit

Sexual science has largely ignored the integrative and transformative aspects of sexual experience. This is another area that remains unexplored in sexual science because it is impossible to count or measure. Even for those who have experienced these integrative and transformative aspects, it may be difficult to find language to describe them. ISIS survey respondents continually use phrases such as: "This is beyond words" and "I have no way of expressing my feelings about this."

By way of illustration, ISIS respondents use decidedly non-scientific language to express this merging when they refer to sexual experience as "a revelation," "a sacrament," "luminescent," "mind-blowing," "sacred," "holy," filled with "spontaneous healing." For some it feels like "making love with the universe." All-encompassing sexual experiences such as these can be life-changing in the most positive sense. Some clients report a problem with so much positive change, however. They say they feel "crazy" because they have no frame of reference for it, and often little language. These experiences may leave them feeling alienated from themselves and their partners instead of close and connected. It is essential that therapists recognize both the joy and the disequilibrium that can result from ecstatic experience, and gently encourage clients and their partners to incorporate into their lives delicious feelings like hope, ecstasy, and a sense of connection with the universe.

Contemporary psychological science has also largely ignored the integrative and transformational aspects of sexual experience, as there is no place for it in the realm of evidence-based practice and cognitive behavioral therapy. That said, consider Abraham Maslow's theory of peak experiences and self-actualization in the mid-twentieth century (in his *Toward a Psychology of Being*); more recently, Mihaly Csikszentmihalyi's book *Flow: The Psychology of Optimal Experience*; and, far more recently, sex researcher Peggy Kleinplatz's explorations of optimal experiences—see her edited volume *New Directions in Sex Therapy* (2012).

For a breath of fresh air, enter twenty-first-century brain research. I draw particularly on the work of Barry Komisaruk and Beverly Whipple, along with their various collaborators who have contributed over the years to the studies that culminated in *The Science of Orgasm*. Their laboratory studies with women show that sexual stimulation and orgasm activate multiple regions of the brain—not just the centers of physical reward and gratification but also (and most importantly for ISIS consciousness) the centers of emotional, spiritual, and cognitive response.

This is a major breakthrough in sex research, for it supports the notion that physical stimulation invokes much more than only physical sensation. It also invokes thoughts and fears, joy and surprise, memories and dreams, pain and pain relief, along with religious ecstasy, discernment, and anticipation of reward and punishment. Moreover, it shows that all of these occur whether or not we are consciously aware that all of them are happening. Since brain studies clearly show the interactivity of sexual response, all of these events are happening in sequence as they trigger one another, though, when they are happening in you, you may perceive that they are occurring all at once.

The bottom line here is that it is imperative that therapists listen closely to clients and affirm their experiences, positive as well as problematic and negative. Expanding the practice of sex therapy means helping clients trust their own experiences. This may involve assisting them to look beyond the lack of scientific information and language about the transformative and integrative aspects of sexual experience. An enormous complexity of events can engage our bodies, minds, hearts, and spirits. Sometimes we notice them all, but much of the time we may not. It is the responsibility and creative edge of the wise clinician to help clients articulate the experience so that they can acknowledge their own erotic perceptions without feeling crazy or isolated, and incorporate them into their lives.

What Our Culture Says About the Merging of Body, Mind, Heart, and Spirit

The problem of feeling crazy and isolated when one opens up to the positive experience of the center is, I believe, based in the sexual proscriptions and prescriptions of our culture, as mentioned earlier in this chapter.

First, the language of ecstasy ("connection," divinity," and so forth) has been relegated to the language of religion. When words like these are used to describe sexual experience, they often create a sense of cognitive dissonance—a contradiction in terms which may negate the nuances of sex–spirit connection. Second, the sex-negativity of our culture dictates that, in terms of sex, shadow language—which focuses on dominance, ownership, and conquest—is more usual than the language of ecstasy. In my experience, this becomes especially problematic for women. For, throughout history, women have found that sisterhood is more easily formed through mutual oppression than through mutual ecstasy (after all, we are the "second sex," as Simone de Beauvoir so trenchantly pointed out). Perhaps a parallel issue for men might be the band-of-brothers bonding on the battlefield and the playing field. I have heard some men describe this as ecstatically and divinely sensual—beyond an urge for specific sexual performance.

Gender differences aside, expanding the practice of sex therapy means helping clients look beyond what our culture says about the transformative and integrative aspects of sexual experience to trust what they experience in their own bodies, hearts, minds, and spirits.

Skills Training for Validating Integration and Transformation

When clients describe experiences that are at the center of the ISIS Wheel, the fully aware sex therapist will need to move beyond strictly evidence-based clinical training and call on some of the qualities usually associated with energy healers and/or spiritual counselors. The qualities I have in mind are the ability to tune in to feelings and the ability to notice shifts in energy.

I do not believe all sex therapists need to possess extraordinary powers. But I do believe that all sensitive clinicians need to be able to accept that there are qualitative differences between performance-based sex and the kind of multidimensional connections some clients may experience—whether these clients' experiences are positive or negative. Being able to acknowledge a client's full experience rather than diagnosing it, limiting it, challenging it, or dismissing it goes a long way toward building client confidence in the therapy process, not to mention the enjoyment of life beyond therapy.

Therapists need to understand that we cannot all have experienced everything in the human condition, let alone be experts in it. So what are we to do in order to exercise our helpful natures? We can refer to other practitioners.

We can encourage clients to explore their connections of sexuality and spirituality through workshops, books, and other means. The clinical skills here involve a combination of acceptance, openness, and generosity. The bottom line for clinicians is: give yourself permission to accept that there is a vast erotic terrain beyond what science and the culture say about sex—beyond intercourse, beyond orgasm, perhaps even beyond sexual ecstasy. And, as always, listen closely to your clients and allow them to be your teachers.

In Part III you will find detailed ways to expand your own practice of sex therapy. The chapters that follow address four core dynamics of ISIS practice, along with practical applications of the ISIS approach in group settings, in therapy sessions with individuals and couples, and in enhancing your own evolution as a therapist.

Part III

THE ISIS PRACTICE

A Guide to Clinical Use

This 15 minutes of ISIS work is worth 15 years of therapy.
ISIS Client

9

CORE DYNAMICS OF ISIS PRACTICE—AND WAYS TO IMPLEMENT THEM

The ISIS approach to sex therapy is based on four core dynamics: creating and holding space, directing movement, creating ritual, and concretizing abstract concepts. The purpose of these core dynamics is to externalize clients' problems in order to change the story. The processes by which these core dynamics work include raising awareness and providing both rationale and method for encouraging clients to find their own solutions, rather than having therapists focus on pathology and prescribe treatment. These general purposes will be recognized by therapists who practice narrative therapy.

Because ISIS practice evolved from the medicine-wheel tradition I practice, its core dynamics are rooted in spiritual practices that have been used in many cultures over the ages for personal growth and transformation. The essential elements of these practices translate into contemporary clinical language and into distinct strategies that today's clinicians can use to expand their practice of sex therapy. In this chapter, I focus on these therapeutic strategies. For readers interested in exploring the spiritual principles of ISIS practice, I refer you to a sequel to this book that I am currently writing: *Sex Therapy Meets Shamanism*.

Core Dynamic #1: Creating and Holding Space

A fundamental role of the sex therapist is to create and hold special energetic space for clients. By this I mean a space that offers clients permission to explore the depth and breadth of their sexual experience. Equally, I mean a space that provides a defining boundary for clients, a safety net so they do not fall off the edge of their known world no matter how far their therapeutic journey may take them. For some clients, this space can feel like stepping over a threshold into another world—a world of insight, inspiration, fluidity, and sometimes fear of the unknown. In psychoneurological terms, this is called liminal space. For some, this space is filled with magical transformations. For others, it is a place of safety and acceptance, often more than they have ever known before.

77

For others it is simply a relief—a place to stop running—physically, emotionally, mentally, spiritually. In the words of a recent ISIS traveler, such space can also serve as "a harbor that takes the wind out of fear and suffering."

Our therapy offices, in themselves, provide a great degree of special energetic space, insofar as our sessions are protected from intrusion, are confidential, and are focused on the well-being of the client. The ISIS approach can augment those energies by including the ISIS template, which is conductive of transformative energy and which can help clients focus and expand their issues in some extraordinary ways. Below are some processes to consider.

Clearing and Aligning the Space

I think of clearing a therapy space much as I think of preparing a garden for planting, to ensure an abundant harvest. Begin with the obvious. Make sure your office is neat—free of empty pizza boxes, wilting plants, and teetering piles of mail. You would be amazed at some of the therapy offices I have entered in my life, as a client, a colleague, and a supervisor. Also, make sure your office is welcoming to the clients who come to you. For some therapists, this means comfy chairs and soft light. A supervisee who works with adolescents keeps jars of candies and other goodies around to make her "kids" feel at home—which is fine as long as she makes it clear that this is a therapy space, not a coffee shop.

It is important to disperse the energies left by former clients—even if you take just a minute to open a window for fresh air, play some music, or imagine or intend clarity. If you are presenting a talk or workshop, your working space may be a shared room or a hotel conference room. This offers an added challenge for your clearing intentions. Make sure the room is clean, organized, and well aired, and do what you can to clear the energy of former inhabitants— and be grateful that people no longer smoke cigars in public places.

Aligning therapeutic space is closely related to clearing it, and can be equally powerful. Aligning space can occur spontaneously, but more often it takes meticulous attention to detail. Recently, at an ISIS training program at Kripalu Institute, we had just completed a movement exercise around the Wheel, and our chairs were strewn all over the room. Our training that afternoon included the core dynamic of creating space, so this was an ideal time to demonstrate how we could refocus our energies simply by bringing our chairs back into a perfect circle, in alignment with one another, which allowed everyone direct eye-contact for communication. I asked one of the participants to orchestrate the circling of our chairs and to enlist the whole group in helping. It took some minutes to get it right, and the group was amazed at how instantly our conversation flowed as a result.

When I set up an ISIS Wheel for a workshop or training, I will take an hour or two, if time is available, to make sure the space is clear and all elements of the Wheel are in happy relationship with one another. This is more than an exercise in OCD behavior. Its strong intention is to align and focus our collective energies so that our process can flow.

Clearing and Aligning Yourself

As important as clearing the therapeutic space is clearing yourself—to meet your clients and to bring together your attention and emotions for the best interests of those clients. Most therapists intuitively develop their own ways to clear themselves, including physical exercise or yoga to refresh their minds and energize their bodies.

If you are pressed for time, clearing and aligning yourself need take you no more than a few seconds of clock time. A couple of quick ways of clearing energy are washing your hands in cold water and taking a few deep breaths, especially emphasizing the exhale, with the idea of letting go of that which is not needed. If you are about to enter an especially difficult session, make sure you allow yourself extra time to clear and align. You can use intention, meditation, or visualization.

Grounding

It is always helpful to ground yourself, no matter what your situation. And with clients who are anxious, or who live perennially in their heads, it can be essential to ground both yourself and them so that you can inhabit the physical plane and access the vast intelligence of your bodies. You can offer grounding exercises at the beginning of a session and maybe several times during the session.

A basic grounding exercise involves a four-part process. First, breathe in and out. Next, feel your feet firmly on the floor. Third, as you exhale, imagine sending any tension you feel deeply into the earth. Finally, as you inhale, imagine drawing those earth energies back up through your whole being, opening up your heart and mind to the full support of the natural world. You can repeat this sequence for as long as time permits. Notice any thoughts, physical tingling, or emotional movement as you continue. You can stay with the sensations for as long as it seems right.

Confidentiality and Other Communication Guidelines

Communication guidelines can help clients feel safe—often safe enough to express feelings they may have held onto their whole lives. The need for such guidelines varies with the situation. How you present them may be quite different in individual sessions, couples sessions, and group sessions or presentations.

In individual sessions, you will have explained confidentiality issues at the beginning of your first meeting, and you can work out specific guidelines as you get to know each other's communication patterns.

When you are working with a couple, it is vital to let each partner know that any information they reveal to you in confidence will be kept in confidence by you and not reported to the other partner. This is especially important when a client's sexual issue involves the kind of secrecy that may surround affairs, kinky fantasies, or covert sexual desires and practices. Note that this is my personal modus operandi about confidentiality. I understand that there are therapists who feel they should keep no confidences of this nature. You will need to be guided by your own training and conscience. The important thing is to let clients know what they can expect from you.

Also in couples sessions, it is often crucial to set communication guidelines that allow each member of the couple to speak with equal voice. Not only equal voice, but a voice that furthers forward-moving communication—no interruptions, put-downs, blames, name-calling, hissy fits, etc. You can be both firm and friendly as you deliver these guidelines. Your directness will help couples notice their habitual patterns, which is a crucial step in their growth and transformation.

At this point, it may also be crucial to let couples know that, for successful therapy, each partner needs to take responsibility for his or her own feelings. With couples who are used to blaming each other or deferring to each other, you may find yourself exploring multiple ways to explain and demonstrate the importance of making "I" statements and the intricacies of active listening.

As part of creating and holding space, you need to let both partners know clearly that you are there for both of them. Effective couples therapy cannot occur if either partner feels you are taking sides. Nor can it occur if the couple believes they can run "good-cop bad-cop" dynamics to lure you into taking sides. Granted, you may feel more open to one partner than the other. Here it is important that you remember that this is your clients' relationship, not yours. Your job is to hold space for their conversation, whatever that may be. If circumstances dictate that you confront one or both partners (for insupportable issues such as physical abuse of each other or sexual abuse of children, for instance) then you will have created a potent space in which to engage in that difficult communication.

In sexuality groups, and even in some of my talks, I ask for a vow of confidentiality—a show of hands, where each participant agrees not to reveal outside the group any personal information that may be offered by anyone in the group. I also routinely review the use of "I" statements, active listening, and giving positive feedback, along with any additional communication guidelines group members may ask for. It is most effective if you deliver all of these guidelines as friendly reminders, not as protracted lectures or finger-wagging threats.

Along with communication guidelines, I feel it is important to let your clients know at least briefly what training you have, along with the kind of help and support you are able to offer and the kinds you are not able to offer. This way, your sessions begin with a clear idea of what participants can expect from you. Note that I am not suggesting that you recite your entire CV or list your academic awards; you are not applying for a job, you are letting your clients know that you have some experience that can help them.

A note on cell phones, which is an increasing issue in this era of insti-omni-indelible communication: Suffice it to say that cell phones have no place in the therapy room, and that it is important for clients to understand that unplugging is part of your policy. Colleagues handle the cell phone issue in a spectrum of ways, from a simple, friendly statement to requiring clients to leave their cell phones (ringers off) in a basket by the inside of the door, so they will be sure to reclaim them on their way out. How you decide to handle it is your call (pun intended, because sometimes we need to inject humor into our therapeutic demands).

Naming—To Create Inclusion and Safety

I find that another aspect of creating special space is *naming*—in order to acknowledge and honor all of the people who are present. This is most relevant in group sessions, but with some couples, or even individuals, the process of naming can prove powerful.

In groups of fewer than about 50 participants, I might go quickly around the room asking each person to say their name—I begin by saying my own name to model what I mean, and then offer an open hand to each person to cue them and keep the process moving swiftly. This exercise takes a minute or two, welcomes everyone into the room, and creates a buzz that energizes the group. With larger groups, I might take two or three minutes to ask participants to introduce themselves to a person or two that they have never met before—which also creates a buzz and energizes the group. If latecomers enter, it is good to ask them to say their names as their way of entry and inclusion.

Equally important, the naming of participants engages each person in the room and sets the stage for collaboration with the therapist or group leader, since everyone in the room is named, not just the therapist or leader. It also helps establish a boundary for the group—an esprit de corps, a sense that what happens in the session is special to this particular group.

Viewing the Large Picture

Another important aspect of creating special energetic space is to establish an atmosphere that enables clients to see the large picture—beyond the performance aspects of sex, and sometimes beyond the boundaries of their own stories that may have them locked into hopelessness and immobility. The purpose of enlarging the picture is to expand your clients' field of options for positive growth and change. There are various ways of achieving a wide view, and my strategy of choice is to use the template of the ISIS Wheel.

The ISIS Wheel enlarges the field through its four quadrants of experience as a visible container for clients' sexual stories. The template of the Wheel serves as a clarifying map through which clients can connect sexual experience with the rest of their lives: body, mind, heart, spirit; past, present, future; metaphor, myth, and archetype—in fact, all the dimensions that also invest optimal sexual experience with interest, juice, and pleasure. The underlying energetics of the medicine wheel template invokes an ancient lineage of aware-ness, growth, and change, which for some clients (and therapists) imparts a particular sense of awe, mystery, even magic.

A participant from an ISIS weekend writes eloquently of the significance of the large view. She sees her overall experience as one of communal magic, reflecting the combined energies of the stories of all the women in our group. Her story also reflects that the healing and affirming energy of the circle contin-ued to affect her even after she returned home, and how the space from the "magical" circle translated to the relational space with her partner.

> On my ride back home yesterday afternoon each of you was on my mind and in my heart. I kept hearing your words, kept seeing your radi-ant faces, your tears, your smiles—and I realized I wanted to write and tell you how much I appreciated what each of you brought to our circle this weekend. I shifted from a place of tremendous anxiety and sense of alienation Friday night (and most of Saturday) to a deeply fulfilling sense that I was seen and heard and held in love by Saturday evening. And by Sunday morning the community we had built in just a little more than 36 hours felt so solid and yet so buoying that as I rode home to my beloved I felt as if I were flying. This is how powerful our circle was: as I related to my partner the events of the weekend, he was so moved that he, too, began crying. He told me later that hearing about what had happened for us gave him hope for his sisters and for all women.

Holding Space

I am often asked what I mean by the phrase "holding space." This is a difficult concept to explain precisely, because it is not fully possible to put a tangible description on an intangible issue. But let me try.

At one level, holding space is the ability for therapists to stay current with all that is going on in the room and to keep the conversation productive for the clients. This may mean using the conversation and dynamics to focus attention and keep your clients safe from outside intrusion—including the cultural message that they may be doing something wrong by daring to change their attitudes about sexual experience. The ability to hold space in this way requires that the therapist be fully awake and alert to everyone who is present as well as to all the elements discussed above: clarity, confidentiality, naming, enlarging the picture, and how these are affecting the process at any given time. Keeping track of all of these is a skill all therapists can develop. I began to learn it in my training as a family therapist, where the task was to focus on everyone in the family, not only one individual. Some clients have asked if I have eyes in the back of my head.

At another level, holding space means attuning to subtle energies as well as to overt statements and body language. By this I mean allowing space for all the feelings in the room, including fear, anger, neediness, tension, and joy. One aspect of attunement means noticing what age clients seem to be when they embody their issues. Are they their chronological age of 38 or 59? Or do the issues they express take them to adolescence, or age five or three—"when I was so small and my brothers were so big and so mean," in the words of one client.

Finally, holding space means being open to your own inner guidance and intuition as well as to the guidance of your clients. Call it multitasking, a sense of "presence," or what you will; in ISIS work it is crucial to hold space for all of these elements. For when space is safely held, clients feel it. They report a sense of light-heartedness, expansion, enthusiasm, creativity, and also flashes of insight.

When space is not safely held, clients feel it, too. They report a sense of insecurity, of being "let down," of "flying off the handle," or of "losing it." "It's like energy pouring out of the room." At worst, clients can be retraumatized, plunged back through their carefully constructed defense systems into events in their lives that were—and may continue to be—terrifyingly out of control. I am reminded of the lines by the poet William Butler Yeats that describe the brutal anarchy during the Irish revolution in 1919.

> Turning and turning in the widening gyre
> The falcon cannot hear the falconer;
> Things fall apart; the centre cannot hold . . .

Such a sense of brutality can exist in therapy as well. For instance, expressive therapies such as bioenergetics and psychodrama may powerfully invoke traumatic memories. The results can be impressive and valuable in cracking defensive blocks so that stuck energy can finally move. But when stuck energy moves, it is imperative that therapists offer boundaries for clients, along with methods to help them transform their moving energies into new insights, strength, and focus. Holding space in this way allows clients to progress forward on their paths rather than regress backward or fall into a bottomless black hole. By providing a natural boundary and also a larger picture, the ISIS Wheel creates a space to explore old traumatic events in relative safety.

Core Dynamic #2: Directing Movement

For many people, a crucial component of great sex is the capacity to flow between body and spirit, between past and present, between time and space. In ISIS work, physical movement around and within the Wheel initiates emotional, mental, and spiritual movement among the concrete and imaginal layers of clients' sexual stories. It also suggests the kind of intention and fluidity that makes for optimal sexual experience.

Moving Around the Wheel

In its simplest form, I ask clients to move to each quadrant to stand and speak. In this way, they can experience the physical differences in how they feel when they tell aspects of their stories from the perspective of each quadrant. Moving around the Wheel allows for another form of fluidity—a flow between time past and time present. For some clients, memories may emerge spontaneously, shedding light on and giving direction to an issue that is difficult to resolve in the present.

A 64-year-old woman relates: "I've spent my whole life as a wife and mother and doing for others. Now it's time for me!" She said she had been seeing a therapist for some years but could report no forward movement. Her sessions had focused around a litany of complaints about her husband, her children, and the community librarian, who was her volunteer boss. As this woman allowed herself to move out of her chair and step into the emotional quadrant of the ISIS Wheel, her story began to change. The voice that emerged was not that of wife, mother, and do-gooder, but of a whiny five-year-old whose mother had died of cancer, leaving her to be the "strong little woman" of the family—no crying allowed. Once she reconnected with her abandoned and misunderstood five-year-old self, she could wade into the years of unshed tears and begin to heal the grief that kept her stuck being a good girl. This story and many others encourage me to get clients moving so that their physical movement can help precipitate movement on all fronts.

To engage physical fluidity, I suggest clients become aware of openings and resistances in breath and posture as they stand in each quadrant.

To engage emotional fluidity, I encourage a full range of feelings as clients reveal different facets of their stories.

To engage cognitive fluidity, I ask clients to consider the cultural and religious messages they received about sex and intimacy, and to relate how these messages affect their present lives—physically, emotionally, mentally, and spiritually.

To engage spiritual fluidity, I encourage clients to see the large picture as they move around the Wheel and to use active meditation and envisioning to enhance their sense of sexual connection and meaning.

Allowing clients to play out their dynamics in multidimensional movement can be a powerful way to help them explore which realities are present, which are past, whose voice is speaking, what the cultural messages are, what the emotional blocks are, and so forth. Here, the task of the therapist is to be alert for nuances. The therapist's task may also include "stage directing" various interactions to help clients focus on the crux of their issues and expand their stories rather than slip back into an old shorthand rehearsing of the story, which too often becomes an endless loop.

Within each quadrant I often encourage clients to express their experience in movement as well as words. Movement can be as simple as walking around the Wheel to tell a story as it changes from quadrant to quadrant. Or it can include permission for the body to speak in eloquent ways. The body is intelligent, and for many clients a balled-up fist or stamping foot will signal the pent-up rage that has so far not dared express itself in words, or even thoughts. Other clients find themselves literally running back and forth between the emotional quadrant and the mental quadrant as they try to sort out the feelings and thoughts that are turning their bodies off from desiring sexual pleasure. All of this movement provides new information for both clients and therapists.

Moving one's story around the Wheel—and moving with one's story—provides permission for clients and therapists to explore a sexual issue from multiple points of view. It is a means for clients to describe multiple nuances of their sexual stories. It is a visible and kinesthetic way of connecting physical, emotional, mental, and spiritual experience about sexual issues. Once clients get out of their chairs, the possibility of surprising discoveries grows incrementally. In short, by asking them to move their bodies, you are asking them to initiate their own power. A take-home advantage is that the potential for power and agency may be reinforced every time the client takes a step.

Dancing the ISIS Wheel

My colleague Kamara McAndrews is a professional dancer and certified dance teacher as well as a marriage and family therapist and sex therapist. She teaches with me at ISIS groups and trainings at Esalen Institute, and she is constantly developing new ways to take the ISIS process into body experiences for clients. Because she is so attuned to physical movement, she is able to help participants notice the sometimes extraordinarily subtle stories their bodies tell. Plus, she encourages clients to engage in creative movement in each quadrant to activate those stories.

Kamara was of particular support to an ISIS participant who is also a dancer, enabling her to take her story into each quadrant with raw power. Kamara encouraged this woman to trace her journey as a terrified immigrant to the US when she was a small child, caught between languages. Working in this way, without relying on words, helped her weave her early history into and around the Wheel through dance movements and express her intense sense of alienation and subsequent fears of any kind of intimacy. This woman has since moved forward in her own journey by creating a series of movements to explore each quadrant of her personal Wheel more deeply.

Moving to the Center

My colleague Chelsea Wakefield offers another option for exploring the Wheel when she incorporates the ISIS template into her "Luminous Woman" weekends. She invites each woman to step into the center of the Wheel and to speak from there—from her unique place of strength and "luminosity." It is from this place that Chelsea invites each woman to explore the quadrants of body, mind, heart, and spirit. The choice to ask them to begin from a place of strength creates a new trajectory for women's lives. In Chelsea's words: "We connect with the places inside where wisdom, strength, fullness, and power reside and create a touchstone for returning there regularly."

Core Dynamic #3: Ritualizing Ordinary Activities

Ritual differs from everyday habit or routine because it is mindful and focused and because its purpose is to underscore and heighten ordinary experience rather than to go through repetitive motions. For instance, healing rites are used to melt pain or exorcise traumatic memories, graduation ceremonies infuse energy and purpose, special prayers and holiday stories bring families together and imprint precious memories.

In spiritual practices, rituals are used to create environments in which the unseen or "non-ordinary" world of spirit can become apparent and familiar. Such rituals might include playing music, dancing, burning incense, eating special foods, lighting candles, laying on of hands, and anointing with oil. Interestingly, many of these spiritual and religious rituals parallel the kinds of sexual rituals that are designed to open human beings to desire and pleasure. Music, dancing, perfumes, preparing a luscious meal, lighting candles in the bedroom, and massaging with sensuous oils may be sexy in themselves and can certainly become an invitation for deeply engaging sexual experience.

In ISIS work, it is possible to introduce a variety of rituals designed to underscore and heighten therapeutic experience for clients. Many of these rituals come from spiritual traditions. But, to remove the mystery factor, most of these rituals are actually exercises about awareness, mindfulness, and reminding clients to notice where they are, where they are going, and who and what is around them. Ultimately, these rituals are to highlight the crucial element in any kind of therapy: helping clients remember who they are.

My Swedish colleague Tina Nevin has developed a practice of rewarding clients who acknowledge what they want, stand their ground, and decline to do someone else's job or take responsibility for someone else's problem. She offers them a candle for each time they stand firm on what she calls "a good No." With this simple ritual she concretizes the crucial point that we must often say "No" in order to clear the way for "Yes"—both in the bedroom and beyond.

Rituals for Clearing Energy

One of the ritual elements of ISIS work includes clearing clients' energy before they enter into the process of therapy and offer their stories. This can be a verbal clearing, such as a recurring statement or a short meditation. It can be a physical clearing, involving breathing, stretching, a welcoming handshake— whatever you feel is appropriate. For many clients there is a ritual clearing involved in simply stepping into your office and sitting down in the chair they have claimed as their own. For, in so doing, they are entering into liminal space—stepping over the threshold of everyday reality and into an arena of change. Clearing rituals represent a letting go of the past, whether the "past" is a childhood filled with terrors, an argument with a spouse, or the bus ride they took to get to your office.

Naming Rituals

Although the importance of naming has already been discussed as a method of creating and holding space, there is also a deeper significance of focusing on naming. In ancient cultures, enormous power was carried by the Name. Names carry power today, as well, although powerful names are most often associated with media stars, sports heroes, politicians, and other celebrities. In ISIS work, part of the point is that everyone is a star. So I find that an important ritual element for meaningful therapy is to ask clients to speak their names in special ways—both to announce themselves and to bring their particular energies into the room.

In a group, I might ask each person to introduce himself or herself to another group member they are meeting for the first time. Or I might go around the room asking each person to say his or her name out loud for all to hear. If the group is circled around an ISIS Wheel, I might ask clients to blow their names and their intentions into the center of the Wheel. In addition, I might ask them to call in the names of energies they want in their lives, and to greet these energies as if they are already friends. I elaborate on all of these naming rituals in chapters 10 and 11.

Rituals to Create New Traditions

In ISIS work, I emphasize that we are creating our own environment, with our own rules—as distinct from the Mars–Venus world we inhabit at other times, where the habitual sexual messages include "Good girls don't," "Real men score," and "God forbid you should feel sexual after menopause." New environments need new traditions—traditions whose purpose is to build self-esteem over the lifespan, and also to build community, establish boundaries, and create a container of safety and inclusion for everyone involved.

One enormously effective tradition in ISIS groups is for participants to introduce themselves in a unique way—a ritual in which individuals reveal a part of their sexual stories they want to keep and enhance and another part of their sexual stories they want to move beyond or release. This ritual opening offers an equal starting place for all of us, whether we are seasoned veterans of ISIS work or nervous newbies. It serves to empower the group by putting everyone on the same page. At the same time, it allows each individual equal time in which to speak both sides of their stories and provides a protected space in which to be clearly heard.

I find that ritualizing even ordinary activities such as walking can be effective to use with clients who feel stuck, especially if they present as rigid, defended, resistant, confused, or more attuned to past experience than to the present. For instance, when I ask clients to walk around the ISIS Wheel, I ask that they take each step intentionally and that they walk in the same direction—clockwise, or "sunwise"—to keep energy flowing in a positive way. The therapeutic message here is not about walking in a certain direction. Rather, it is to clarify consciousness. It is about creating an instant way for clients to pay attention to where they are moving and to feel a sense of personal agency regarding the flow of their positive energy.

When easily achievable rituals like these are presented as a mindful practice, invoked in safety and suggested without rigidity, they serve to free movement in all four quadrants of sexual experience, and they may offer surprising paths out of deeply rutted patterns of behavior. The effect of introducing these rituals into therapy sessions and groups often frees up the therapeutic process for therapist as well as client, for, when clients are stuck and immobilized, therapists may be stuck and immobilized as well. When this occurs, the whole process of therapy becomes frozen in place.

In addition, introducing these kinds of rituals may free up clients' approach to their own sexual rituals that have become routine or boring. For instance, if backrubs and bubble baths have become ho-hum for couples, they can try skinny-dipping in a nearby lake, or playing with body paints, or (a favorite suggestion of mine) finding ways to make love to each other for an hour without ever venturing above the ankles. Ritualizing in this way is not so much about performing a specific activity as it is about choosing how to enter into activities that create pleasure, and about what these activities mean in clients' lives. Mindfulness and attention can enhance sexual interactions, from flirting and courtship to putting on condoms. They can help clients find new ways to say "a good No" and to ask for what they really want.

Core Dynamic #4: Concretizing Abstract Concepts

By "concretizing," I mean giving tangible form to thoughts, feelings, ideas, and situations. The ISIS approach focuses this notion in a personal and individualized way, by inviting clients to choose objects that hold special qualities that they want to explore. These objects are more than just a metaphor. Although they may contain the illuminating power of metaphor, they are also tangible. Clients can feel them, hold them, and move them. They can choose where to put them and what to do with them. A client might grapple endlessly in therapy with an enormous issue like love or rejection; choosing a physical object to represent issues such as these may interrupt a repeated story and suggest new images, new points of reference to consider, a whole new therapeutic trajectory.

Concretizing abstract concepts about sexuality is valuable because it allows clients to explore their problems without pathologizing them and may offer surprising information about what clients want and do not want. Also importantly, concretizing provides tangible take-home possibilities for growth and change beyond the therapy session.

I typically ask clients to bring two objects to place within the Wheel. One object is to represent a part of their sexual story they want to keep, enhance, or embellish. The other object is to represent a part of their sexual story they want to let go of or move beyond. The reason for bringing two objects is to make both sides of a story available for exploration. This allows clients to explore their sexual complexity and to experience how their sexual stories are neither all good nor all bad. Equally important, exploring the whole spectrum interrupts the trajectory of a story that a client may have told for so long in the same way that the story itself has come to carry the defining authority of myth. When this occurs, the story cannot change. It is frozen in time, like an old photograph embedded permanently in memory, or like the proverbial fly embedded in amber. With repetition over time, a story like this becomes an imprint in the brain that may wield more power than the actual experience it describes.

Another important rationale for exploring many sides of a story is the neurobiological one. Initiating complexity can initiate new neural pathways, which opens up space for new stories, new behaviors, new horizons. The science of neurobiology is vital and complex, so, without going into the brain chemistry, I liken exploring all aspects of a story to making new deer tracks in the woods—an image for which I thank my colleague Tammy Nelson. A crucial point for therapists to remember is that, once these new neural pathways are created, it is essential for clients to reinforce them through continued practice. Otherwise, like exploratory deer tracks, they will lose their definition. The underbrush will take over and traffic will revert to the paths most traveled.

What Clients Bring

The objects clients bring to the Wheel vary tremendously. One woman brought a ripe mango to represent the juicy lushness she felt with her lover; she also brought a strip of plastic "danger" tape to represent the gang rape that traumatized her as a teenager. Another woman brought a pink teddy bear to represent her innocent (and needy) child-self; she also brought a mirror—so that she could see herself as an adult able to make positive (and desired) sexual choices. Other clients have brought telephones—for communication or lack of communication, and musical instruments—for harmony or lack of harmony. They have brought watches and clocks, flowers, books, drawings, stones, scarves, cameras, whips, rulers, spike-heeled shoes, vibrators, and sexy underwear. Objects like these take on the aura of "power objects" or "medicine pieces" that contain potent seeds of a whole story—memories, myths, "irrational facts," and, most significantly, the possibilities for transformation.

To put this another way, think how instantly and completely an engagement ring may evoke the many facets of sexual desire and hope, or how a legal envelope containing a divorce decree may evoke the chill of sexual loss and dread. Like metaphor, these objects stand for the whole story. Yet these objects are no longer stored in the memory. They are out in the open for all to see. To handle the actual objects and move them around allows the story they contain to emerge tangibly in each quadrant of the Wheel.

What Concretizing Achieves

Concretizing in this way allows multiple layers of a story to emerge at once, visibly and clearly. In so doing, it calls up events, reactions to events, the history of events, even the projected future of events. Choosing and working with objects offers a unique way for clients to focus their stories, reconceptualize them, and try out various scenarios until they find ones that work for them. Clients take their objects home with them, which offers possibilities of extending the usefulness of these objects well beyond the session.

A colleague speaks of the ISIS work she recently did with a couple in their early sixties—heterosexual, committed, and generally happy with most aspects of their lives. Their issue was what she called "a middle-class, mid-life crisis of desire"—the kind of problem sex therapists might find in their offices any day. He (call him Roger) wanted more sex than she (call her Louise). Louise's desire for intercourse had waned considerably since the onset of menopause, partly— and perhaps mainly—because her vaginal mucosa was growing increasingly dry and fragile, and the intercourse she had once enjoyed playfully and plentifully with Roger was painful, even though she kept it as brief as she could manage.

My colleague had determined that, with the exception of their desire discrepancies and also their recent sad visits to Roger's father in a nursing home, the relationship between Roger and Louise was relatively free of strife. My colleague had also determined that it was not appropriate for Louise to take hormones for her vaginal dryness, as she had a family history of breast cancer. My colleague suggested lubrication. The couple experimented, and found that some lubes helped Louise's pain "a bit." But sex "still wasn't really fun."

At this point in the therapy, my colleague was stumped, and decided to introduce the ISIS Wheel as the next step with Roger and Louise. She explained the process of the Wheel and how helpful she thought it might be to provide new information they could all work with. She modified the two-object ISIS exercise and asked them each to bring into the office next time one object that expressed what they really wanted in their sexual relationship. Roger brought a can of green chilies, "to keep sex hot and spicy." Louise brought a Raggedy Ann doll, to signify that she would like sex to be "more playful."

As my colleague helped Roger and Louise explore the meaning of these objects in the context of the whole Wheel, it was the doll that took on the greatest power as a medicine object. As the story evolved, it was revealed that this doll had been given to Louise by her mother when Louise was 23. Her mother had said, "You never liked dolls when you were a kid so maybe you can appreciate one now." Six days later, her mother died of a heart attack. The Raggedy Ann doll was the last gift Louise ever received from her. My colleague writes:

> Roger and Louise both spoke from each quadrant and explained how in each quadrant they could feel either more hot and spicy or more playful. In the spirit quadrant, Louise broke down in tears to tell her story, and I asked Roger to join her there. There she looked into his

eyes and let him know that she felt her purpose and meaning in life was to be his wife and lover. That she was born to help him heal the suffering he endured as a child.

What follows next speaks to the powerful connection between the body, spirit, and emotions. My colleague writes: "After this session, Louise's vagina suddenly wasn't hurting any more."

Looking back on this ISIS Wheel session, the Raggedy Ann doll served as a bridge for Louise between her past and her present. Holding the doll enabled her to connect with the energy of her inner child, grieve the loss of her mother, and open her heart—and her genitals—to the relationship with Roger that nurtures her now. Plus it brought out crucial information about the young Roger, the 13-year-old altar boy initiated into sex by the parish priest—years before the notion of priest sexual abuse was commonly recognized as harmful. Roger, too, was moved to tears as he walked the Wheel. This exercise helped this couple open their hearts to each other in a new way. It was "a liquid way," as they tell it. Their liquidity has lasted, and they describe the richness in their relationship now as way beyond spicy—certainly way beyond a can of chilies. For this couple, love acted like an aphrodisiac.

The potency of concretizing may be magnified in a group, as you will see in chapter 10. The collective energy heightens and supports the work with individuals' stories. And, as illustrated in cases that follow in other chapters, the objects clients bring may develop lives of their own, gathering enough energy to galvanize clients into action.

Taking the Objects Home

An essential aspect of therapy for the successful use of concrete objects with an individual client, a couple, or a group is that clients reclaim their objects at the end of the session and speak about what changes may have occurred during the session, stating what they will do with their objects when they get them home. I ask them to make a commitment to own fully these objects and all their characteristics. You, the therapist, never assume responsibility for these objects, any more than you would assume responsibility for the client. Moreover, the taking of objects home often extends their usefulness beyond the session. Examples will abound in the next chapters.

How each clinician chooses to create and hold space, initiate movement, incorporate ritual, and concretize abstract concepts will be shaped by the inclination of the therapist, the nature of the therapy, and the needs of the client. Effective ISIS practice can occur without ever creating a physical Wheel. It may be as simple as welcoming a client into your office and using the Wheel and core dynamics as your own mental construct to help you guide therapeutic inquiry. However, my experience in training therapists indicates that working with an actual template of the Wheel, using actual objects, and actually moving around the Wheel invests the practice with increased meaning and power.

In the next chapters, I will elaborate on ways therapists can use the core dynamics of ISIS Wheel practice to help expand the practice of sex therapy in group work, in individual sessions, and in couples sessions.

10

USING THE ISIS WHEEL IN TRAINING SEMINARS AND PERSONAL GROWTH INTENSIVES

In ISIS work, there is a great deal to be discovered in group processes that can be carried over into sessions with individuals and couples. So even if in your practice you deal only with individuals or couples, I urge you read this chapter about using the ISIS Wheel in groups. A number of the processes are repeated in the next chapter on conducting ISIS sessions with individuals and couples, but the ideas are informed and enriched by the ISIS group experience.

Perhaps it is a bit of an overstatement to say that everything I learned about expanding the practice of sex therapy I learned in ISIS groups. But the truth is, the ISIS process that is outlined in this book has been developed during more than fifteen years of adapting ISIS ideas to group seminars and personal growth intensives. And ISIS is still a work in progress—I learn something new every time I meet with another group. I learn from the participants. I learn from supervisees who co-lead with me. I learn from my own responses to each group.

This chapter takes you through the major procedures—from preparation and setting space to creating the ISIS Wheel and guiding the participants.

Preparing for the Group

Clearing Yourself Before You Begin

Before setting the space for the group session, wash your hands and do whatever else you need to do to clear your own energy. For me this usually includes personal grounding and opening myself to guidance that first of all I will do no harm. Then I focus on the group I am about to conduct. I visualize the group and imagine a circle of engaged participants in a highly energized space.

Clearing the Space Before You Begin

I cannot emphasize too strongly how important it is to clear the energy of the space in which you are going to conduct an ISIS group. I have been in hotel meeting rooms that buzz with electronic vibrations. I have been in church basements cluttered with chairs from last night's choir rehearsal. I have been in rooms through which helpers are passing to prepare the lunch our group will eat that noon. Unless distracting energies from scenes like these are cleared, they tend to stick to the space and make for a discordant workshop experience.

I have conducted trainings and groups in wonderfully clear places too—Esalen Institute, in the round stone house built for Fritz Perls at the height of the human potential movement; at Rowe Conference Center, where the resonance is so strong you can sometimes hear the hum of energy in the room; at the Casa de los Artistas in Boca de Tomatlan, Mexico, where our meeting space has three sides open to ocean, river, and jungle. The Goddess Studio in San Diego is another amazing space where we met for an ISIS group. Its walls are hung with massive goddess paintings created by its owner, Amalya Peck. I immediately got the message that I needed to ask permission of each of these goddesses to enter their sanctuary. At the feet of one particularly fierce goddess I was moved to place a pomegranate as a gift of appeasement.

Wherever you conduct a group, it is important that you be aware of the space around you—with all of its attributes and limitations—so that you can meet its energy and prepare it to receive the ISIS Wheel and the group that will surround the Wheel.

It is also important to differentiate between a group whose primary purpose is clinical training and a group whose primary purpose is personal growth. Although both of these kinds of groups are invariably therapeutic, I do not refer to either of them as therapy groups. I introduce them both as arenas for change and transformation.

When I clear space for an ISIS group, I begin, wherever possible, by walking around the area of the room and getting a sense of how the room feels to me. If any parts feel energetically dense, dark, or sticky, I attempt to open the energy in a variety of ways. If it is appropriate, I use my spiritual tools—described in my forthcoming *Sex Therapy Meets Shamanism*. If the room is in a public place such as a hotel or a classroom, I use the power of intention, silently asking that the space be clear enough to facilitate movement of energy for all concerned.

Creating a Group ISIS Wheel

The physical ISIS Wheel you create sets the tone for the group. Make sure you create it with care and with intention for the well-being of the particular group you are conducting. To create your group ISIS Wheel you will need:

- a groundcloth of some kind. The groundcloth is the foundation of your ISIS circle: it creates visual focus throughout the group; it delineates sacred space for the group and for the items that participants bring in to explore; and it carries energy from group to group. For ISIS groups I use a very old, very beautiful Afghan tribal cloth that measures almost 3 feet square. You may have something similar, or perhaps you have a favorite scarf or sarong you can fold or other material that will feel just right. Whatever you use, reserve it for the special purpose of space holder and energy holder for your ISIS groups.

- dividers to delineate the quadrants. I use four woven strips of material that are about 3 feet long. I have also used embroidered ribbon. You can use whatever you like as long as it goes with the groundcloth you are using.
- markers for each quadrant and the center. I use cards labeled "Physical," "Emotional," "Spiritual," "Mental," and "Center." You can make your own cards. I once used file cards folded in half, like place cards, though now I use cards designed by an artist friend.
- meaningful items to bring special energy to each quadrant. If the situation is right, I may add a stone for the physical quadrant (to represent the earth), a shell for the emotional quadrant (to represent water), a feather for the spiritual quadrant (to represent air), a candle for the mental quadrant (to represent fire), and a crystal for the center (to represent clarity and trans-formation). Use your own judgment as to whether items like these will encourage your clients to open up, or whether they might seem unfamiliar or alien enough to trigger resistance.

Opening the Group: When Participants Arrive

Clear Participants

Clearing energy is a prerequisite for effective healing of any kind. This state-ment is broad, but, if you think about it, it is natural for therapists to focus on their clients as a way of preparing for an upcoming session. In ISIS terms, a clear, aligned, and balanced mind, heart, spirit, and body facilitate the trans-mission of positive energy for both clients and therapists.

I routinely clear participants before and during a group. The clearing may vary depending on the makeup of the group and where the group is held. Just as in clearing space, it is effective to use the power of intention—asking that participants be clear enough to open up to the growth and change they want and need. When it is appropriate, I also use a variety of spiritual tools—I describe these in *Sex Therapy Meets Shamanism*.

Welcome Participants

My welcome to participants usually includes an outline of what they are likely to expect during our group meeting. This is a time to greet, distribute hand-outs, and answer questions about logistics.

Disclosing Information About the Wheel

If this is a personal growth intensive, the group will enter to find the ISIS Wheel and an air of mystery in the room. Where fire laws permit, they will find a circle of votive candles around the Wheel—unlit, one for each participant. If we are not allowed to use candles, they will find the Wheel surrounded by votives holders filled with water, into which they will place a flower (described below).

I mention the sense of mystery, and say that I will wait to disclose information about each quadrant until after participants have placed their objects intuitively.

If this is a group seminar for training professionals, we may or may not begin with the ISIS Wheel in the center. For training purposes, I emphasize the cognitive aspects of the Wheel before focusing on the mysteries and often open with a PowerPoint presentation showing ISIS research and diagrams of the ISIS Wheel. With or without a PowerPoint, I usually begin a training group with an introduction to the quadrants of the Wheel and an outline of how we will be using this information in our training. There is more information about this in chapter 15, "ISIS Training for Professionals."

Ensure Confidentiality

Whether the purpose of the group is for training or for personal growth, I always ask for a vow of confidentiality. I explain that what I mean by confidentiality is that no personal information that has been shared in the group goes beyond the group. I state that participants are welcome to share their own feelings and learning outside the group, but that they agree never to identify personal information shared by any other of the group's participants.

I ask each participant to raise his or her hand in agreement—and I check to see if there is something participants do not understand or do not agree with. Some individuals need to be doubly reassured that their personal information will not be revealed. I have learned over the years to keep the conversation short and direct, because fears about confidentiality can become a focus for participants' anxiety about sex itself and discussion about confidentiality can become a smoke screen to mask the real issues. I invite members to revisit the issue of confidentiality if and when an occasion arises.

Taking a group vow of confidentiality serves several functions. It elicits an all-important "Yes" response at the beginning or our meeting. It requires physical action that energizes the group. It offers a kind of safety that encourages permission to share deep feelings. And it provides an initial bond of trust among group members which usually grows exponentially as the workshop proceeds.

Set Communication Guidelines

In beginning each group, I find it is essential to review at least a few basic guidelines for how we are to communicate, even if the group is comprised of trained professionals who teach communication skills themselves. Again, the spirit of offering these guidelines is to set a tone of safety and to foster group cohesion. Three basic communication guidelines I mention are:

- Use "I" statements.
- Listen without interruption while others speak.
- Speak from the heart—that is, from direct experience, rather than speaking for others or repeating messages that may come down through the culture.

Additional guidelines are as follows:

- Giving advice is a no-no. I usually mention that, for some people, it may be difficult to resist the temptation of offering helpful advice to others in the group, and I remind them that the most useful information is that which comes directly from sharing their own experience.
- Ensure equal opportunity. I address the inevitability that some group members are apt to talk longer than others and that it is important to give everyone the same opportunity to speak. In the distant past, there have been groups in which I set a kitchen timer, and others in which I have asked for a volunteer to keep time for each person who speaks. Now, I tend to allow the group to take responsibility for monitoring itself. I may say something like:

   There are 33 of us in the group. It's 8 o'clock in the evening, and this conference center asks that we end our session by 9:30. You can do the math here. I want to make sure everyone has a chance to say what needs to be said by way of introductions, so it can help if you organize your thoughts before you speak. A great deal can be communicated in two minutes' time . . . .

Finally, I remind everyone that group is an arena for change, and that this is their opportunity to practice new thoughts and behaviors. This kind of change can feel risky, as if one is leaving behind all the rules of convention and safety. By way of encouragement, I often quote a Native American saying:

   As you go the way of your life, you will come to a great chasm.
   Jump. It is not as wide as you think.

Bring Participants into the Wheel

I offer a specific format for introductions: "Speak your names out loud, then breathe or blow your name into the center of the Wheel." I invite participants to speak in any order they choose. This format establishes three things right from the beginning: first, that when to speak is the choice of the speaker, not the leader; second, that our breath is connected to our thoughts and feelings; and, finally, that we begin to create an intimate relationship to the Wheel through offering our breath.

Ask Participants to Place Their Two Power Objects in the Wheel

This is a major exercise, based on one of the core dynamics described in chapter 9. It functions to introduce participants, interrupt stuck stories, and engage the entire group in movement. The way I introduce it in groups is first to model it myself or ask my assistant to model it: I state my name and blow into the center of the circle, to connect my name to the circle with my breath. Then I place the objects I have brought into the circle—clearly stating what each represents, what part of my sexual story I want to nurture and expand, and what part I want to release and move beyond. Note that the spirit behind this kind of sharing is to include myself as part of the group rather than to set myself off as a remote leader, expert, or judge.

Wait—Does the Group Leader Really Place an Object into the Wheel?

When I conduct ISIS groups, I always put myself into the circle. I believe it is integral to this ISIS process that I place enough of my issues into the circle that I become a part of the group and not apart from it. This is part of my philosophy about collaborating with clients rather than playing the role of all-knowing therapist. I remind the clients that the Wheel is the therapist, in the sense that it is in the honest offering of all of our issues that growth and change occurs.

I share my objects briefly, but significantly and from the heart. I might bring (for instance) an empty plastic water bottle to signify that I sometimes plunge into deep feelings of worthlessness that stem from early childhood abandonment issues, and that when I feel those signs coming on I have to remember that I'm a grown adult with skills. And I might bring a flute to signify that when I feel most open and clear I experience an ability to reach out in a way that touches others' hearts and souls, and that I would like to nurture and expand the part of me that is connected with clarity and openness.

There is an essential difference between my placing my objects (as leader) and the workshop participants placing theirs. My motivation is to complete the circle by joining the group, not to focus on my personal issues (overtly anyway) but on the issues brought by the workshop participants. ISIS participants do focus on their issues, of course.

I understand that the issue of sharing as a therapist is hotly contested among professionals, so let me offer a caveat here. Whether or not you opt to share your issues and objects in an ISIS group, your conduct is solely up to you and your comfort level. It is not mandatory for you to share in the way in which I have described. I do not share in this way in sessions with individual or couples.

Ask Each Participant to Light a Candle (or Place a Flower)

After each participant blows his or her name into the center and places the two objects, I ask that he or she lights one of the candles—to signal a willingness and ability to "light their own fire." After lighting a candle, each person then walks around the group with the fire-lighter until the next person opts to introduce him or herself. Where fire laws do not permit, I have used votive candle holders filled with water and asked each person to choose a flower from a central vase to place in their individual holder—to bring an intention to bloom.

When all the participants have introduced themselves, placed their objects, and lit their candles (or placed their flowers), we are sitting around a ring of fire (or blooms) with the energy of all of our stories vibrating in the center. The ring of flowers, while less dramatic, also provides energy and a living container. This powerful setting becomes the theatre for whatever will unfold as the workshop continues.

A note on candles and flowers: At the close of each session in an ISIS group, each participant blows out his or her candle (or returns his or her flower to the common vase), then relights it (or replaces the flower) at the beginning of the next session. This creates repeated opportunities for activating personal commitment and also for signifying closure.

Invite Participants to Walk Around the Wheel

When all the objects have been placed, I invite participants to walk around the Wheel to see all of the objects in relationship to one another and to offer all participants the opportunity to move their objects if they wish. This is a preamble to an open invitation for participants to move their objects at any point during the workshop, so that they can try them out in various quadrants of the Wheel. The only caveat about moving their objects is not to disturb somebody else's object in the process.

Walking the Wheel also introduces an invitation for participants to locate which quadrant they feel most drawn to after they have placed their objects. It is important to the unfolding of the ISIS process that they locate this quadrant in a physical way, using the intelligence of their bodies as well as guidance from their hearts, minds, and spirits. A major benefit of this seemingly simple exercise of walking the Wheel is that it gets participants up and moving and puts into practice another of the core dynamics of ISIS work: movement.

To reiterate what is spelled out in chapter 9, physical movement around the Wheel initiates emotional, mental, and spiritual movement among the concrete and imaginal layers of participants' sexual stories. Further, the act of moving and walking helps to activate body intelligence and expand participants' consciousness, even at a symbolic level. Walking around and among the quadrants of the Wheel suggests the capacity to flow between body and spirit, past and present, time and space.

The invitation to move also suggests the kinds of intention and fluidity that make for optimal sexual experience—whether the fluidity concerns the flowing in of sensual energy or the letting go of tension, anger, or other forms of stuck density. For instance, one ISIS participant addressed the Wheel in fury during the Saturday afternoon of a weekend workshop. She picked up my metal Tibetan bowl and clanged it repeatedly as she shouted her frustration: "I can't reach the center of the Wheel! I can't reach the center of my life!" The surprising outcome came to her from guidance she received during the Saturday evening drummed journey. She found herself shapeshifting into a being small enough to walk through all the objects in the Wheel as if she were walking through a magic forest. This image gave her something to work with in her life: namely, to slow down, breathe, and, in her words: "jump-start my heart to enter the beautiful tapestry of sexual experience."

Teaching the Quadrants

After participants have placed their objects and circumnavigated the Wheel, I offer a teaching about what each quadrant of the Wheel may hold. This teaching is based on the makeup of the Wheel and the placement of the objects and issues the group has brought into it.

For a weekend group, this teaching typically falls on the Saturday morning following the Friday night introductions. If the group is one day long or shorter, this teaching can be woven into the schedule either before or after participants place their objects. For training groups, I usually begin with teaching the quadrants, when I provide a detailed handout (which you can obtain free by writing to me via my website).

I begin by walking around each quadrant and describing the kinds of issues that may manifest in each—as outlined in earlier chapters. In the physical

101

quadrant, I describe issues of sensation and numbness. In the emotional quadrant, I describe issues of love, resentment, and angst. In the mental quadrant, I describe issues of choice along with messages and judgments. In the spiritual quadrant, I describe issues of connection and disconnection, along with taking the large view. I describe the center as the meeting and merging of all these issues—a transformational state of ecstasy, or of despair.

As I make my teaching round of the Wheel, I invite individuals to join me and to place themselves in quadrants that exemplify the issues they have already stated. For instance, a woman embroiled in a nasty divorce might step into the emotional quadrant, a menopausal woman complaining of vaginal dryness might step into the physical quadrant, and so forth.

This invited participation allows the issues in each quadrant to come alive with personal stories with which the whole group can begin to identify. By the time I have completed this part of my teaching, there is most likely vital activity and movement around the Wheel. Some group members are already involved in asking questions and deconstructing their own issues; others are engaged in empathic listening, holding space, or moving into the circle to create a kind of ad hoc group psychodrama—stepping into the role-play of mothers, fathers, and ex-mates or acting as alter egos to participants who may have a hard time speaking up. Still others spontaneously add their own stories to the stew as they are triggered by the stories of other group members.

Out of this seeming chaos emerge the seeds of organic order—where words are said, movements are enacted, personal connections are made, and the ISIS Wheel comes to life, containing the germ of deep insight and healing for many of the participants.

Is There Such a Thing as Too Much Information?

I am of two minds about how much cognitive information about the quadrants is optimal for individual growth or for group process, and therefore I make sure to tailor the teaching of the quadrants specifically for each group.

For personal growth intensives, I usually refrain from teaching cognitive material until after participants have intuitively placed their objects into the Wheel and then been invited to move their objects. Allowing clients to make their own choices without direction from the therapist can have extraordinary effects, as in the story of Curtis and Elsa, in the next chapter.

In professional training seminars, I usually introduce the Wheel at the outset, so that, by the time they do the exercise of placing their objects, participants are already aware of what each quadrant represents. In individual and couples sessions, as you will see in chapter 12, I invariably describe the Wheel and the quadrants before asking clients to place their objects.

Exercises and Activities to Introduce During an ISIS Group

After the initial teaching of the quadrants is the time to offer a series of exercises and activities to focus questions and deepen the experience for clients and students. Some of these are outlined earlier. Others are below, organized via the quadrants you will explore in group: physical, emotional, mental, and spiritual. I invite you to use these as suggestions to create your own sequence of events, which can take numerous forms, depending on the group purpose, participants, issues, and the time frame in which you are working.

Although each of the activities described below can be used as a stand-alone exercise, each can also be used in conjunction with the major ISIS activity where clients bring objects to the Wheel to represent multiple parts of their sexual stories. The activity of placing objects is so basic to the ISIS process that it is part of the core dynamic of concretizing, outlined in chapter 9.

Activities to Help Expand Sexual Experience in the Physical Quadrant

To expand the practice of sex therapy, we need to help our clients engage their bodies in the process. There are conference centers where I teach that are an ISIS practitioner's dream because they invite physical experiences that naturally connect with mind, heart, and spirit. Rowe Conference Center has a magical mossy labyrinth that invites a ruminative walking journey through all aspects of our sexual stories. Esalen Institute is at the edge of the ocean in Big Sur, California, with hot springs where participants can float and steam as the otters play in the waves and the sun drops into the sea. But even in more ordinary settings it is possible to engage the body in activities that awaken and transform.

Throughout this book, I suggest using the breath, for energizing, grounding, and enspiriting one's self. In chapter 5, I focus on the genitals and beyond— exploring your own extragenital matrix. In chapter 9, I outline the importance of physical movement to the ISIS process, especially when a client's story is stuck. Below is another activity that works wonderfully to engage the intelligence of the body. This one is especially great for a rainy day, and particularly if you need to loosen up a group and get them out of their "shoulds" and "oughts" or out of their analytical heads. Allow at least an hour, and two hours if you can.

Creating Yourself on Paper

Materials to have on hand: big rolls of paper at least 2 feet wide, scissors, pens, markers, crayons, glue, glitter, magazine ads, bits of fabric, and anything else that would thrill a pre-schooler. The directions to give your group are as follows:

1   Choose a partner for the exercise.
2   One of you lie on the paper, the way kids do in nursery school, while your partner in this exercise traces the outline of your body onto the paper. Then switch, roll out more paper, and trace the outline of your partner's body.
3   When each of you has been outlined, cut out your outline, decorate it, write words and stories on it—do whatever you want with it. You can spend an hour or more doing this, and letting yourself feel the stories as you begin to write and draw them on your body.
4   Share your experience with your partner.
5   Everybody come together into the large group, holding the paper you in front of the real-life you, and share the experience you have had. Speak as your paper body if this works for you. Alternatively (or additionally), tape the paper bodies to the wall and introduce them in a show-and-tell session.

Questions to consider:

• What did you learn about yourself?
• If your body could speak, what would it say?
• What will you do with your paper body when you get home?

Be aware that there is something about the little kid aspect of this activity that evokes primal feelings. Participants may cry, or pout, or find themselves hoarding scissors and crayons. And, through it all, insights surface to transform the sexual, sensual adult. Here is how one woman integrated the experience. She had come to the weekend to "get a handle" on her low sexual desire.

> I learned from that exercise that I saw my body through my mind, not my emotions, and nothing to do with pleasure. My paper-doll body was covered in words, but the images that I most strongly related to in the group were other women's paper bodies covered with glitter and color and pieces of yarn. The thing is, I couldn't access those parts of my body the way I had written on it.

The paper body she had scrawled all over became a living metaphor for her low desire—so much so that she resolved to change her behavior and try to engage her husband in a playful way. Her first act when she got home was to re-create the experience with him. Her husband retraced her real body (not on paper this time) and they both had a wonderful time. "He decorated me—in all my glory."

Activities to Help Expand Sexual Experience in the Emotional Quadrant

Sex therapy clients very often have issues with knowing what they want, asking for what they want, receiving what they want, distinguishing what they want from what they don't want, expecting what they want to be given to them by others, and on and on. It can be helpful to offer several "what-you-want" activities in the course of a group. In chapter 5, I detail how you can use "Ad for a Lover" and its companion "Letter to an Abuser," activities that can take a variety of forms, from a writing exercise to a focused introduction for group sharing.

Below is another activity you can adapt in many ways, for use in large audiences or small groups, and also with individuals and couples. My colleague Esther Perel tells me she teaches it all over the world—an affirmation recently confirmed by an Israeli ISIS participant. I found a clip of Esther teaching this "turning off and on" activity on You Tube—and she does a fabulous job!

Turning Off and Turning On

First, ask participants to choose partners. The partners may be real-life partners. This exercise works wonderfully to help couples update their desires, but it also works wonderfully even with partners who do not know each other.

This is a sentence completion exercise. Explain that each pair of partners is going to speak antiphonally—that is, back and forth. When Partner A has completed the sentence, Partner B completes the same sentence stem in her or his own way, then Partner A again, and so on.

The first sentence to complete is: "I can turn myself off sexually by . . .." Be sure participants understand that this is an exercise about self-responsibility and power, not about blame—that is, how their partner or someone else can turn them off.

Do a short demonstration with someone in the group to model how the exercise works, so that everyone understands what you mean by going back and forth with sentence completions. Remind them that each person is initiating each sentence from their own desires, not responding to what the other person just said. For example, you might say: "I can turn myself off sexually by staying up till all hours working on the computer." Your partner in the exercise might respond: "I can turn myself off sexually by eating junk food and feeling too yucky for sex . . . "—and so it goes, back and forth. Time the partners for about five minutes, then ask them to switch sentence stems.

The second sentence to complete is: "I can turn myself on sexually by . . .." Possible sentence completions are: "Remembering about a fabulous time we made love by the ocean . . . " or "Exercising so that my body feels energized and ready to move . . . ." Time the partners for another five minutes, then ask them to share with each other what they noticed about themselves.

You can deepen the impact of this exercise by asking participants how and when they are doing those activities that turn themselves on. Then (if you are in a group or demonstrating in front of an audience) open the sharing to the entire group.

This simple and direct activity has opened many hearts and changed many minds about the complex subject of what you want and how to initiate it in ways that help your success rate.

Activities to Help Expand Sexual Experience in the Mental Quadrant

Throughout this book I talk about sexual messages—messages that seemingly come straight from our DNA and lodge in our brains to affect our experience of sex, pleasure, and intimacy. Chapter 6 outlines various activities regarding taking a sexual history. Below is a simple, effective way of expanding awareness about the kinds of messages that drive our sexual attitudes.

Retrofitting Your Sexual Messages

You can offer this retrofitting exercise as a whole group activity and ask participants to share "popcorn" style, or you can ask them to form groups of two, three, or more—depending on the size of the group and the time you have to spend. The basic question is: What messages did you receive about sex, pleasure, and intimacy when you were growing up, or throughout your life—from family, friends, school, church, doctors, television, or elsewhere? (You can offer a few examples, such as "Good girls don't," "Real men score," "Sex goes downhill at midlife.")

- How do you find yourself incorporating any of those early messages into your life today?
- What are the messages you want to keep?
- What are the messages you want to let go of?
- Is there anything about how you incorporate those messages that you would like to change?
- What is your first step toward making the change you want?

Depending on how the conversation goes, you can take this into ISIS Wheel movement—asking participants to stand in the quadrant from which their disempowering messages came and move to the quadrant where they can rephrase and revamp those messages to become empowering and juicy.

Activities to Help Expand Sexual Experience in the Spiritual Quadrant

Spiritual activities abound in this book, from guided imagery, meditation, and energy balancing to Tantric techniques. All these are effective ways to help clients and students explore spiritual aspects of their sexual experience. In addition, I often use stories, poems, and sayings to help participants particularize or expand the meaning of a situation. Poems by Rumi or Mary Oliver are tailor-made for this. I love the question Oliver asks at the end of her poem "The Summer Day:" *"What will you do with your one wild and precious life?"* The Native saying quoted in the previous chapter bears repeating here, as it engages participants at a level of imagination and meaning, encouraging them to reach out beyond their comfort zone: "Along the way of your life, you may come to a great chasm. Jump. It is not as wide as you think."

Along with inspirational words like these—and you will choose the ones most moving to you—I offer the activity below. Its purpose is to help participants open and trust their imagination and intuition. This activity takes about 10 minutes to complete, another half hour to process, and provides endless openings for discussion afterward.

Opening Your Doors of Perception

Ask participants to pair up into partners—preferably with someone they do not know, or at least someone whose history they do not know well. The instructions are simple:

"Sit opposite one another, introduce yourselves, look into each other's eyes.
"Now each of you close your eyes. Breathe and ground your own energy." (Be explicit about how they are to breathe and ground.)
"Now, I'm going to ask you to see each other with your eyes closed. Yes, it is possible to do this—through visualization."
"I'm going to mention a series of images that I'd like you to visualize for your partner in this exercise. You'll have a short time to play with each image before we move to the next. Just stay with the images silently. You'll have a chance to share with each other at the end of this activity."

After this introduction, you offer up a string of images, giving about 30 seconds for each, and ask them to breathe between each image.

The images below are favorites of mine, but you can substitute ones of your own if you like. The point is to start with fairly generic, easy images (flower, tree) and move to more complex and personal ones (young child, old person, energies you put out into the world).

107

- See your partner as a flower.
- See your partner as a tree.
- See your partner as a landscape.
- See your partner as weather.
- See your partner as a house.
- See your partner as a kind of machinery or electronic device.
- See your partner as a work of art—a painting or sculpture.
- See your partner as a famous lover from history.
- See your partner as a very young being.
- See your partner as a very old being.
- See your partner's legacy to the world—the culmination of his or her work and dreams.

It helps to accompany these "see your partner as" instructions with some kind of relaxing gentle music. Instead of music I like to use a frame drum, with gentle, rapid rhythmic beats. This is a kind of drumming that has an ancient history as a prime healing modality to help expand insight and overall connection. Modern science reveals that rhythmic drumming activates the pineal gland, which sits near the center of the brain between the two hemispheres—just behind the "third eye." The French philosopher René Descartes called this the "seat of the soul."

Opening Your Doors of Perception is a feel-good exercise. It increases clairvoyance, and your participants will amaze themselves at what they are able to "see." Most participants feel expanded—both deeply seen and also powerful, like seers. It can be particularly effective to do this exercise in the evening, as darkness or gloaming adds to its mystical quality. It can also be an enlightening activity to adapt as a part of couples therapy, as long as you choose just the right moment for the couple—so they have an opportunity to see each other in a positive and supportive light.

Ending an ISIS Group

Beginning to End the Session

When the time has come, I start by announcing that this is a moment for each participant to begin reflecting on the learning that has occurred for them. I affirm that this is learning that may continue forever, but right now it is time for us to begin to bring to a close this particular time we have spent together.

Then I prepare participants to reclaim each of their objects, literally unwinding the ritual process with which we began the group. By way of initiating the unwinding of the Wheel, you can suggest the following directions.

- Enter the Wheel one by one, in any order, as the spirit moves you.
- Pick up all the objects you have placed in the Wheel (note that participants may have added new objects during the course of the group).
- Briefly state what you have learned by working with your objects during this ISIS experience. ("I've learned that I can say the word 'vibrator' so I'm not as timid as I thought.")
- State specific steps you will take as your commitment to ongoing growth and change. ("I will speak up for what I want.")
- State what you are going to do with your objects when you bring them home. ("I'll put this sacred vibrator back in my bedside table drawer—and I'm gonna use it! I'm also gonna introduce it to my husband!")
- Pick up a take-home gift that you will find in the center of the Wheel. (In groups, I routinely provide a gift from the Wheel, so that each person can go home with something tangible, something more than they brought, something they can keep to help them remember their ISIS experience and anchor it in their consciousness.)
- Blow your commitment to continued growth and change into the gift you have chosen. (I routinely ask participants to blow their commitment into their gift and then into the center of the Wheel to connect them with the energies of the whole group. Using the breath is one way participants can connect outside ritual with their own bodies.)
- Express gratitude to the group. (For the last session, I often place chocolate kisses in the center and ask participants to take a kiss and then blow a kiss to the whole group—see my comments further on.)
- Blow out your candle (or move your flower back to the communal vase).
- Walk around the Wheel until the next participant stands up to reclaim his or her objects.

It is best that you prepare for this ending to be powerful, especially if you remind participants to speak their closing statements from the heart and not from some pre-planned notion they may have of saying what may please you as the leader. Even in ISIS work which focuses so intently on collaboration between client and therapist, a power gap between client and therapist sometimes surfaces like an old bugaboo, and it is important to keep returning the focus to the clients and participants.

When you are doing ISIS work in a group, it can be extremely effective to frame these suggestions within the core dynamic of ritual, so that they are incorporated into the overall ceremony you have created. For instance, an overall theme in one ISIS group was ancestor energy, especially the energy of the participants' mothers and grandmothers. So, as a way of initiating the ending, I asked the group collectively to call in their ancestors. Anyone could introduce a name, and all of us chanted that names three times. The presence of these ancestors acted as unseen helpers, assisting at the completion of our weekend.

These kinds of examples are only suggestions as to how to proceed, as some participants will have a spontaneous response as soon as they pick up their object. Note Julie's story, below.

A Note on Gifts and Gratitude

A powerful way to create ritual at the end of a session is to provide a take-home gift and a process for receiving it, such as asking participants to blow their commitment into the gift to energize it. These gifts from the Wheel are often stones I have collected from mountains, oceans, or rivers that have spoken to me. I love to bring East Coast stones to ISIS events in San Diego or San Francisco and West Coast stones to East Coast workshops, as it seems (to me at any rate) as if this is a way to widen the circle, making connections with the natural world that go beyond just our group. At the very least, we are connecting ourselves from coast to coast.

One winter, when my partner and I were driving through a town in East Texas, we came on a pond filled with a huge convocation of Canada geese. The field next to the pond had feathers wafting about everywhere. In just a few minutes I gathered a large handful of glossy feathers and found that these were a natural give-away for a later ISIS group that met in Toronto, Canada—as if I were bringing these feathers back to their source.

In groups I also ensure that the closing ritual involves an opportunity for all participants to offer gratitude to all the group members—including themselves. Managing ample time for these gratitude offerings has become a problem I have encountered over many years of conducting workshops. By the end of a workshop, participants are often so open-hearted that their expressions of gratitude could go on forever, and threaten to fill the entire last session. While this may be extremely warm and fuzzy, it also means we would have to eliminate some of the important ending work that needs to take place, especially when workshops are held in conference centers that have a strict time schedule. My solution to this has been to offer a bowl of chocolate kisses—and ask each participant to blow kisses of gratitude to the entire circle as part of their final statement. Again, this encourages using the breath to connect us all, even as we are all going our own separate ways.

... and Then Put Out the Light

If you have asked your participants to light their way in and out of the circle with candles, this is the moment to ask them to blow out their candles as they reclaim their objects—again, a use of the breath. And, again, a moment of responsibility and choice, this time signifying closure . . . not of the issue they came in with, but of this session or workshop. If you have used flowers instead of candles, each participant replaces the flower in the common vase.

For participants who have difficulties with endings, this can be a powerful moment, as it involves their own agency in closing, owning their experience, and actively moving on. As each object is reclaimed and each candle is blown out (or each flower replaced), we are all returned, at least visually, to where we began. I sometimes compare this experience to a Tibetan sand painting, which is elaborately created, only to be intentionally erased in a spirit of non-attachment.

Despite the visual sensation of returning back to where we began, for most participants there is a sense of being in a different place energetically. For some groups this is a magical moment. Some groups spontaneously hold hands or circle up with their arms around each other.

We often end with a poem, or a saying, or a song. In one workshop the women held hands and called in the lineages of their mothers and grandmothers—I am Linda, daughter of Ruby, daughter of Beulah, daughter of . . . and so on, back as far as they could remember.

During the final two minutes I ask us to let go of each others' hands and to scoop up the energies from the center into our hearts, then blow them back into the center, then scoop these energies up again and blow them out to all people who are ready to receive them. Finally, I ask the circle of group members to hold their arms in front of them at shoulder height and clap on the count of three. It is done. This is another example of the use of ritual as a core dynamic of ISIS work.

Re-entry: Extending the Group Experience

For most participants, the ISIS experience expands their hearts, minds, and spirits, opening up avenues to buried memories and also to possibilities for new sexual and relational connection. In addition, many ISIS participants become intensely bonded to the group, even in the space of a weekend. All of this opening, expanding, and bonding can generate issues for some individuals as the group is drawing to a close.

One issue is separation anxiety from the intimacy of the group. Another involves individuals' concerns about the return home to their former lives. Some participants feel so radically changed by their ISIS journey that they are plunged into a kind of cognitive dissonance, a sense that former thoughts, feelings, and values no longer hold firm. To anticipate these issues with re-entry, I address them during the final session by offering at least two strategies.

The Pyramid of Protection

Over the centuries, certain geometrical forms have proved to serve different purposes. For instance, the circle is admirably suited to communication and the pyramid is suited to protection from outside forces. Calling down the Pyramid of Protection is an instant strategy for keeping one's self safe from energetic assault, such as the kinds of disbelief that you will invariably meet in the world outside the rarified atmosphere of an ISIS group. It is an especially useful strategy when tender feelings are new-born, so it works admirably for re-entry.

The directions are simple. Begin with a clearing breath to align your energies. Place your feet firmly on the floor and close your eyes if that helps you feel aligned. Then, with your intention for the highest good of all concerned, you are going to visualize an energetic pyramid that surrounds every part of you, from beneath the soles of your feet to over the top of your head. You are able to see through this pyramid, and you can communicate through it. But no physical, emotional, mental, or spiritual harm can reach you for as long as you keep it in place.

To activate your pyramid, say: "I call down the Pyramid of Protection to surround me." Anchor these words with a snap of your fingers or some other physical action that you will keep for this purpose. Notice what happens when you call down your pyramid. Are there physical, emotional, mental, or spiritual changes? The effects may be dramatic or subtle. As you continue to invoke your pyramid in times of stress, what you notice may shift and change.

When you are new to this kind of activity, it helps to practice it out loud at first and to practice using a voice of command, one that will catch the attention of the multitudes. As you become more adept at invoking your pyramid, you may find you can do it silently or just with a snap of your fingers. You may find yourself calling it down to protect almost every venture you take, including your airplane on take-offs, or your car every time you turn on the ignition.

A Follow-up E-mail Group

A second technique for addressing end-of-group angst is to offer options for participants to join a private e-mail listserv, so that group members can remain in contact with one another if they wish. There is no pressure to be part of this listserv; opting in is entirely voluntary, via a piece of paper I pass around toward the end of the group.

The ability to stay in contact has proved to be a wonderful device for positive reinforcement. It is a way for participants to tell one another of their insights on the way home, share their re-entry stories, and generally stay in touch for as long as they want. Here is a typical share:

Dear ISIS Sisters,
I don't know that I've ever participated in anything where I felt the immediate connection and trust with the whole group that I felt with you. I'm profoundly grateful for the experience and for all the heartfelt follow-up.

112

Here is another share about re-entry:

> The night I returned home, my partner and I got into a conversation (not even about sex) that eventually took a wrong (for lack of a better word) turn. What I thought was my attempt at communication, my partner saw as my picking a fight. It struck me that there's a way of communicating in the circle that needs care in its translation to daily life. This made me remember my first spiritual retreat. When we left, we were cautioned about returning to the world of "spiritual Muggles." So, I was so pleased the next morning to see that Gina had sent us an e-mail on the topic of "re-entry" (a much better frame). I also understood in retrospect why Gina had given us the "Pyramid of Protection" strategy as we prepared to leave. Re-entry is no small thing.

Bringing the experience home is no small thing, indeed. It is a commencement, a commitment to continued growth and communication. Much more about this subject is in chapter 14.

11

STORIES OF TRANSFORMATION

How Sexual Dysfunctions Are Transformed as a Result of ISIS Groups

Below are three cases of sexual dysfunction and how they were approached during weekend ISIS intensives. Each of these participants has given permission to tell their story. Confidentiality has been maintained by altering names and other identifiers. As you will see as the stories unfold, the ISIS process is more than just a collection of techniques. It takes all four core dynamics plus the resonance of the group. In other words, to create the change each client wants, it may take a village.

Una: Long-Term Vaginismus—Releasing Body Memory

Una, a lab technician from Missouri, placed in the ISIS circle a steel knitting needle. This was an object she had brought to represent what her mother had tried to abort her with some 50 years earlier. She had come to seek help for chronic vaginal spasm and pain which was so severe that she was unable to experience anything approaching pleasurable intercourse with her fiancé. She had been in sex therapy with a medically oriented sex therapist. Dilation techniques assigned as homework had not helped her, and the telling of her story during our group revealed why. As Una's story unfolded, it became apparent that her pain and spasms were deeper than just genital. They were embedded in her whole history as an unwanted child. It appeared that she had quite literally absorbed her mother's pain into her body—the guilt and despair of a working-class Irish Catholic woman in the days before *Roe* v. *Wade*—for whom a knitting needle seemed to be the only option for ending yet another pregnancy.

Our group held Una's story with attention and compassion, along with the stories of the 36 other women present. The group held compassion for Una's mother, too, as several others in the group shared anguished tales of their own abortions and miscarriages. I believe it was the resonance of this group that inspired Una to unwind her tangle of feelings back to when she had absorbed her mother's dilemma so empathically, so specifically into her own body—as if her mother's prayer for rejection and death had surged through her own placenta to lodge in Una's vaginal muscles and mucosa even before Una was born.

Una shared with us that the Gaelic meaning of her name is "starvation."

Our ISIS weekend included a drummed meditation in which each woman was invited to dive beneath the radar of cultural expectations to explore her own imagination. This particular meditation guided each individual to meet the inner Keeper of the Flame of her sexual energy. (This meditation, including the rationale for using a drum, is detailed in chapter 19 of *The Heart and Soul of Sex*.)

Una had never meditated before. Yet she received extraordinary inner guidance—again, I believe, aided by the resonance of the group. During her meditation she received a specific directive to make peace with her mother, whom she had not contacted in over ten years, and who was now languishing in a nursing home with mid-stage Alzheimer's. A week later, Una followed the directive in every detail. She knelt by her mother's wheelchair, called her by her Irish name, presented her with a pot of shamrocks, placed her father's wedding ring on a chain around her mother's neck, and for the first time in her life opened her full heart to her mother in understanding and compassion rather than in raw neediness and anger. She knew her message had been received when a tear spilled down her mother's cheek. Una gathered her mother's tear onto her right thumb and placed it gently onto her own eyelids.

The unfolding of Una's story transcends all logic. The outcome transcends logic as well, and clearly there was no predicting it by any clinical standard we may project for sexual diagnosis, treatment, and recovery. But ultimately it all worked. As Una opened her heart, her vagina opened too. Intercourse at last became possible. Even more than possible: it became the lushly sensual lovemaking Una had always yearned for. "Mind blowing doesn't even begin to cover it," she e-mailed our group a month after our ISIS weekend. "Most amazing was the fact that I experience absolutely no vaginal pain. Let me assure you the pain has left the planet."

Una's story is a stunning example of how trauma that occurred in our past may determine our present, and then, given the right conditions for transformation, that very trauma can morph into positive possibilities neither the individual concerned nor a therapist could have imagined. I take her story as a deep lesson about the power of cultural control, intergenerational memory, and body intelligence. The "irrational facts" of the story are that Una's willingness to identify her past emotions and release them released her vagina from its chronic spasm and pain during intercourse. This is a place where conventional sex therapy had not been able to take her. Una's experience reinforces my belief that effective sex therapy often incorporates more than a "best-practices" formula that includes (in Una's case) the use of graduated dilators.

The ISIS Wheel learning I take from Una's story is that providing an emotional and spiritual container gave her permission to seek options beyond the cognitive and behavioral levels of therapy and to receive support from the group. Finally, the Wheel and the core dynamics of ISIS practice provided a new arena in which she could suspend her disbelief and allow an outcome none of us could have predicted by using evidence-based medical criteria.

Kim: Low Desire and Inhibited Orgasm—Releasing Childhood Abuse

Kim, a 43-year-old bisexual art therapist, attended an ISIS weekend to explore the repeated sexual traumas of her childhood, the memories of which she said years of talk therapy had not been able to erase. To represent these traumas she brought with her a fist-sized black rock. She expressed her pain to us with a depth of sobs that evoked tears from almost every woman in the circle: "My father took my desire away. He took my orgasm away. I have never had an orgasm without experiencing shame." As she told us her story, she paced the circumference of the ISIS Wheel like a caged tiger. At the spiritual quadrant she stopped, breathless. "I enjoyed it," she whispered. "I've never said this to anyone before. I felt so turned on by my father."

As her story unwound, Kim revealed that the years of sexual seduction by her father had occurred in the family cabin at the edge of a lake, a place she had avoided visiting for almost three decades. Like Una's ISIS journey, Kim's journey extended beyond the group, and it, too, evolved into action that was uniquely her own.

After the weekend, Kim took her black rock and revisited that cabin by the lake. She stood outside and looked through the bedroom window where her father had had his way with each of his daughters. She allowed herself to feel the helplessness, the fear, the seduction—all feelings she had resisted every day for decades. But peering into that window she felt something else, too, and it astonished her. She was flooded with memories of warmth and nurturing. Above all, she was filled with a sense of *belonging*. She breathed deeply and allowed every cell to remember how she had secretly welcomed her father's special attentions in the dark, which, as she finally confessed to us, had excited her as much as they repelled her and shamed her.

It wasn't until Kim had run through her entire range of emotions that she fully comprehended the mind-numbing rage she'd been holding onto all these years—about being overpowered, forced, trapped, seduced into enjoying those orgasms her father generated. She yelled and ranted and cried and growled and laughed about the "boundary-hopping invasions" that had robbed her of her childhood and of a significant part of her adulthood, too. She looked at the black rock in her hand and knew what she needed to do to loosen the grip of those memories so she could move on.

Kim sent a letter to our group after what she calls her black-rock experience. Here is an excerpt, printed with her permission:

> I get really clear that the rock belongs in the bottom of the lake. I blow into the rock and I bind all of that negativity into it, and intend for each and every person who violated me to take back their own energy, and I walk to the shore of the lake and hurl that blessed rock out into the middle of the lake in a sure-fire act of release and letting go.

Hurling her rock of negativity into the family lake was a symbolic act. But for Kim it was also a concrete act of trust and hope. It was transformative for her because it released from her body and spirit what she says years of psychotherapy had never been able to dislodge. "Negative long-standing energy blocks and memories have been removed, and I indeed feel like a whole new person."

Kim's story interweaves all the ISIS elements of concretizing, ritual, and movement. What gave her power to transform was her ability to embody her experience into the concrete—blowing her complex responses into the black rock in which she had transmitted all her early abuses. Her casting of the rock into the lake echoes an ancient ritual for healing from trauma. The shamanic healer Alberto Villoldo eloquently recounts just such a ritual in his 2007 book *The Four Insights*.

But Kim was not simply harking back to old traditions. Her action arose spontaneously from her emotions of the moment. What gave her courage to move was the expansiveness and boundary offered by the ISIS Wheel, by the core dynamics of movement and concretizing, and by the compassionate, non-judgmental witnessing of her story by the group.

Curtis and Elsa: A "No-Sex" Couple—Making It Concrete and Releasing Control

At an ISIS workshop for couples, the transformation began almost immediately, during the placing of objects into the circle. Curtis, a literary agent, and Elsa, a family physician, had been childhood sweethearts. Now married for some 39 years, they cared deeply for each other, bickered cruelly, and mourned the almost total loss of a sex life that had once rocked their souls. Curtis revealed a core element of their discontent when he placed a well-worn Webster's dictionary into the circle—in the emotional quadrant, the place of the heart. With tears in his voice, he stated that this book contained words of love, of which he wished to say many more to Elsa, and that it also contained words of sarcasm, of which he wished to say many fewer. Elsa brought a screwdriver to the circle to represent her habit of controlling, fixing, and, she admitted, screwing up their intimacy. To represent her intent to open up more spontaneously and generously to Curtis, she brought a fuzzy red heart she'd bought in a candy store. She placed it directly on top of Curtis's dictionary.

After the first go-round of introductions and placing our objects, I ask group members to walk around the circle to see if their objects feel as if they are in the right place, or if they need to be shifted to a different quadrant or placed nearer or farther away from the center. On his first pass around the circle, Curtis slid his book out from under Elsa's red heart and plunked it on top. A moment later, Elsa came by, slid her heart from under Curtis's book, and plopped it firmly back on top of the book. Here was a teachable moment if I ever saw one. I stopped the action.

"Does anyone notice what is happening with the heart and the book?" I asked. A laugh of recognition rippled through the group. Puzzled looks from Elsa and Curtis. "Can anyone describe a dynamic they just saw?"

Others in the group commented on the power cha-cha they saw playing out between heart and dictionary and spoke of the gender wars in their own relationships. Elsa lit up in a glow of comprehension that wiped 40 years from her face.

Elsa: "Oh noooooo. I didn't mean that as a *power grab*. It's just that I believe so strongly that the conversation about love and sex begins in the heart— without the heart, all our words are just empty."

Curtis: "It wasn't a power grab for me either. But words are so important. To me, it's the words that convey what I feel. That's what I was trying to say with the dictionary."

Here was another teachable moment—this one about interpreting other people's experience rather than asking them to describe it for themselves. I asked Curtis and Elsa if they would be willing to act as a demonstration model for the group. When they accepted, I asked them to stand in the mental quadrant and repeat their strong opinions. Elsa began, and was clearly displaying emotions as well as thoughts. This was a moment to ask: "Is there *feeling* there?" When she indicated "Yes," I asked her to move to the emotional quadrant to continue speaking from the place of her heart. When she shifted back into *thought* ("The heart should come before words!"), I asked her to move back to the mental quadrant, to clarify her stance. She shuttled back and forth many times between mental and emotional experience. The conversation finally morphed into Curtis moving to the spiritual quadrant to express what he saw as meaningful: "The important thing is that we love each other. It doesn't matter who comes first. Let's stop arguing and start listening to each other."

I recognized this statement as a teachable moment as well, one that interrupted the story Elsa and Curtis presented to the group, as a couple whose continual disagreements were part of a basic power struggle. I also knew that asking them to talk about listening to each other could well touch off another unending argument. So I returned their attention to their two objects.

I asked each of them to pick up their objects without speaking. Together we walked around the Wheel. I pointed out the obvious in their relationship as demonstrated by the dance between dictionary and fuzzy heart: that they were in great agreement about their goals, and that in their zeal to care about each other they tended to leap to conclusions about what was best for the other. In the process they fell into a pattern of continually trampling on each other's most tender feelings. Elsa concurred. "Sometimes it's hard for us to know who's on top."

"If you were each to place your book and heart in the circle to please yourself and not the other, where would you place them?" I asked. Elsa and Curtis wordlessly placed them side by side in the emotional quadrant of the Wheel. And side by side is how the heart and the dictionary remained throughout the weekend. It was that direct and that simple. (Note that the process of transformation is not always that direct and simple, but with ISIS work it often is.)

More importantly, and most amazingly to them, these objects acted as a metaphor for their relationship, just as the Wheel and the group acted as their arena for change. Curtis and Elsa stopped bickering. They expressed curiosity about each other's opinions. They looked at each other. They laughed. They held hands. And they began to make love again—and they say this has lasted. After the workshop, they sent me a photo of the heart and book resting side by side. "This 15 minutes of ISIS work is worth 15 years of therapy," Elsa wrote.

When I use Curtis and Elsa's photo for ISIS training in core dynamics, I call it "Concretizing 101." Clearly, the transformative quality of their story began in the realm of concrete objects—the dictionary and heart they brought to the circle. Unlike Kim's rock story, the transformation occurred in the circle itself, with both movement and ritual. As the group circumnavigated the Wheel and witnessed the drama being played out between book and heart, Elsa and Curtis were inspired to listen to each other and also to ask new questions. The effect was an intervention that interrupted their stuck story about themselves and each other. The outcome was that they allowed curiosity, transformed their patterns of relationship, and began making love again.

12

USING THE ISIS WHEEL IN
INDIVIDUAL AND COUPLES
THERAPY

The purpose of using the ISIS Wheel with individuals and couples is to help them become aware of clearly discernible connections between physical, emotional, mental, and spiritual experience. Organizing the connections in this way encourages clients to make distinctions, clear confusion, and open new options for communication. It also engages clients in their own therapy and allows therapists to collaborate with them rather than only diagnose and treat them.

Before addressing particulars about how to use the ISIS Wheel in individual and couples sessions, it is important to point out that the ISIS approach complements many other therapeutic models with which you may be familiar.

Use the Techniques You Know

The ISIS approach is compatible with other approaches, including behavioral sex therapy. As clients delve deeply into their stories, you will use all the therapeutic techniques you know to help facilitate the journey. This idea is spelled out in chapter 15, "ISIS Training for Professionals."

If you are using the ISIS Wheel as part of ongoing therapy with an individual client or couple, you do not have to confine them to using the physical Wheel for every session. You can use the Wheel as one of your many ways of expanding your own practice of sex therapy. You might use it for an assessment session and return to it from time to time to explore particular issues. You may find that some clients take to the ISIS Wheel quite naturally and want to use it over and over again in the course of their therapeutic journey. One client called recently and said, "Put me on the Wheel! I feel safe and open there."

There are some clients for whom an invitation to work with the Wheel seems to provide an instant sense of safety, initiation, and transformation. Other clients are skeptical at first. Some clients resonate to the language of spirituality or ceremony; others do not. Some are intrigued by the sense of being in a circle;

others are reticent to join in. Yet, for any clients who engage with the Wheel, moving to and speaking from different quadrants activates innovative ways to describe both desires and problems. It also opens the way to solutions that allow for "both/and" language rather than "either/or" language.

How the ISIS Approach Can Help Couples

For couples, working with the Wheel provides a special function. Movement around and within the Wheel can show partners exactly where each locates him-/herself when expressing the details of a story to a partner. Equally important, movement around the Wheel shows when the partner is speaking from a physical, emotional, mental, or spiritual place. Concretizing both desires and problems with tangible objects clarifies choices, as clients are able to see and work with the objects they have chosen to embody those choices. Concretizing also helps dislodge entrenched story lines by encouraging physical, emotional, mental, and spiritual movement. When concretizing is combined with movement around the Wheel, it can produce extraordinary insight and change very quickly, as illustrated earlier in the story of Elsa and Curtis.

Appropriate uses of the Wheel necessarily vary from client to client. For instance, with stalemated and/or desire-discrepant couples, encouraging movement to all quadrants can help open new avenues of communication and a safe space to practice new language for what each wants—again Elsa and Curtis constitute a prime example.

With couples who are at a volatile juncture in their relationship, it may be helpful to introduce the Wheel to the partners one at a time before bringing them together, so that you can fully explain the nature of the Wheel with one-on-one focus. For instance, when a couple is fully entrenched in the dynamic of blame, they may automatically use the Wheel as another avenue to project their disappointments and problems onto their partner and bypass responsibility for themselves.

A colleague who was using the ISIS process in a therapy session for the first time was chagrined when just such a blaming couple brought in the two objects she had assigned. Their objects were pieces of paper containing written details of all the things their partner was doing "wrong." My colleague experienced their response as a setback until she found she could—without ascribing blame to either member of the couple—use their response to the assignment as a shining example of how they kept their disagreements alive. She asked them to reverse roles and own some of those "wrongs" for themselves. Then she assigned each of them to bring in objects for the following week, to represent what they wanted in their relationship as distinct from what they did not want. This time she gave crystal-clear instructions. Experience with the objects helped this couple (and the therapist) clearly see their dynamic, so that they could begin their climb out of the depths of blame.

Another way to smooth the way for volatile couples is to ask them to limit their statements to one sentence while they are placing their objects into the Wheel. It may be necessary to repeat communication ground rules many times. The most useful rules may be to use "I" statements, rather than speaking about or for one's partner, and to keep comments positive, in the interest of moving toward solutions rather than going over old ground.

Preparing to Use the ISIS Wheel in Individual or Couples Sessions

Many of the suggestions below are consistent with those for conducting ISIS groups as outlined in chapter 10. There are, however, some practical differences as far as the use of space is concerned. There are also some intrinsic differences relating to the personalized therapeutic focus of individual and couples therapy as distinct from the kind of resonance created in groups.

Introduce Your Clients to the Wheel

In some instances an ISIS session may arise organically from a session you are engaged in with a client. But it is usually important to talk with clients in advance to let them know what to expect. Not only does this preparation serve as a warm-up, it may spur clients to do a good deal of their own work before the session, so that they arrive in a more aware place.

A good way to begin is to show your clients the diagram of the Wheel, so they get the picture. Explain why you think working with the Wheel may help them. Perhaps couples communication is the issue. You can describe how working the Wheel offers a map to help each partner identify where their arguments about sex originate—old messages, remembered slights, too many kids. Perhaps a new husband needs to understand the childhood sexual abuse his wife survived . . . and so forth. Whatever the situation, use this time to clarify the clients' issues and engage their commitment to growth and change.

Describe the format of the session to your clients. Let them know that you may be asking them to stand, to move around, to bring objects into the session, and to relate to these objects. Let them know what these activities may require of them and how you think such activities might help them move toward their stated therapeutic goals.

It is often most effective to introduce ISIS concepts slowly and carefully, leaving time to address any questions respectfully and thoroughly. Because the

ISIS process integrates so many levels of consciousness and behavior, it is especially important to offer your clients a cognitive frame for what they are about to engage in. You may need to find several ways to describe the template of the Wheel, along with your rationale for suggesting they use it.

The important thing is to elicit a "Yes" response from your clients, so that once you are engaged in the ISIS process they are curious and enthusiastic rather than skeptical or resistant. While many clients light up at the notion that you have a process that will help them, others are more reserved. If you meet stiff opposition, you may decide that ISIS is not the approach for these particular clients—now, or perhaps ever.

Extend the Usual Time Frame for Sessions

It is a good idea to plan extra time for ISIS sessions. Feedback from ISIS practitioners suggests allowing at least one and a half hours for an initial individual session and somewhat more for an initial session with a couple. If you can arrange to schedule an initial session as your final therapy session of the day, you can offer a somewhat open-ended time frame, which will remove pressure for both you and your clients.

The reasons for allowing extra time are various. First, ISIS work represents a departure from what clients have learned to expect from therapy sessions— that is, sitting in a comfortable chair and talking with a therapist. ISIS sessions will probably be more physically active than that, and possibly full of surprises. Clients need and deserve some preparation for this shift in format, even if you have described the Wheel in advance.

Aside from these reasons for allowing extra time, consider that ISIS work is designed to go deep. Once clients are engaged, they may reveal material that surprises them, and those surprises may need to be processed before the session is over. For instance, walking the Wheel may trigger responses that take clients back to childhoods and childhood traumas. You may need to help these clients differentiate between the adult who entered the office and the child who suddenly emerges and needs to be acknowledged and allowed to speak. In addition, consider that the responses evoked as a client explores the Wheel may be pre-verbal or otherwise beyond verbal articulation. When there are no adequate words to describe feelings or situations, clients need extra time, understanding, and encouragement to process their responses.

A supervisee reported to me that one of her clients' initial responses to her guiding him around the Wheel in her office were so intense that he actually dissociated when he reached the center. The good news was that this raised information about his history that he and the therapist had been trying to get at for many months. But the session needed to be extended for almost a full hour extra in order to attend to (in his words) "thoughtful downloading and rebooting" before he went home. His story is outlined in the following chapter.

Be Aware of Anxiety and Resistance

Some clients feel anxious about trying something new and "strange"—that is, moving beyond the sitting-and-talking model of therapy. This anxiety may manifest in resistance of various kinds, from not wanting to get out of their chair to statements such as "I'm not good at role-playing." Other forms of resistance include jokes and sarcasm ("Do you charge extra for making us work?"). Still others involve evasions, especially projecting their feelings onto others ("My husband would never be comfortable doing something like that."). A form of resistance I encounter fairly regularly is a flood of questions: "What do you mean by two objects?" "I don't see what this has to do with my issues." "You mean if I want to stop being crabby I should bring a crab into the office?" "Can I keep the objects after the session or do I have to leave them here?"

With some clients it is most effective to allow them to talk on until they run of out of arguments. Some clients will begin to answer their own questions. Most will feel better just having the sense that they are being heard and not manipulated.

Trust in the Process

The ISIS process is based on sound research—results of a nationwide survey along with many years of hands-on experience with the core dynamics of creating safe and liminal space, ritual, movement, and concretizing abstract concepts. It also draws from evidence-based practices such as performance-oriented sex therapy, cognitive behavioral therapy, and more.

On another level, the Wheel is based on an ancient template for awareness and transformation. When I am guiding clients in ISIS work, I can rely on both the clinical and the spiritual aspects of the Wheel to help clients expand their own stories and find directions they need to explore. Most often these directions are about connection: connecting past events and feelings with the present; connecting body, mind, heart, and spirit; connecting partners who have lost the ability to communicate fully with each other; and connecting individual clients with their own deep desires.

Clear Your Own Energy

Every therapist accumulates energy from the issues clients bring into the office. Sometimes this energy feels good and inspiring—the joy of connection, the flow when a client begins to move in a forward direction. This is positive energy we might take into a next session to inform clients that follow, in the same way that group energy resonates with other members. Often, however, we accumulate dense energy, whether this is leftover sadness or anger from the last client we saw or a build-up of tension from a day or week or month of attending to the painful problems clients bring us.

There are various methods of clearing energy between sessions. At the simplest level, wash your hands between each client (cold water is a great diffuser). Then take some deep breaths, breathing out whatever your last client brought into your session and breathing in a full heart (exchanging oxygen and carbon dioxide is a great diffuser). Some therapists take a few moments between clients to clear their minds and emotions with meditation. Others clear their bodies with exercise or yoga postures. One colleague I know keeps her iPod handy and plays five minutes of meditation music between clients to help her shift from problem-solving mode to a more open place of listening.

In addition, you can practice some grounding exercises to align your energy so that you feel fully supported by the earth. Basic instructions for personal grounding are in chapter 9, as part of the core dynamic of creating space. For many more suggestions, see the exercises in *Full Body Presence*, the wonderful book by my colleague Suzanne Scurlock-Durana.

What if you are tempted to use the precious time between clients to answer phone messages, check your e-mail, and balance your check book? Remind yourself that all of these tasks are important and may help distract you temporarily from the problems brought by your clients, but that they are not conducive to centering your energy or opening you to the sensitive work of the ISIS Wheel.

Clear the Energy of Your Room

Once you have cleared yourself, it is important to clear the space in which you see clients. As we have discussed throughout this book, one of the immediate differences between ISIS therapy and the usual talk therapy has to do with the visual space and also the liminal space—the energetic space that you cannot see. The action of clearing helps you begin to take charge of the session energetically even before your clients enter.

In chapter 10, I suggest a variety of ways to create space before beginning ISIS groups. For individual or couples therapy, it is important to take the same degree of care, though the actual preparation will be different and will be dictated by the configuration of your room and the particular clients you are seeing.

A crucial step is to set the space carefully and intentionally to help sweep away any leftover energies from earlier clients. You may do this by opening windows or playing music, letting the resonance of the sound permeate every corner of the room. One colleague says that, after a difficult session, she uses the client's chart like a fan to move the energy out of the room. In fact, there is no one definitive way to clear space, so the choice is yours. It is mainly about intention and does not have to be an overwhelming or time-consuming task. For many other ideas, see Denise Linn's *Sacred Space*, which is filled with suggestions from simple housekeeping to using sounds and scents and visualizations to clear dense energies from the room.

Visualize Your Client(s)

Once you have cleared yourself and your space, visualize your client and tap into your imaginal senses to understand what might be the most effective way of clearing him or her right now. What comes to you may be something quite doable, such as a brief meditation or simply a warm greeting as your client enters the room. Or you may visualize something quite un-doable, such as immersing the client in a rushing waterfall. Images such as this are important to acknowledge, and, if it seems right, you can actually perform them in your imagination—it takes no more than an instant.

If you are not sure where to begin as you visualize where your clients could use some clearing, try jump-starting the process by adapting the exercise in the previous chapter called "Opening your doors of perception." This will prompt you to ask yourself questions that will help you visualize many aspects of your client.

Set Up the ISIS Space

Now that you have a clear You and a clear room, and have visualized your client(s), you are ready to prepare the details of your session. If you are not going to create an actual Wheel on your floor, there are numerous other options for setting up ISIS work with both individuals and couples, and these are spelled out farther along in this chapter.

If you are going to set up an ISIS Wheel in your room, make sure you have all of the elements that are important. These include those elements listed in chapter 10 and repeated here:

- a ground cloth of some kind. For meetings with individuals and couples, I use a colorful napkin about 12 inches square. You may have a favorite scarf or other material that will feel just right. Some supervisees have found that squares of woven material meant for pillow covers work beautifully.
- dividers for the quadrants. I use four woven strips of material that are about 18 inches long. I have also used embroidered ribbon. You can use whatever material you like as long as it goes with the ground cloth you are using.

126

- cards to mark each quadrant and the center. I use clearly written file cards folded in half, like place cards: "Physical," "Emotional," "Spiritual," "Mental," and "Center."

- meaningful items to bring special energy to each quadrant. For sessions with individuals and couples I usually keep it simple and use nothing at all, so that the ISIS Wheel showcases their objects only. If the situation is right, I may add a stone for the physical quadrant (to represent the earth), a shell for the emotional quadrant (to represent water), a feather for the spiritual quadrant (to represent air), a candle for the mental quadrant (to represent fire), and a crystal for the center (to represent clarity and transformation). If you want to create a more obviously intriguing or sacred space, you can add candles and flowers, as you might for setting an ISIS Wheel for a group.

Use your own judgment as to what kinds of items will encourage your clients to open up. Be aware that some kinds of items might seem so unfamiliar that they raise questions and even trigger resistance.

Activate the ISIS Space

If you have created a Wheel, this is a time to activate it—that is, to focus on it and on how it can help your clients. You can bring offerings to the Wheel such as candles, flowers, and special objects of your own, especially if these relate to the issues your clients are bringing in. This kind of focus goes beyond clinical dictates, and there are extended suggestions for activating ISIS space in *Sex Therapy Meets Shamanism*, the forthcoming companion to this book.

Set a Clear Intention for Your Client

Finally, it is crucial to set a clear intention for the well-being of your clients. You can do this by visualizing your clients and remembering their issues. Use a tenet of humanistic psychology and see your clients and their issues in their healthiest, most vibrant light—as creative, resourceful, and whole. Some therapists bring clients' energies into the room by placing client notes or objects belonging to a client in or near the Wheel. Others visualize their clients' goals and an open path leading to these goals.

Preparing Clients for an ISIS Wheel Session

As you have already introduced your clients to the idea of the ISIS Wheel, they know that they are opting for something out of the ordinary before they arrive. There are still more preparations that will enable your ISIS sessions to help your clients.

Clear Your Clients' Energy

To help your clients center themselves and settle into the room, make eye contact and check in with them about where they are in that moment and what they want from the session. For clients who are willing, I might suggest a deep and intentionally clearing breath—breathing in a sense of spaciousness and breathing out tension or whatever else is not wanted. Again, for clients who are willing, I might also offer a very short meditation—less than a minute—to suggest openness to exploring body, mind, heart, and spirit.

For clients who are open to methods of clearing that are based in spiritual traditions, see further suggestions in *Sex Therapy Meets Shamanism*.

Share Your Therapeutic Intention with Clients

When your clients are comfortably in the room, and aware of the Wheel, let them hear from you how you imagine the Wheel might help them. For instance, for a man who has difficulty knowing what he wants, you might suggest that the Wheel can offer a safe space to practice articulating his wishes from each quadrant. For a client whose rage feels out of control, you might suggest that the Wheel can offer an equally safe place for her to explore the origins of her rage and begin to gain some awareness and understanding. Moreover, it can offer a practice that she can take home with her—not to negate the rage, but to encompass it in a safe template with boundaries that keep it from flying out of control.

Hear Your Clients' Intentions for Themselves

After all this prep work it is crucial that you bear in mind that the session is about the client, not about doing the ISIS Wheel.

What are your clients' issues? What do they want? How do they rationalize, divert, obfuscate, self-sabotage, block the ways to satisfaction? How do they open up and hope ISIS work may help exploration and change? Listen with utter attention and respect. Refer to your clients' intentions as the session proceeds. Also, note that clients' intentions may alter in the course of the session as their expectations expand and change.

If there should be a shift in intentions, ask questions and make the shift overt. Be sure to point out the change you notice and ask your client if this is true. In other words, keep checking in with your client to make sure you are on the same page.

Ensure Confidentiality

In group work, I routinely ask each member for a vow of confidentiality—a show of hands to promise that sensitive material stays within the group. I feel it is equally important in doing ISIS work with individuals and couples to reiterate whatever confidentiality contracts you have already set in place in the course of your therapy agreement. Even though your individuals and couples may assume all that they say and do in your office will be held in confidentiality, repeating your contracts with them may serve a couple of purposes. First, it can help to relieve some of their anxiety about entering new territory where they may fear what they are about to discover—like the man who dissociated as he did an initial go-round with the ISIS diagram. Second, it may give them permission to bite the bullet and look "foolish"—a fear they may have in attempting something new.

Introduce Your Clients to the Idea of Power Objects

An effective way to introduce clients to the Wheel is to ask them to bring objects to represent parts of their sexual stories on which they want to work. I describe the use of power objects in chapters 9 and 10.

The basic instruction is: "Bring in an object to represent a part of your sexual story you want to keep and expand, and another object to represent a part of your sexual story you want to release and move beyond." You can tweak these instructions to reflect whatever you and your clients have agreed to work on. For example, an author client wanted to explore her relationship to the book she was writing, and we decided she would bring in the manuscript as a single object for her to explore from every quadrant. Ultimately she discovered that the juice of her message was in the spiritual quadrant, which explained to her why she was struggling with the academic issues in the mental quadrant. Another client felt it important simply to bring himself into the Wheel without any objects so that he could monitor his own body as he moved from quadrant to quadrant. Above all, working the ISIS Wheel is a collaborative venture between client and therapist. Your sessions will be most powerful if you listen to your clients and make the decision together.

An interesting byproduct of asking clients to bring in objects is that they may do a great deal of processing of their issues before they ever arrive in your office. Many clients have shared with me that the most significant part of their ISIS work was choosing their objects, because it forced them to remember, to think, to feel, and to reflect on the meaning of their experience.

The choosing of objects does even more. I said this before, and it, too, bears repeating: the act of choosing the objects interrupts the patterned story lines that clients spin about the progression of their lives. The interruption helps them see their stories in a different way and in a different light. In the choice process, the clients have already begun to learn a new skill—like swimming or riding a bicycle. The next step, actually bringing these objects into the ISIS Wheel, may seem easy by comparison.

129

Make Sure Clients Have Brought Their Objects

Before clients enter the room you have set up, ask them if they have brought the objects they want to work with during the session. If they have their objects, invite them into the room and proceed with the session—first clearing their energy as described earlier, and following the suggested sequence below. Of course, feel free to use another sequence that works more naturally for you and your clients.

If your clients have not turned up with the objects they agreed to bring, this is the time to find out the story. The intention is not to chastise or shame them but to uncover information that will inform the therapy. Again, it is crucial to stress that ISIS Wheel work is never about performance. It is about process. To tease out the process, the most effective stance of the therapist is curiosity rather than judgment or control.

Have your clients neglected to bring their objects because of lack of initiative on their part? You can use this moment to open up discussion about how important therapy is (or is not) to this client. How important is their sex life to them? Are they in therapy to please a partner? If so, what is in the session for them? Is it the expectation of your clients that you will do all the work? If so, what do they expect you to do? This is your opportunity to point out that therapy is a two-way street and that you do not have all the answers they need.

Perhaps they have "forgotten" to bring their objects? Again, you can use the time to discuss their consciousness—about therapy and about their life. This is an opportunity to help them discover just how awake they are and how awake they want to be. Chronic forgetfulness has its rewards for some clients, especially for those with partners who pick up the pieces. Forgetting is also a classic way of burying dark and painful memories. Exploring the reasons clients resist bringing in objects may evoke more material for discussion than the objects themselves.

Were they afraid to bring their objects? Sometimes clients find their objects so intrinsically scary that they are not ready to face the objects themselves. I am remembering a client who said the object she *would* have brought was a hand grenade. Although we did not enter into a formal ISIS session on that day, this client's admission opened up an extended discussion about her fears, especially her fears about her own rage, which had roots deep in her infancy.

Other clients fear you might ridicule them for the objects they might bring. I am remembering the buttoned-up male economist who wanted to bring a teddy bear but feared I would think he was effeminate. In his corporate world, men do not work with teddy bears. Again, the information he provided led to an "extremely profitable discussion" (his words).

So any and all of these omissions create valuable openings for discussion of the topics that sent clients into therapy in the first place. You can choose to bring the discussion into the Wheel without using objects. Or you can use stand-ins for the objects they might have brought. (The woman who would have brought the hand grenade chose an orange from a bowl of fruit in my office. It served as a safe and adequate repository for her anger for the time being.)

You can also bypass the Wheel and simply talk about the issues, saving the actual Wheel work for another time. The truth is, however, that this neglected-object moment may present a most valuable opportunity for discussing dynamics that may never have otherwise surfaced—because you are right there with the client's guilt, feelings of failure and inadequacy, distrust of authority (and perhaps of you), and whatever else the client may be carrying with them instead of the objects they agreed to bring.

Set Communication Ground Rules

Again, as in group sessions, emphasize the importance of using the language of feeling as well as the language of thinking. I routinely stress the strategy of using "I" statements and speaking for one's self. This is especially important in couples sessions, where partners may have fallen into habits of making assumptions and speaking for each other (see the story of Curtis and Elsa in chapter 11). There may be specific communication guidelines for specific clients. With one woman, recently, I asked that she speak loud enough so that I could hear her. Part of her defensive posture was to mumble and speak with her hand covering her mouth. As I have some hearing loss, it was impossible for me to know what she was saying; I could not even read her lips. We used this opportunity of sharing our mutual idiosyncrasies as a springboard to help guide her gently from her inaudible self, where she was emotionally stuck as a good girl who was supposed to be "seen and not heard," to the a self-confident, articulate adult she wished to be.

Bring Clients into the Wheel

Ask clients to speak their names out loud. Then (if it feels appropriate) ask them to blow their names into the center of the Wheel—as if they are blowing a kiss. Using breath in this way is a simple and powerful technique that can connect clients' bodies to their thoughts and intentions. Naming themselves in this way becomes more than a kind of classroom exercise. Breathing themselves into the Wheel also helps to establish their intimate relationship to the Wheel. Further, it represents a kind of "yes" response that lets you know your clients trust you enough to be willing to proceed in directions that may be unfamiliar to them, and perhaps to be able to step outside of their comfort zone.

Ask Clients to Place Their Power Object(s) in the Wheel

Working with power objects is a major exercise that has been described in chapters 9 and 10. Suffice it to say here that each client needs to state clearly what each object represents, and what parts of their sexual story they want to nurture and expand or release and move beyond. Without the interactive energy of the group, it is especially important for you, the therapist, to hold space while the client speaks. Holding space is a core dynamic that encourages clients to explore the depth and breadth of their sexual experience, as outlined in chapter 9.

Introduce Ritual Elements (if Appropriate)

If your choice is to use ritual with this ISIS session, now is a good time to begin—with candles or other ritual articles. With some clients, it is entirely appropriate to ask them to light candles once they have placed their power objects in the Wheel. With other clients, candles would be entirely inappropriate. It is your call. In support of candle-lighting, you can use this as a wonderfully effective and graphic way for clients to play out the willingness and ability to "light their own fire," which is a concept they can take home with them. If candles feel over the top, or are deemed a fire hazard in your building, consider bringing nature to the Wheel in the form of flowers, or even just a bowl of water.

Review the Wheel with Your Clients

Before beginning the actual work of the session, briefly review the Wheel with clients, explaining each quadrant. Depending on the clients and your relationship with them, this may take a few focused minutes or may be as little as a word or a short phrase.

The properties of the quadrants are spelled out in chapters 3 to 7, along with some suggestions for how to think about each quadrant in terms of your clients. Leave them some space to fill in the blanks with their own experience. There is a delicate balance between dictating to your clients the definitive word on what each quadrant is supposed to mean and offering enough information to allow them to think and feel and intuit for themselves what each quadrant means for them and for their lives.

The truth is, it is impossible to paint an absolute picture of each quadrant because so much of what belongs in each one arrives there from memory or feeling or intuition or some other intangible source. Plus, much of the richness that informs ISIS work comes from parts unknown, perhaps directly from the limbic system rather than from the cognitive centers of the brain. A neurobiologist colleague calls these unknown places our "hedonic hotspots."

It bears repeating ad infinitum that the ultimate content of the ISIS Wheel is unique to each individual, and that it may constantly shift and change depending on what is happening in their brains, their lives, or even in your therapy office.

The bottom line here is for you to use your own judgment about how to describe the quadrants in a way that will allow your clients to see them as a fascinating landscape to explore. On first seeing the Wheel, one man exclaimed, "What a playground!" With this kind of reaction, you know that you have gone way beyond the realm of the rational thinking mind to help open your clients to their own limitless imagination.

Invite Clients to Speak About Their Objects

Once clients have chosen where they will begin their journey on the Wheel, ask them to speak about the objects they have brought. Or, rather than asking them to speak about the objects, you can ask them to speak about themselves in relation to their objects, or ask them to speak *as* their objects, or ask them why or how they chose these particular objects. It is your call as to how to bring in the conversation about the objects.

Clients might start speaking spontaneously. If not, you can gently coach them. "What does this book/vase/ring represent?" "And what does it say about this quadrant you're choosing to speak from?" "What is it about this object that you want to keep—or move beyond?" "What would you like to say to this object?" "What would you like to do with it right now?"

It is also important to determine with clients whether they are speaking from experience that is in their past, their present, or their future. For instance, a client may pick up an object and begin to sob. If you suspect that those sobs come way back from childhood, you might ask, "How old (or young) do you feel right now?" If she says, "Five years old," then you can follow gently with a suggestion such as, "So, if you're willing, just hold that object right now and speak as a five-year-old . . . . How about moving over to the emotional quadrant?" If she has a problem beginning, you can gently prompt her by saying, for instance, "What was the name you were called when you were five?" or "What did you call your mother when you were five?" In other words, offer her some prompts, but don't put words into her mouth—especially about a subject as sensitive as sexual abuse, even if you strongly suspect this is an issue she needs to articulate. Always allow specific content to initiate from your client. And remember that moving back and forth in time can move your client into a state that is akin to a hypnotic trance, in which verbal directions are taken very literally.

In terms of trance states and hypnotic induction, it could be important for you to know the relatively recent history of US innovators, as familiarity with their work will enhance and expand your own practice of sex therapy. Psychiatrist Milton Erikson, founding president of the American Society for Clinical Hypnosis, pioneered some of the definitive material on hypnotic trance in the mid-twentieth century (see *The Nature of Hypnosis and Suggestion*, 1980). Erikson trained the philosopher and anthropologist Gregory Bateson (*Steps to an Ecology of Mind*, 2000 [1972]). Bateson's work heavily influenced Richard Grinder and John Bandler (*The Structure of Magic*, 1977), the innovators of Neurolinguistic Programming (NLP). NLP was a forerunner of today's effective treatment for PTSD: Eye Movement Desensitization and Reprocessing (EMDR), developed by Francine Shapiro (the latest version of this technique is in her 2012 book *Getting Past Your Past*).

Invite Clients to Walk Around the Wheel

You can facilitate your client's journey around the Wheel in a number of ways. For those who need (or would value) support, you may accompany them on their journey as a guide. One client put it, "It feels like you're being Virgil to my Dante through the circles of purgatory." Indeed, this journey can some-times feel scary and confusing, like entering the "dark wood" that begins Dante's *Divine Comedy*. You may find yourself walking with a client around the perimeter of the Wheel once or several times. It is usually helpful to describe the properties of each quadrant each time you walk past, to orient the client to what qualities draw each individual to begin the sexual journey—physical, emotional, mental, and spiritual.

During this walk, I may walk beside clients or behind them—either way, letting them lead the journey. Or I may simply stand aside with attention, holding energy for them with my presence and my voice. The idea here is to support your clients absolutely, but without seeming to lead them or do their work for them. Again, it is your call in terms of what is appropriate for each individual client.

For clients whose stated (or unstated) need is for independence, it may be most helpful to stand aside and allow them to find their own way around the Wheel and into it. You can offer verbal encouragement, guidance, or questions:

> "So what do you notice as you stand in the emotional quadrant?"
> "Is it different for you when you move into the place of spirit?"
> "Notice what's happening for you as you move in and out of the physical quadrant."
> "Try moving back and forth again and say what you feel."

Some clients know exactly where they are headed, and they go there like hom-ing pigeons. Others are less sure, and they rely on your guidance. Yet others may vacillate wildly. I remember more than one client who literally ran back and forth between mind and emotions, between the thinking self and the feeling self. Allowing this vacillation to play itself out may be an extraordinarily useful exercise in awareness—an opportunity for clients to witness themselves playing out an inner dialogue that may never have been fully articulated until that time. As one woman reported after she had raced repeatedly from quadrant to quadrant: "Now I know why I'm always too tired to have sex!"

Invite Clients to Begin by Choosing a Quadrant

Often the easy way to introduce the Wheel is by asking clients to choose where they want to begin to tell their story. For instance, a woman whose presenting problem is negative body image might begin in the physical quadrant. But she may begin in another quadrant as well. She might see her negative body image as an emotional issue, or a cultural one, or a spiritual one, in the sense that it keeps her from letting go into realms of connection with herself and her partner. The point is that, in introducing ISIS, you are placing the client in a position of choice. You do not have to diagnose her or him.

Invite Clients to Speak from Other Quadrants

When clients have spoken from one quadrant, it is important to invite them to speak further from other quadrants—to expand their story and to help you expand your sense of who they are and how you can help them. You can be quite proactive, even directive, about asking them to branch out. If such directness is a challenge for you (or your clients), you can explain that you are being directive so that you can utilize this ISIS template as a teaching tool to raise their awareness—and yours.

When urging clients to explore their own relation to the Wheel, suggest they start where their current story takes them. For instance, if body issues are what they need to explore, encourage them to move into the body quadrant to see how that feels—similarly with the quadrants representing heart, mind, and spirit. This can be especially effective if they choose to explore the quadrant that represents what is most uncomfortable for them.

"How Do I Know When to Suggest that Clients Move?"

This is a question colleagues regularly ask me, as if I am in possession of some kind of prescient magic. Really, there's no magic at all. It is a question of opening yourself to what is happening in the room and picking up your clients' cues—both the verbal and the non-verbal ones. Let's go through the quadrants one by one.

Moving to the mental quadrant When you hear clients use judgmental words, such as "should" and "ought," this is a moment to suggest they tell the story from the mental quadrant, which is the place of judgments and cultural messages as well as of discernment and choice. Another clue to moving to the mental quadrant is when clients get so caught up in their stories that they can't stop talking, and you (and they) have a sense that they are "stuck in their heads."

Moving to the emotional quadrant When clients express strong feelings, you can suggest they move to the emotional quadrant to speak from there about their love, fears, hopes, rage, longings, and whatever else is in their hearts.

Moving to the physical quadrant When clients indicate body pain or pleasure or longing, or describe joys or difficulties with sexual performance, you can suggest they speak from the physical quadrant, the place of sensation.

Moving to the spiritual quadrant When clients are searching for meaning and/ or life lessons, this is a moment to suggest they move to the spiritual quadrant and speak from there. They may resist moving into this quadrant by saying things such as, "I don't have words for this" or "I'm not spiritual because I don't belong to any religion."

You can reassure them by pointing out that the realm of spirituality often lacks concrete language. You can also offer the information that spirituality does not necessarily involve belonging to an organized religion. In ISIS terms, religion often belongs in the mental quadrant, as so many religions contain "shoulds" and "oughts" about sexual expression.

Further, you can note that many human beings are even more shy about (or afraid of) speaking about spirituality than they are of speaking about sexuality. This is my observation over almost four decades of sex therapy practice, though I have never seen this discrepancy documented in the scientific literature. If you suspect this fear, you can invite your clients to bypass linear language and go straight to images. Such images might include colors, metaphors, dreams, fantasies, and memories. One client described spirituality via memories of his grandmother, who protected him from his crack addict parents. Another client likened spirituality to the rising and swirling flames in a campfire that seemed to speak courage to her. Another could relate to the concept of spirituality through the sensation of swimming in the ocean and feeling part of "all that is."

Invite Clients to Reposition Their Objects in the Wheel

You might suggest that your clients explore their objects by placing them in different quadrants or that they investigate how it feels to place them closer to or farther away from the center. If there is time and opportunity, I encourage clients to move their objects to every one of the quadrants, to re-explore and retell their story in each of them.

The reason for suggesting this is to allow clients to pinpoint and particularize exactly where, to which quadrant, their objects (and their issues, and they themselves) belong. Note that the moving of the objects is not a scientific experiment in which you are measuring exact distances. It is an opportunity for your clients to explore nuances of feeling and meaning without having to stumble through the usual editing processes that limit their story to themselves and to others.

A more global benefit of clients moving their objects around the Wheel is that this activity involves all four of the core dynamics as outlined in chapter 9. It involves use of space, because clients are moving their objects in space. It involves ritual, because using the Wheel is ritual. It involves concretizing, because you are asking clients to relate to their objects. It involves movement, because clients have to get out of their chairs or off their backjacks or pillows in order to navigate the Wheel. It is in physical action that the metaphor becomes real. Once your clients move, they are literally in a different place than they were a minute ago, an hour ago, or a lifetime or two ago, if this idea fits into your cosmology.

When Walking Is Not Feasible

Not every therapist's office is set up to accommodate a physical ISIS Wheel. And not every client (or therapist) is comfortable setting up a special ISIS Wheel on the floor. If this is your story, you can still do the exercise of "walking the Wheel," but in a different way.

Rearrange Your Office Furniture

Some colleagues arrange their office furniture so that there are four chairs, one to represent each of the quadrants. One colleague puts file-card labels in the chairs to indicate body, mind, heart, and spirit, so that clients can point to them to indicate where they are. Others ask clients to move from chair to chair to indicate from which quadrant they are speaking.

Use an ISIS Handout

The simplest method of using the ISIS Wheel is to show clients a diagram or drawing of the Wheel, to describe the quadrants, and to ask them to indicate their experience by pointing to the quadrants—letting their fingers do the walking. This method is simple on paper, but it can have profound results.

One colleague showed the ISIS diagram to a 46-year-old male client who found it impossible to talk about his feelings in therapy beyond an occasional "fine" or "OK" in response to her direct questions. His presenting problem was that he was unable to initiate an intimate relationship in his life. My colleague hoped that using the diagram might inspire him to relate more of his story. His response on seeing the diagram was to begin writing all over it—with such interesting results that I have obtained my colleague's permission to share his responses here, with details changed to preserve confidentiality. The colleague includes this session in her own ISIS story, which is in chapter 15.

First, this client renamed the Wheel to put his own interpretation on it. He crossed out "The ISIS Model of Sexual Experience" and wrote in: "The Manipulation Model of Broken Sexual Experiences." Then, he proceeded to fill in the quadrants as follows:

Emotional Story
    Fear—overpowering terror of being out of control
    Obsessing—do the right thing—or else
    Shutting up—not talking
    Self-defense—hidden, whatever you do, you can't take me
    Simple boyish love—need for acceptance
Physical Story
    Weak, small—dominated by the Big Boys
    Broken—Sad—Hurt—Indefensible
    Self-hate
    Live life from a distance
Mental Story
    Take myself down with my smarts
    OK—Not OK
    Winner—Loser
    Lost day-dreaming about Nothingness
Spiritual Story
    Grandma—special love
    With her No matter what
    faith, cherish, forgiveness,
    all Emotions Realized

As you can see, an enormous amount of material emerged from this seemingly simple exercise. It was as if the diagram of the Wheel gave this client the organizational template that allowed him to articulate issues that had been knotted in his consciousness and which he had not been able to discuss with anyone, including his therapist.

As my colleague processed this "model of broken sexual experiences" with this client, what came to the fore was his uneasy balance between over-control and spinning out of control. In her words:

> He stated that it was very powerful and helpful to write this out, but as we talked about his experiences he clearly began to dissociate. I moved to help him be in the moment by focusing on mindfulness, a concept he is familiar with, in order to get him more in touch with his surroundings. Fortunately, he was my last appointment of the day, so I could go slowly with this.

Note this colleague's need for extra time to process this exercise with her client. The evocative nature of ISIS work often means spending extra time, especially at first, because the ISIS process can raise so many issues so fast.

> Once I was sure my client was fully present again, I told him that I appreciated the hard work he had done and thanked him for sharing such a powerful emotional expression with me. I assured him we could work through his feelings slowly, at his own pace, as he seemed a little out of control—which was one of the fears that he had expressed— and I felt it was very important to him to feel controlled and "put together" before he left the office. Especially, I felt it was important for him to experience and understand that it was possible for him to move back and forth between control and out-of-control, so that he could begin to move through his fear. He was able to discuss his feelings for a period of time, and we discussed ways he could take care of himself when he left the office. What an intense session.

Ending the ISIS Session

Drawing an ISIS session to a close with individuals or couples is fully as important as drawing a group session to a close. Closing an ISIS session is not only about tying up loose ends into a nice bow before you send clients out the door or about "closure"—in the sense of "Well, that's that; time to get on to something else." It is more about honoring the notion that this session may be over in terms of clock time and also acknowledging that its energy may remain to spark awareness for an immeasurable amount of time to come. For some clients, a particular session may represent a kind of base camp, to which to return, or a launching pad, a place to move on from.

As a follow-up to an ISIS session, one woman held a ritual burial for a wedding ring that she felt carried "evil energy" from her ex-husband. Another client, who despaired of ever finding a lover, decided from her ISIS experience that it was time to open herself to the world of pleasure. She staged an elaborate ceremony where she married herself—surrounded by five of her closest friends, who had all chipped in to buy her a world-class vibrator. The vibrator did not remain her significant other for long. One of those five friends stepped in and became her partner.

Stories like these affirm for me that it is no accident that school and college graduations are called "commencements." As a wise spiritual teacher used to say, "Before beginnings there need to be endings." And remember Christiane Northrup's phrase from chapter 5: "The greatest predictor of great sex is a new partner. *So become that new partner!*"

I go about ending sessions with individuals and couples with the same intentions and often the same strategies I use in group sessions—so please read chapter 10 on groups even if you intend to use the ISIS Wheel only with individuals or couples. As in other aspects of ISIS work, I place the clients front and center and leave time and space for something unexpected to occur.

Steps to Ending the Session

In terms of what I actually do: First, if clients have brought objects to the session, I ask them to reclaim each of their objects. I begin by asking them to pick up their objects, hold them, and state what they are. Next I ask them to state the learning or insights or energy they are taking home from the session. Then I ask them to say specifically what they will do with the objects.

Where will they put their objects? On the bedroom window sill? On a personal altar? And so forth. How will they continue to relate to them? Look at them? Talk to them? Touch them? Continuing a relationship with their objects after the session is a crucial phase of ISIS work and how it may expand the practice of sex therapy. The long-term relationships clients develop with their objects become a tangible take-home message. Its intricacies are outlined in the next chapter.

To help them connect their objects with the larger energies that are present during ISIS work, I routinely ask clients to state their learning and to blow this learning into their objects and (if we have used a Wheel) into the center of the Wheel. Just as they used their breath at the beginning of the session to blow their names (and spirits) into the Wheel, this reminds them to align their minds, hearts, bodies, and spirits.

If the ISIS session has not involved using physical objects, I ask clients to reclaim their experience using the most creative language they can—stating their learning and their intentions about continuing that learning once the session is over.

You can of course vary this sequence and any details, depending on the client. Some clients will have a spontaneous response as soon as they pick up their object or begin to end the session without an object.

Finally, where it is relevant, I ask clients to state their commitment to taking specific steps to growth and change—again, using the most creative and personal language they can, not simply repeating what I might have said.

It is supremely important to guide clients to speak from the heart and not from what they think you want to hear. Even in ISIS work, which focuses so intently on collaboration between client and therapist, a power gap sometimes surfaces. It is essential to help clients be aware that they are speaking from their own desires and on their own behalf. In this commitment beyond the session phase, it is especially important that clients are making these commitments for themselves and not just to be compliant clients, to please you, their therapist.

To close the session formally, do what you usually do about making a follow-up appointment and saying good-bye for now.

13

A STORY OF TRANSFORMATION
IN INDIVIDUAL AND COUPLES
PRACTICE

This is a story of how the ISIS approach can work in both individual and couples therapy. It is mostly Annette's story, with a note about a follow-up couples session with Annette and her partner. The clients involved have given permission to tell their story, and confidentiality has been maintained by altering their names and other identifiers. As with the stories of using ISIS in groups, you will see that the process is more than just a collection of techniques. You will also see the value of using the ISIS template as a strong and safe container for allowing the core of clients' stories to emerge in order both to set a stage for deep and lasting healing and to allow that healing to take a direction that might surprise you.

Annette: Journey Beyond Trauma and
Post-Traumatic Stress

Annette is a 48-year-old graphic artist who had previously attended three ISIS weekends. She had found that participating in the groups had helped her understand the implications of her childhood sexual abuse. Most importantly, her participation had given her practical tools to help manage some severe PTSD symptoms in many relational areas of her life: she said she could now relate to friends and co-workers without retreating into a fog of anxiety and depression. But she finally felt ready to reach beyond what she called "the safety" of her celibate life to enjoy an intimately sexual relationship. She called to say "HELP! I need an individual session on the Wheel. I've finally fallen in love. But whenever I feel desire or get sexually aroused I feel pain everywhere—in every joint, in my vulva, *everywhere*." I set aside two and a half hours to work with her.

We stood before an ISIS Wheel in my office. With a new client I would have explained how the Wheel works and why I thought the ISIS process, as distinct from a behavioral or pharmaceutical intervention to manage her pain, could help her. But Annette already understood the ISIS approach from her intensive group work, so I simply asked where she would like to begin.

She headed for the physical quadrant. This is where many clients begin their stories, because they are conditioned to regard sex as primarily physical, and it is in their bodies that they first notice something amiss, whether it is numbness, disease, distorted body image, or a DSM-categorized sexual dysfunction such as pain, anorgasmia, vaginismus, or problems with erection or ejaculation. Annette's story began with physical pain.

Annette's Physical Story: From Arousal to Pain

In the physical quadrant, Annette described her pain as both sharp and crippling—shooting sensations "that come whenever I have a sexual feeling." She also said, "They frighten me a lot." As she stood in the physical quadrant and spoke, she seemed small and fragile, almost as if she were trying to disappear. I asked her how old she felt at that moment. She said she was seven. Stepping into the Wheel had already deconstructed time for Annette, so that her past had become most evidently present. This fluidity of clock time was a major clue to affirm what both of us had discussed on the telephone: that her issue with sexual pain was probably linked to trauma from her childhood abuse.

"What's happening when you are seven?" (In keeping with Gestalt practice, I addressed her as if it was present time.)

"My family is passing me from hand to hand."

"What do you mean by 'passing you from hand to hand?'"

"They're all having sex with me: 'You're seven. It's your birthday. How about sex?'"

Annette looked inward and offered nothing more here. With another client I might have pressed for many details. Or I might have suggested doing a sexual genogram to determine the cast of abusive characters in her family constellation. With yet another client I might have discussed referral for a medical workup to explore diagnosable sources of her pain. But with Annette, who is still a shaky, downcast age seven as she stands in the physical quadrant, I took care not to do any of these. I felt that pressing for details of her childhood abuse might have restimulated old trauma without furthering our search for her source of present pain and her route to pleasure. I also felt that a prescriptive conversation about how to manage her pain would have given her a strong cue to escape into her head, which is one of the ways she had learned to cope with the pain of her childhood. Either way, I felt that stopping her at this juncture would have resulted in a detour from finding the body–mind–heart–spirit disconnection that we had both agreed was our quest.

I accepted her seven-year-old story as a matter of fact, and asked if she wanted to stay in that place of age seven to explore it further. She shook her head, "No." Given this indication that Annette was ready to move out of her childhood space, I asked, "What do you need to do right now to grow your self back up to the present—to your 48-year-old self?"

I felt confident in using this shorthand language with Annette because we had worked together, and I knew she understood what I meant. Were she a new client, I might have suggested that she be aware of her breathing, feel her feet on the ground, feel her body growing through various ages and stages of her life—and possibly stopping along the way to explore other stuck spots. With Annette, I skipped these steps and simply suggested that she follow her breath back into this room, into present time, standing in the physical quadrant of the ISIS Wheel, where we could focus on the sleuth work for which she had asked for help. And I asked her to make eye contact with me as a way of grounding herself in the here and now.

Annette spent a minute doing her own version of shifting into the present, and when she made eye contact with me I asked, "Are you fully here now?" She nodded, "Yes." At this point, I suggested she move to the emotional quadrant to speak from that place to explore further aspects of her story, as I imagined more information would emerge.

Annette's Emotional Story: Terror and Visible Turn-Off

When Annette moved into the emotional quadrant, there was an immediate visible change from the fragile seven-year-old child to the put-together adult with whom I was familiar. Her spine was straight and tall, but the adult she presented had almost no emotional affect. Standing in this quadrant, she related the story of how she had spent three years after college in a psychiatric hospital—"dissociating" —and two decades after that in therapy, which enabled her to talk about the abuse now without "losing it." I asked if her therapy ever addressed any of the positive aspects of sex and intimacy. "No," she said.

She spoke of Chris, her new lover, as caring, patient, funny, a gifted editor. They had known each other for years. Annette lit up a bit when she shared that their sexual interest had burst upon them in the past months, as if they had been lying in wait for each other. But mostly her statements and blank affect reinforced for me the extent of her disconnection and how deeply her physical pain was linked to disrupted attachment and bonding.

We discussed how a sudden flood of desire such as she felt with Chris could generate pain through a high state of neurological sympathetic arousal—that is, fight or flight activity. I also reflected that the route to healing such confusing physical messages is often through the emotions, and not through pharmacology— hormones, pain-killers, and so forth.

In the emotional quadrant I might have invited other clients to do Gestalt work, family therapy, energy healing, recovery groups, EMDR—or whatever we agreed might help them fill in missing information and encourage deeper intimacy with themselves and their partners. But I knew that Annette had already engaged in decades of therapy. I shared with her that, in her case, at this moment, I felt the task was not to ask her to re-experience the pain by entering into yet another therapeutic modality. I felt she was ready to move forward, not backward, and that our task was to seek a way that was strength-based and more immediate for her. But we needed some more information. We were both curious to see what light the mental quadrant would shed on her issues, and she moved over there spontaneously, with no direction from me.

Annette's Mental Story: From Judgment and Doubt to Discernment

Here in the mental quadrant, Annette displayed the same lack of affect she had shown in the emotional quadrant. From this place of discernment and judgment, she affirmed that sex was absolutely to be feared. Not surprisingly, her mental story was one of negative judgment, shame, and doubt—beliefs injected into her by her family rather than instilled by societal or religious messages, as happens with so many clients. She expressed concern that her lack of information about healthy sex had resulted in missed cues and terror of desire throughout her adult life. I agreed that her assessment was undoubtedly true, and we took a few minutes to discuss readings and films that might help update her knowledge. But mostly, Annette and I agreed, the information that could help her through the pain that haunted her desire and arousal was not based on research data, academic theory, how-to books, or erotic videos. For her, the answers resided in her relationship with Chris, and especially within herself.

In hopes of gaining access to those connections and meanings, I asked Annette to move into the spiritual quadrant, the realm of connection and meaning.

Annette's Spiritual Story: Connection and Meaning

It was in the spiritual quadrant that Annette came fully alive. Her body relaxed, her breath flowed, her energy shone brightly. "When things got bad, this spiritual place is where I used to go to feel safe," she said, referring to her years of abuse and also psychiatric hospitalization. "This is also where I meet Chris. Our relationship is as much spiritual as it is sensual, and this is why I trust it so fully."

For Annette, spirituality was not about religion; it included much more. Like many ISIS respondents, she described spirituality as an intimate sense of connection, both with herself and with a power beyond herself—God, Goddess, Higher Power, wolf, tree. In the spiritual quadrant, she said she felt like a clear channel to all of these: "When I stand here, I am open like a flute. I can feel the music of the spheres pouring through me."

From witnessing Annette's comfort, strength, and joy in this quadrant, it was evident to me that she had spent much time in spiritual realms. I guessed that she had probably learned in infancy to bypass pain by propelling her consciousness out of her body and into her spirit. Indeed, she had learned how to dissociate herself from the abuse she suffered in her family, which is probably what had saved her from a future of personality disorders, substance abuse, suicide, or all three. A problem for her was that her dissociative skills had been diagnosed and treated as dysfunction, certainly during her years of hospitalization. In this way, Annette had been (at some level, anyway) retraumatized by the mental health system that was trying to help her.

For clinicians who have been trained to predicate their interventions on evidence-based data that can be counted and measured, it may seem off the charts to assess or even admit the existence of spiritual states. Yet there is much in the established psychological literature to affirm the essential role that spiritual consciousness may play in optimal states of mental health—from Abraham Maslow's theory of self-actualization to Jung's assertion that human experience is characterized by "irrational facts" that are beyond quantification. It has been helpful to me to be able to cite cognitive back-up that so clearly supports my own clinical observations with ISIS work over the decades, even when these observations may run counter to traditional sex therapy.

Relevant to Annette's presenting problem for this ISIS session is that her sexual experience involved her body as well as her mind, emotions, and spirit, and that when she finally fell in love she needed to make peace with her body instead of vacating it. Her body was, in fact, yelling at her to pay attention. At age 48, she finally had to find a way to re-enter her body, with pleasure. We identified our next step as "Mission Impossible."

The question before us became: How can Annette experience pleasure without pain? Or perhaps the question was: How can Annette incorporate pain into pleasure? Or put another way: How can Annette send new messages to her autonomic nervous system that both minimize pain and maximize pleasure? Put in ISIS terms: How can Annette find a pain-free path that allows her to move back and forth between her spirit, in which she experiences such pleasure and joy, and her body, in which she experiences such hurt and pain? I shared these questions with her without presuming to suggest answers.

At this point, Annette had a light-bulb moment. She asked me if I would be willing to take her on a drummed journey. This is a transformational kind of meditation she had experienced with me during our groups. I have written about this kind of meditation in chapter 19 of *The Heart and Soul of Sex*, "Invoking Your Keeper of the Flame," and describe it further in *Sex Therapy*

Meets Shamanism. Suffice it to say here that the purpose of this kind of meditative journey is to shift levels of consciousness beyond cognitive reality in order to help clients access their own deep inner wisdom.

This particular intervention has evolved from shamanic practices, and I acknowledge that it is not appropriate for every clinician to use. The point here is that Annette was asking for my assistance in helping her fly under the radar of cognitive thinking so that she could access a pain-free path to sexual arousal and intimacy. In a similar instance, I invite you to use whatever meditative or consciousness-shifting methods work for you and your clients.

I trusted Annette's intuition that a drummed journey was exactly what she needed right then to help her connect spirit and body. I also trusted that at this profound level of her story Annette would discover unique routes to understand her wounding and find her own ways to what she needed.

To prepare for her journey, I asked Annette to lie on my office carpet beside the Wheel. My direction to her was that she begin by breathing deeply and that she follow her breath to a place inside her where she felt safe, open, and clear. From this place inside herself, I asked her to send her consciousness into the very center of the ISIS Wheel—the place where body, mind, heart, and spirit merge and meet. I felt confident Annette could do this, as I knew that projecting her consciousness was a skill she possessed.

I then offered her a positive injunction. This is a transformative technique outlined in the work of Milton Erikson and others, and which I have found to be supremely effective when a client is open and ready. The injunction I offered Annette was directive and clear:

> In the center of the ISIS Wheel you will receive inner guidance about how you will be able to connect your highly evolved spiritual sensitivities with your wounded heart, mind, and body. This is the place where you will discover whatever you need to learn about sexual pain and sexual pleasure.

When I could see that Annette was breathing regularly and deeply, I began to beat softly and rhythmically on a frame drum for about 15 minutes—until Annette indicated that she was ready for me to stop.

Annette's Journey to the Center: Integration and Transformation

Here is Annette's story as she related it when she returned to the here and now, after her journey to the center of the ISIS Wheel.

At first during her inner journey she experienced her pain as a river—a Ganges—with all its complexities, from providing sacred clarity and fecundity to being a conduit of refuse and garbage. In short, she discovered that pain was not everything, but that it was a part of everything. She also understood that pain was part of the sacred flow of life. Moreover, she realized that there was a way through it. In her journey, she found a boat, a vessel that helped her travel this river safely, and ultimately with great pleasure. It was a solid vessel with huge, colorful, billowing sails. She saw the name written on the prow of this vessel. That name was "Prayer." Prayer was a practice Annette instinctively knew how to do.

When she returned from her inner journey Annette reported feeling radiant and relaxed. She had a clear direction. She no longer felt afraid that physical pain would keep her away from the relationship she wanted with Chris, and she felt certain that she could discuss these extraordinary insights and experiences with Chris, who would understand, and help.

As part of Annette's re-entry into the world of clock time, I suggested that we schedule a follow-up session with Chris, as I felt it could be crucial for Chris to understand the complexity of Annette's sexual responses, and that it might help if she could experience the ISIS Wheel as an organizing principle. A month after this session Annette and Chris came for a session together. I set aside two hours to see them, with the intention of leaving enough time to explore whatever arose.

Annette and Chris: A Follow-Up Session with the Couple

To orient Chris to the ISIS approach, I asked Annette to introduce her to the Wheel, describing the quadrants and the center in her own words. Then I suggested that Annette retell her story from each quadrant—her story of sexual arousal and pain, as she was experiencing them in the present, and also as she had been experiencing them a month ago.

Annette Retells Her Story

As Annette told it, the basic issue remained, but with differences. She reported that she still felt some physical pain on sexual arousal, though she described an increased ability to anticipate and enjoy sexual feelings. She attributed this shift to two factors. One was her new awareness of why and how she had separated her physical and spiritual experience. The other was her discovery that she could use prayer as an ally. When Chris and I asked Annette exactly what she meant by prayer, she said that prayer for her was not about invoking a deity; it was more about appealing to her own well-honed dissociative skills to move her from physical pain to spiritual safety—and now from there to sexual pleasure.

148

Chris Responds by Moving on the Wheel

To offer Chris a way to listen to Annette's story in an active way, I directed her to stand in whatever quadrant expressed her response as Annette was telling her story. That is, if she felt a surge of anger when Annette was describing the early sexual abuse, she could move herself to the emotional quadrant. If she experienced spiritual connection when Annette described her inner journey, she would join Annette in the spiritual quadrant, and so forth.

The purpose of suggesting such movement was to help both of them organize their responses about this complex issue. Another purpose was to enable each of them to manifest their responses so that they could see where each other stood—literally—on the Wheel. Still another purpose was to offer both Annette and Chris practice in using the template of the Wheel as a safety net, to support the trust they felt with each other. A crucial take-home purpose of using the ISIS Wheel with Annette and Chris was to offer both of them a tangible device on which they could rely if the issue of Annette's pain, or Chris's responses to her pain, became confusing or upsetting when they were making love. They could bring the ISIS Wheel into their bedroom as a way to guide their discussion.

I explained that there was no right or wrong in where either of them moved on the Wheel, and that I would be attending closely to both of them, asking clarifying questions if warranted. If either of them wished to stop the action at any point to explore their responses, I invited them to do so.

An interjected note here on using the ISIS Wheel in couples therapy: Had this been a different couple with a different story, it could have been important at this point to help call forth parts of the partner's story, especially if anger, rejection, or communication differences were in the picture. In that case, in the interest of clarifying any points of contention that existed in the couple, I might have offered Chris an invitation for her to speak her own story as she moved from quadrant to quadrant, perhaps even allowing her story to take equal focus with Annette's.

But no such points of contention were apparent between Chris and Annette. Consequently, our focus remained on Annette's story and on Chris's ability to respond with empathy and understanding. Throughout this session, my stance as a therapist was to support both Chris and Annette as they showed each other their responses by moving into various quadrants of the ISIS Wheel. (Again, with a different couple with different issues, I would have adapted my stance by being more or less directive, albeit equally supportive.)

If a single moment stood out for me about this session, it was when Chris placed herself in the physical quadrant and reached her hands across to Annette, who was standing in the spiritual quadrant describing her struggle to step fully into physical pleasure. Chris's gesture was one of pure invitation to connect.

Eloquently and without words, it showed her understanding of Annette's quandary and an ability to move beyond her own immediate needs to reach out to Annette. It was a gesture that carried the energy of the prayer that had so powerfully moved Annette during her inner journey.

It was time to close this session—with affirmation for the couple's ability to hear each other and relate to each other, and with an invitation for them to return for another session if and when they wished.

Reflective Thoughts

A year later, Annette called to say that she and Chris were now living together and that they were planning their wedding. She said that sexual desire and arousal had become a joyous part of both their lives. In the increasingly rare instances that Annette experienced physical pain, both she and Chris were able to acknowledge its presence as an invitation to undertake a new level of sexual curiosity and discovery—body, mind, heart, and spirit.

Reflecting on this ISIS story underscores for me that helping Annette and other clients make the subtle connections between sexual pleasure and pain generally lies beyond the scope of cognitive-behavioral sex therapy. In fact, helping clients fully engage in these subtleties may involve every one of the skills a therapist has acquired in the course of developing a practice: psychotherapy and sex therapy along with sensitivities that incorporate energy healing and even spiritual counseling.

Our use of the ISIS Wheel in this collaborative way served several therapeutic purposes. First, it offered Annette a cognitive frame through which to reconsider the threefold belief that she was irreparably damaged by her childhood abuse, that she was sexually dysfunctional, and that she was "disordered" by the dissociative abilities she had developed to survive her abuse. Bringing Chris in on an ISIS session reinforced these positive reframes and added the element of Chris's understanding, support, and active communication.

For Annette to retell her story through the template of the Wheel allowed her more than a cognitive reframe to negative beliefs. It offered her an embodied sense that the paths to healing lay deep within herself rather than through an imposed theory or regimen. Following these sessions, Annette said that, on the occasions when her pain recurred during sexual excitement, which it inevitably did, she consciously used her dissociative skills to call forth her vessel with billowing sails to help her glide into her body instead of away from it.

In these ways, Annette was able to create a constellation of safe ways to move through the pain, which she now identified as the toxic flotsam of her early life. With Chris, she began to allow herself to explore the entire flowing river of adult loving sexual experience, opening herself up to delight and ecstasy as well as to moving beyond fear and resistance. Annette described her pain on sexual excitation as finally beginning to disperse, like a monsoon mist on the Ganges.

Note that this entire ISIS story evolved without using power objects to concretize the abstract concepts of pain, pleasure, and abuse. Also note that other ISIS core dynamics played major parts. Movement was important to help Annette locate parts of her story on the Wheel and also to help Chris and Annette communicate where they each stood as Annette retold her story. Ritual was an important part of Annette's drummed meditation and her extraordinary inner journey.

The core dynamic that played the largest part was creating and holding liminal space—by locating Annette's and Chris's concerns within the multidimensional structure of the ISIS template. The ISIS Wheel offered Annette the sense of safety and direction to explore her complex issues along with a dependable place to land when she returned from her journey into the center. For the couple, the Wheel offered a blueprint for clear communication about the potentially explosive and divisive issues involved in sexual pleasure and pain. Annette's summary: "It helped us trust each other."

14

TAKING THE ISIS
EXPERIENCE HOME

For many clients and therapists, the ISIS experience does not stop with the end of a workshop or therapy session. These are only the beginning. The ISIS experience continues to generate awareness and growth through the Medicine Wheel template, through the core dynamics, and through the objects that represent various aspects of our sexual stories. Although it is important to acknowledge hurdles clients may experience in the re-entry process to their homes and workplaces, that is only part of the story. In chapter 10, I offer specific strategies for lowering the hurdles. This chapter looks at positive strategies to help clients take the ISIS experience home.

Taking Home the ISIS Template

Most ISIS Wheels are created in communal spirit. Their characters are determined by the objects and offerings clients bring to explore. When the session is over, much of the physical creation of the Wheel disappears—gone, like a Tibetan sand painting. But the template of the Wheel remains, as the structure that has held the energy of each particular session. Moreover, the spirit and energy of the ISIS Wheel live on, with the potential to inform all who have been a part of any or all sessions.

What individual clients take home with them from the ISIS template varies. For some it is the sense that there is a container for their stories, no matter how complex or convoluted those stories might be. The Wheel has served as an organizing principle for participants telling their stories—to their therapists, their friends, their partners, and, most significantly, themselves. The story of Annette in the previous chapter is a prime example of this. Others take with them the beauty and energy of the Wheel, and many re-create that beauty in their homes and offices, sometimes quite spontaneously, out of what is at hand. This is what occurs for the woman below.

What you said is so true . . . about the importance of having a container when you go on those difficult journeys. The night after our closing, I made an ISIS circle out of the crocheted eight-point star doily next to the bed at the B&B—and at home I have made one out of a similar doily my grandmother crocheted . . . .

Others identify with the ISIS Wheel in a new consciousness of the circles and wheels all around them—in nature, in mandalas and labyrinths, and in the multidimensional components in almost every situation in their lives. All of these call up the ISIS experience and remind them that there are ways to explore their stories, and their lives, from different perspectives.

Practitioner colleagues bring ISIS Wheels into their offices in diverse ways. One has made a poster of the basic template, which she hangs where clients can see it and where she can refer to it. One keeps an ISIS Wheel diagram under the glass on the coffee table in her office, so that she and her clients can use it whenever the time is right. Several colleagues keep stacks of ISIS diagrams they can use in the office and give clients to take home with them. Others keep an "ISIS-to-Go" kit in the office so they can create a simple Wheel on their office floors when it is needed. Others use ritual elements to create sacred space in their offices—their ISIS Wheels include candles, shells, stones, and other special objects. Two colleagues created "God's-Eye" ISIS weavings with sticks they gathered together at an ISIS training. All of these inform the office space, whether or not therapists are actively engaging clients in ISIS work.

Taking Home the Core Dynamics

An extraordinary aspect of ISIS work is that it shifts long-held patterns—physical, emotional, mental, and spiritual. Core dynamics of the ISIS process contribute to these shifts, and the core dynamics themselves may become part of what colleagues and clients take home.

One core dynamic of the ISIS process is creating a sense of liminal space. This means the ability to make the environment a safe and vital arena for change—a place of power, connectivity, resonance, and expansion. For many ISIS graduates, this sense lasts far beyond the sessions around the Wheel. Colleagues bring this sense of liminality into their offices. Clients bring it into their homes and bedrooms. They are able to create a powerful container through clearing energy and through focused intention, as described in earlier chapters.

Another core dynamic is movement. When ISIS practitioners ask clients to get up out of their chairs and walk around the Wheel to notice their experiences from multiple perspectives, something takes place that does not happen when there is no movement. There may be a simple shift of expectation—that the therapist actively wants to listen and understand rather than offering a diagnosis or "fix." Or there may be a shift of focus—the novelty of telling a story from different perspectives makes the story fresher, more expansive, less by rote.

For many, there is a sense of embodiment. Clients have described the activity of getting up and moving during therapy as helping them form a new relationship with their bodies—even when no overt body work is done. The simple act of walking the Wheel taps into the body's innate intelligence. What clients take home with them from ISIS sessions remains in the memory of muscles and skeletons and cells, as well as in minds and emotions. Numerous clients have mentioned literally incorporating the powerful action of taking a step out of an impossible situation or stepping into a situation they *do* want. Beyond the sessions, the take-home potential for shift is present every time clients move their bodies. One client describes it as follows:

> I uncovered the hidden beliefs I had about myself and you helped me release them so I could fall in love with myself . . . finally. I can't tell you the freedom I've enjoyed since then. I left feeling a door had opened up and that I could just step back into my perfect flow.

Core dynamics of ritual and ceremony are also processes that travel beyond ISIS sessions. These may include slowing down, breathing, walking intentionally, lighting candles, calling in the spirit of what you want, and, perhaps above all, noticing the world around you and the world inside you, body, mind, heart, and spirit.

Taking Home the Power Objects

When clients have reclaimed the objects they activated in the Wheel, it can be extremely helpful for them to continue to relate to these at home, as "power objects" or "medicine pieces." These objects hold the nuances of the stories with which the clients came in. Now they also hold the energy of the circle, plus any momentum that clients may have experienced in the ISIS Wheel.

One way for clients to engage actively in their own experiences of growth and change is to develop a relationship with their power objects at home. For some clients it is a revelation to find that they can continue opening up on their own without guidance from a therapist or coach. This may be a revelation to some therapists, too. It can be humbling in the most productive sense to find that your clients can get along without you and thrive on their own. For both therapists and clients to learn and assimilate this lesson effectively roots out the seedlings of client–therapist dependencies before they have a chance to sprout and burst into bloom.

While you are ending your session is an auspicious time to introduce your clients to the idea of continuing to work with their objects. Explain that the objects they have been working with contain new and crucial information that can benefit them—potentially for a long time.

The energy of these objects may feel palpable to your clients. One woman said, "When I look at this picture of myself as a five-year-old it puts me right back in the circle and I remember how my heart suddenly seemed to open up and soften." This is more than a cognitive memory for her. It is also a body memory, and she can access it through breathing and visualization as well as through intellectually recalling the situation. The photograph she activated in the ISIS Wheel provides a tangible way to reconnect with her past, with concrete power to monitor and change her responses to present situations that relate to her past.

For other clients, the energy of their objects may be subtle, perhaps not noticeable at all. The energy quotient will depend on the sensitivity of the client, the power of their story, and sometimes the objects themselves. Objects such as photos, wedding rings, and love gifts typically carry strong memories with specific associations. Natural objects tend to carry intrinsic energy—these include crystals and other stones, which are acknowledged as keepers of memory and wisdom. The individual meanings of these objects is crucial, however. Always allow your clients to state what the special significance of their objects is for them. Build on the meanings they ascribe to their objects, not on what the object may symbolize in the literature, or for you. In other words, this is an opportunity both to resist interpretation, no matter how brilliant it seems, and to listen closely to your clients.

Allowing Objects to Become Teachers

Once you have explained the rationale for taking their objects home, ask your clients to allow these objects to become teachers. Granted, for some clients it is a major stretch to believe that an old gym towel or a broken mirror can have anything more to say to them. The gym towel stood for all the times a 66-year-old woman remembers being laughed at in high school because she had small breasts. Once she brought the towel home from her ISIS group, she found control over the memory (and release for her resentment and rage) by unraveling the towel, thread by thread. The broken mirror stood for another woman's broken dreams of romance; once home, she realized that what was broken were romantic fantasies, not real dreams. She bought a new mirror and pasted affirmations on it.

You may have to suggest ways clients can allow themselves to enter into a willing suspension of disbelief. This wonderful phrase was coined two centuries ago by poet Samuel Taylor Coleridge to prepare his readers for his highly imaginative writing. It means the ability to put aside your fixed ideas about something in order to sense its larger meaning and its context. In ISIS terms, suspending your disbelief involves the ability to move from the mental quadrant of the Wheel, which is ruled by rational linear thoughts and judgments, into the emotional, spiritual, or even physical quadrants, which offer a different, often more fluid sense of the whole picture—in other words, allowing yourself to step into liminal space.

So you are asking your clients to enter into an ongoing relationship at home with their objects, just as they might have related to a favorite stuffed toy or imaginary animal when they were kids. This is a kind of Calvin and Hobbes invitation—to play, to imagine, to make believe. You are inviting them to free up body, mind, heart, and spirit. You are helping them open a door from the world of everyday reality to the unseen world of images and spirits.

Although moving between these different realities is an energy concept, it belongs to the realm of science as well—especially if you understand science as a story that is told to explain what is not yet understood. Contemporary brain research tells us that moving back and forth between linear thought processes and imaginal levels of perception actually creates new neural pathways in the brain. This is the basis of the hypnogogic states reached, for instance, during therapeutic processes such as NLP and EMDR. Daniel Siegel, a professor of psychiatry at UCLA, has written a number of smart readable books about neural integration or, as he terms it, "mindsight."

Gaining at least a rudimentary understanding of how our brains access information helps some clients locate the process of growth and healing in the realm of human possibility rather than of magical thinking. But you do not have to become a brain researcher to recognize a sudden openness to healing when it occurs. I referred earlier to the practical spin on psychoneurobiology by my colleague Tammy Nelson, who refers to this aspect of growth and healing as "making new deer tracks in the brain." And, when we open up these new paths in our brains and in our lives, we must reinforce them.

Finding a Special Place for Take-Home Objects

Suggest that your clients find a special place for their objects in their home or office or yard, or wherever seems most suitable. This could be on an altar, a desk, a window sill, or wherever the client will see their objects often, and where the objects themselves will be happy (remember, you are suspending disbelief here and entering into a world of energy, imagination, and play to expand your own story).

If a take-home object contains negative energy, it may still become a significant teacher. Urge your client to seek out a totally safe place to keep it. It is especially important not to introduce negativity into the bedroom. The transmission of energy does not stop with sleep. It may intensify and burrow into deep levels of your consciousness. Also, I remind clients that the bedroom is a place for making love as well as for sleep. It is best to find another spot for any objects whose purpose is to help you work through your traumas.

Creating a Relationship With Take-Home Objects

Once your clients find a place for their objects, suggest that they carry on relationships with them. One ISIS colleague urges clients to program themselves to dream on their objects—by visualizing them as they are falling asleep and asking for information to be revealed during dream states. Another way to suggest your clients keep the energy alive and meaningful is through developing simple rituals, such as looking at their objects every day, and touching them, and saying: "I remember."

As clients develop an energetic relationship with their objects, they will know if and when the time is right to transform or release these objects, as Kim (in chapter 11) did with the black rock which carried the energy of her childhood abuses. As Kim told the story, this rock she had brought to our ISIS group literally propelled her to seek out the family cottage where those abuses had occurred. Then it literally yelled at her to breathe all of her old hurt and confusion into it, and finally it moved her arm to hurl it deep into the lake.

Other clients have reported shredding, burning, and burying objects that contain toxic energy for them. But it is important to help clients understand not to destroy their objects until they have made conscious the intangible feelings and memories those objects carry. Otherwise those feelings and memories can burrow deep into the underground of the unconscious and continue to spread, just as wildfires spread through the roots of trees. Or, borrowing from the deer track metaphor, they can make mole tunnels deep in our brains.

Many clients keep their objects for inspiration, as Curtis and Elsa (in chapter 11) did with their book and heart, which they say remind them to listen to each other instead of insisting on being "right." ISIS graduates tell me that they sometimes keep their rocks, shells, and other medicine pieces for years: "The lipstick—I still have it in my drawer." "The crystal with my intentions is in the bird's nest I found walking that day." "I framed that photo of me and Harold and keep it on the shelf above our bed." And on and on. Some ISIS grads carry their power objects with them, like the woman below.

> The two stones I worked with mostly live on the ISIS Wheel I made in my office. Though I find I want to keep their tangible energy close to me to remind me to stay centered and strong—so I've been carrying them in my pocket this week.

157

Another perspective is offered by Kiri, who had brought to an ISIS group a red rose to represent her wish for what she called "organic love." It had been part of a vase of flowers her husband had sent to wish her well for the weekend. She writes:

> When I arrived home on Sunday, I noticed that the rose I'd brought to the weekend and that had sat in the Spirit place in the Wheel was significantly more open than the other roses in the arrangement. There may be some botanical explanation for this, but I know what I choose to believe.

The truth is, Kiri discovered that her experience in the Wheel had opened her as well as the rose. Once home, she used the rose to help her reach new sexual connections with her husband, especially to open up their communication:

> When he saw how open the rose was, we were able to discuss that he's been afraid of my passion, and he now wonders what mixed messages he's been giving me all these years in the bedroom. Wow! What a gift this process has been, and continues to be.

Moira is another woman who speaks movingly of the power of the object she brought home—a necklace of fire opals. She had placed this in the Wheel to signify her wish to let go of the pleasure anxiety that felt like an unreasoned resistance to "going all the way" during sex. Moira had been raised Catholic and attended an all-girls Catholic school. She and her husband met when they were both six years old. "In our marriage, I think we were still that age sometimes. We carried on some weird kind of power struggle as if we were kids fighting over a pail and shovel in the sandbox."

So, for Moira, sex was accompanied by a vision of struggling children and disapproving nuns—a vision that delivered a clear "Stop" signal every time she felt excited or began to let go into pleasure. After her ISIS experience, she was able to replace this stop signal with a new vision—one of feeling herself become the mysteriously beautiful and fiery opal necklace secure in the energy of the Wheel.

> Now when I'm considering "going there" with my husband I see that dark, candlelit room with that soft and warm feeling I had and I let it carry me with the same knowing that I can go as far as I want with it. More often than not it's much easier to keep going and have one great experience after another because I feel validated that although the sex is here for me it's up to me to enjoy it (or not).

Moira writes that there's no more fighting in the sandbox at home. Her husband is reacting "wildly wonderful" to her new generosity of spirit, mind, and body:

He's been so present in all the ways I appreciate and it's carried through to all areas of our relationship causing us to feel sooooooo close, which is all either of us ever wanted in the first place. The great sex is just the icing on the yummy glorious giant cake! I am so blessed.

As clients prepare to take their objects home, suggest that they reflect on the ISIS commitments they have made. Ask that they feel the commitments, think about them, and meditate on any changes they notice as a result of their experience in the Wheel.

Communicating about ISIS Experiences

Finally—very important—encourage your clients to talk about their ISIS experiences. This may be difficult at first, because the language of sex is so focused on performance—who did what to whom. But it is worth the effort to try to find words to express feelings and insights that fall beyond the performance paradigm.

Talking out loud helps make these experiences real so that they don't lodge in the memory as far-away one-time occurrences. Talking about them will help them feel current and connected with the rest of your clients' lives. Ideally, clients who have partners would talk with their partners, as long as these partners can welcome the unfolding of potentially sensitive and subtle material—the way Moira's husband did.

Not all clients have friends who are open to talking about the subtle connections inherent in ISIS experiences. Nor do they have partners who are open enough to accept the degree of multidimensionality involved. Some friends or partners are scared of so much openness. Some partners may be open to hearing but simply do not want to change their performance-oriented ways. I have heard of partners who have become angry, even enraged. Clients who have opened up may shut the experience down in self-defense. A woman who had hoped to save her shaky marriage said that coming home to that kind of energy "felt like subjecting a new-born to shaken-baby syndrome." In fact, some clients say it is difficult for them to find anyone in their world they trust to understand the depth of their experience. One woman said: "It's as if I were trying to describe a Hogwarts moment. I live in a land of Muggles."

Introducing a newly opened self into the world is a matter of trust. But we are of the world and we cannot live forever in a vacuum, even an ISIS vacuum. So, however difficult it may be, I strongly urge clients and all ISIS graduates to talk with someone—a friend, a therapist—someone who will listen to them and encourage their opening rather than trying to shut it down.

Part IV

TRAINING AND
INTEGRATION

If the situation is used for truth and sanity, its outcome must be peace.

A Course in Miracles

15

ISIS TRAINING FOR PROFESSIONALS

Health, well-being, and intimate relationships are profoundly affected by sexual issues. Yet most health professionals lack training and supervision to help their students, clients, and patients negotiate sexual choices in safety and pleasure. ISIS training attempts to help fill this lack by offering an innovative model for exploring a wide range of clients' sexual stories about desire, gender identities, sexual orientation, pleasure, dysfunction, aging, abuse, affairs, polyamory, and more.

Like ISIS retreats and personal growth groups, ISIS training sessions for professionals are structured to encourage heightened awareness. But there are essential differences. The training begins with a PowerPoint presentation and involves role-plays, didactic sessions, and case supervision to help health professionals practice and teach the ISIS core dynamics, along with an expanded view of sexual intimacy that includes physical sensation, emotional passion, cognitive discernment, and spiritual longings for connection.

There are several levels of ISIS supervision and training for sex therapists and other health professionals. I offer some of these myself, and others are offered by members of the growing ISIS Network. All these focus on the integrative approach typified by the ISIS process outlined in my books, on my website, and elsewhere.

These training sessions are never tied to only one modality. Besides sexology, they span a gamut of powerful protocols and methodologies, among them family therapy, family systems, Emotionally Focused Therapy, Gestalt therapy, bioenergetics, psychodrama, pychosynthesis, hypnosis, narrative therapy, Imago, and EMDR. A few of the activities I use are outlined below. More will be outlined in the Clinical Workbook to accompany *Expanding the Practice of Sex Therapy*.

Using the ISIS Wheel as a Clinical GPS

When I teach, I use all of the core dynamics of ISIS work: creating and holding space, movement, ritual, and concretizing abstract concepts. When I conduct group training for sex therapists and other health-care professionals, I use the Wheel as a kind of navigation system to help participants locate their clients' issues—and also to guide their clients to locate their own issues.

Pop Quiz

In order to actively engage a whole group of trainees at once, I model the core dynamic of movement by asking them to get out of their chairs. One way I teach is to ask everyone in the class to move as a group to stand together in each quadrant. I then ask them to call out, popcorn style, the issues their experience tells them belong in each quadrant.

I might formulate this as a kind of quiz. For instance, if they are in the physical quadrant, I might ask such questions as:

- What kinds of issues will your clients bring you *here*?
- What are the presenting problems?
- How might the physical issue be related to a client's emotional issues (or mental or spiritual issues)?
- What might you suggest the client do to raise self-awareness?

This exercise is an effective ice-breaker, as it offers a relaxed opportunity for members to share their particular expertise. When I am working with seasoned professionals, there is great scope within each quadrant to answer questions such as these in the variety of ways in which each individual has been trained.

A traditionally trained sex therapist might focus on sexual dysfunction—with homework on sensate focus. A Gestalt therapist might focus on body awareness—encouraging the client to reveal various stories the body tells. A trauma specialist might focus on abuse issues—and suggest a session of EMDR. An Imago therapist might focus on couples communication—and assign worksheets with sentence completions. And so forth. There may be enormous diversity in the answers, including information that I might never have thought of, so we are all expanded.

The beautiful thing about this exercise is that you cannot do it wrong. There is no one right answer, so it can open up infinite possibilities. And there is an opportunity for professionals to ask questions of one another, which enriches everybody.

The beautiful thing about gathering a group of professionals is that they expand the practice of sex therapy by simply being themselves and opening up the conversation.

Naming the Issues

When the group has demonstrated an understanding of the scope of each quadrant, I take them a step further. I ask them to imagine each quadrant as a kind of therapeutic Petri dish in which they can closely investigate certain kinds of sexual issues and dynamics clients may bring in. Their job is to name these issues and to investigate them.

For example, when they are all standing in the physical quadrant, I might ask, "Suppose a client comes in asking about Viagra—is it in this quadrant that you might begin to explore?" "What about clients complaining about vaginismus or premature ejaculation? Might you look in this quadrant for sources of traumatic sexual abuse? Or for the impetus for affairs? Or for a couple exploring poly relationships?"

When the training group is standing in the emotional quadrant, I might ask, "When a couple comes in enraged at each other, is this the quadrant you might suggest they explore first?" "How about a 50-year-old man who confuses his early childhood feelings of worthlessness with his feelings about his wife?" "Or a 34-year-old woman who is still trying to please her angry father who died when she was 10?"

When they are all standing in the mental quadrant, I might ask, "When clients' conversation is full of 'shoulds' and 'oughts', or when a woman can't have an orgasm because she's afraid it's against her religious teaching—is the mental quadrant a place you might begin to explore?" "How might you help them use the mental quadrant to explore their other cultural responses?" "Would you begin here to help a man explain to his partner what it was like growing up in a cult?"

When they are all standing in the spiritual quadrant, I might ask, "Suppose a woman is engaged in a personal journey in search of herself, and her partner feels dismissed—is this a place you might begin?" "Suppose a couple is at war with each other over whether or not to have a baby?" "What about if one of the partners is suffering from severe depression because of job loss or the death of a parent?"

Clearly there are no absolutely right or wrong answers to these questions, either. The object is to help trainees use the Wheel to invoke curiosity about clients' issues—and about their own reactions.

Collaboration Can Help Therapists, Too

As I have said throughout, using the ISIS Wheel may also benefit therapists—in this case, opening up an avenue for collaboration rather than aiming to pathologize, diagnose, or otherwise control each interaction or outcome. The self-assessment process that is part of ISIS softens power imbalances between therapist and client. It also provides an acknowledged partnership between therapist and client that lessens opportunities for sticky levels of transference and countertransference. As the locus of authority shifts to clients, therapists report the ability to witness more, fix less, and become more transparent about teachable moments and other therapeutic choices.

Moreover, as clients find their own ways of moving around and within the Wheel, they sometimes discover options that exceed therapists' goals or even wildest dreams. One of my favorite ISIS stories is told by a supervisee who conducts ongoing group therapy for women who suffer from severe PTSD as a result of sexual abuse. Her supervision issue with me was how to help these women talk about sexuality without restimulating their abuse traumas. In the past, whenever she had introduced the subject of sex as a topic of discussion in the group, the women all started dissociating. In effect, they left their bodies and evacuated the room: end of discussion about sex. This had gone on for some ten years of her running the group.

We reviewed ways in which she could both create ultra-safe space and ask the women specifically what they needed to feel secure enough to discuss sexual issues in the group. We also talked about the benefits of introducing the notion of concrete objects, to help ground the women who attended her group. My supervisee decided to move super slowly with this group. She suggested that one woman volunteer to bring in one object each week. Then the whole group would focus on it and discuss it. The members of her group loved this idea, and the strategy has been working ever since.

My favorite part of the story is about the woman who brought in a cough drop—to represent the numbness she felt during sex with her husband. The group all agreed it would not be right to get rid of the cough drop—just chew it up or throw it in the trash—because numbness (which the cough drop represented) could be useful as well as a problem. So the group decided they would place the cough drop in a glass of water, and each week they would look to see how much it had dissolved. In that way, the women were all able to initiate conversations about their own numbness vis-à-vis sex: what it was useful for, how long they wanted to keep it, and what kind of agency they had over it. And the group as a whole was at last able to find a safe way to talk about sex and sexual relationships.

The point is that using the Wheel and the core dynamics offers therapists a frame to hold space for clients to discover their own paths. Witnessing and honoring their clients' experience can be potent therapeutic strategies. So can suggesting options without trying to fix clients or solve problems for them. I remember hearing master therapist Virginia Satir speak compassionately to a client who was enmeshed in a complex family drama: "I don't have an answer for you, but I want you to know you have a very powerful problem."

As I experience it, this comment from Satir bespeaks enormous trust in the client and in the therapeutic relationship established with the client. I use it here because it illustrates a major ISIS message: Trust in the process. You are dealing with energy here and the paths may be subtle and seemingly indirect. As reflected in the stories in this book, tangible results and outcomes may manifest during a session or sometimes only after the session. These results may surprise your clients, and they may surprise you, too.

Integrating the ISIS Wheel with Other Practices

The ISIS Wheel can be integrated with other therapeutic modalities and approaches, including performance-oriented sex therapy. Clinicians have reported combining the ISIS concept with cognitive behavioral therapy, Gestalt therapy, Imago techniques, meditation, guided imagery, hypnosis, yoga, psychosynthesis, psychodrama, art therapy, Twelve-Step work, Jungian sand tray therapy, and more.

Educators have reported using the ISIS concept to teach a range of sexual options to medical interns, psychology majors, high-school students, and older women. One educator uses the ISIS model to integrate sex education with art therapy, having her students create drawings from each of the quadrants to illustrate feelings. Another uses the Wheel as a roadmap for decision-making around sexual rights for patients in nursing homes.

Therapist colleagues are adapting the ISIS Wheel template to their own practices and innovating new ways to use it. One therapist keeps a stack of ISIS diagrams in her office to use during intakes. Another therapist, who feels her conservative Christian clients would be uncomfortable with a medicine wheel, sets chairs in her office to represent body, mind, heart, and spirit and asks clients to move among the appropriate chairs. My colleague Chelsea Wakefield adapts the Wheel to her "Luminous Woman" circles focused on negotiating an inner peace treaty.

These and other colleagues are using the Wheel to help a variety of clients explore a diversity of issues: a computer programmer trapped in his head—to expand his options for erotic empathy; a priest tormented by what he calls his "carnal desires"—to permit him to express a full range of feelings; a lesbian with emerging memories of abuse—to find coherent ways to connect her past and present life; a gay man whose pattern of cruising is destructive to him and his family—to offer a process for increasing his awareness and empathy without assessing moral judgment; a couple torn apart by an affair—to enter a safe forum for hearing each other and negotiating what each of them truly wants; a chronically fighting couple—to practice more nuanced forms of communication by speaking and listening from different quadrants; a chronically repressed couple—to explore multiple avenues of sensation and emotion; a porn aficionado who wants to interrupt his behaviors—to raise awareness of what parts of him are being fed by his actions, and also to encourage his partner to respond to him sexually in new and possibly more engaging ways; a post-menopausal woman frantic that she has never received enough love—to offer her context in which to rehearse ways she can move into the center of the Wheel, the center of her life, the meeting of body, mind, heart, and spirit.

An ISIS Practitioner Speaks

Professionals are drawn to explore ISIS work for a variety of reasons, each of them unique. Ginger Holczer, a sex therapist from Springfield, Missouri, came into the ISIS orbit because she had read my earlier books, and she hoped that supervision with me would help her find ways to integrate a more spiritual consciousness into her sex therapy practice, which is in a particularly conservative area of the US.

Ginger entered into a supervisory relationship with me and we worked together intensively for two years. Since then, she has opened up her practice to more creative ways of working and is beginning to offer groups and training sessions in her community. Moreover, she and I have discovered a mutual passion for historical sex research, especially regarding women. We are collaborating on an article about the first US sex survey, by Clelia Mosher, an MD from Stanford University, who surveyed 45 wives between 1892 and 1912—opening a new window onto our Victorian foremothers, who were not as "frigid" as they are cracked up to be, with insights into what really turned them on.

Below is Ginger's personal story of ISIS therapy and supervision, to show how a professional's personal journey through the process can benefit her clients. I am so grateful for her permission to include this story here, as I find it both instructive and moving—as well as a testament to the fact that ISIS works in countless ways.

Expanding My Practice of Sex Therapy

Ginger Holczer, PsyD

The instructions were to bring two "power objects" to an ISIS training week with Gina in Mexico in January, 2011. One object was to represent the direction you want to head in your life—or at least what you want from the training; the other object was to represent how you know you hold yourself back from being all you can be. It seemed simple enough, and for several weeks I mulled over the possibilities, not knowing exactly what I was going to bring. The "direction I wanted to head" part was easy. I wanted to move in a spiritual direction, which I felt was lacking in my life. My idea of "spiritual" was a sense of connectedness in the universe, as well as deeper connections with other people, and to represent it I brought a small brass plate with an etching of a tree and various spiritual symbols. It was the representation of "how I hold myself back" that was difficult. The day before I was to get on the plane I settled for a pair of sunglasses. I wasn't sure how I was going to use them, but sunglasses seemed like the right choice.

My sunglasses went into the ISIS Wheel on the first day of the training. I tend to be in my head most of the time, so I put them in the mental quadrant and thought, "Okay, task completed." My opportunity to process my objects came and, surprisingly, I found myself moving the sunglasses around the Wheel into every quadrant—feeling the feelings, thinking the thoughts, making the connections, and identifying with my body. It didn't take long for me to realize why I had made such an appropriate choice: the sunglasses hid a part of me that I did not want others to see—not even myself. How freeing it was to walk around the Wheel with an ISIS therapist who was simply witnessing my story, my emotions, my "Aha!" moments, holding space for me in such a way that I felt safe and nurtured. I was able to see and literally experience my own "process," running around and around the Wheel, trying to find the right place to put the glasses. It dawned on me that I was living my life running around in circles, trying desperately to hide the very thing that would have actually given me what I yearned for—intimate connection.

Not only did I see myself running around in circles when it came to my personal life, but I was also running around in the way that I was doing therapy with my clients. As I am a traditionally trained psychologist, my practice consisted basically of "talk therapy." With some of my clients, I spent week after week trying to make change through a very static process. I felt that it worked for the most part, but I also felt at times that there should be more to therapy than sitting and talking for weeks on end. I realized through my own process with my sunglasses that I was able to "put feet to my work," helping others to find a movement that seemed more conducive to change, without the element of continually mulling over the same story that kept occurring in my clients' lives.

The work I did on my own issues was important in that it not only helped me move forward personally, but it also provided me with a glimpse of the experience of movement on the part of the client. I realized that, as a "witness" to the narrative of my clients with the ISIS Wheel, I was also always a participant—present, holding space, and standing with my client. Without my own experience with the ISIS Wheel, I might have been more apt to direct or try to "fix" the client instead of allowing him or her the freedom to find his or her own "feet" and unique movement around the Wheel, accepting wherever the client is at in any given moment.

This way of processing and honoring my clients' stories changed the way I saw myself as a therapist and helped me to realize that I didn't always have to be an expert anymore. As I told Gina in supervision, sometimes I was so busy being the expert, I forgot to be the student. I needed to spend less time trying to fix my clients and more time letting them teach me what it is like trying to live their stories.

Since the ISIS training in Mexico, I have had the opportunity to try out my new-found intervention with wonderful results. There was the middle-aged male client who struggled with erectile dysfunction. I had worked with him for almost a year with little progress, despite a great deal of work on my part. In fact, when he left the office each week, I felt exhausted. I showed him a diagram of the ISIS Wheel, discussing how we would use the Wheel in sessions to come. He asked to take a copy home and then brought the Wheel back to me, having written over the entire paper. He described his life from each of the quadrants in a very angry voice, which was unusual for this client, who generally reported that "Everything is fine." We were then able to process his pain, anger, and abuse in detail.

Then there was a female client who had difficulty with orgasm. We had talked about sexual abuse, how the abuse affected her life, and how it continued to hold her back, but I felt stumped as to how to move forward with her. I asked her to bring two objects to our next meeting: one that represented a part of her sexual story she wanted to keep and one that represented a part of her sexual story she wanted to move beyond. The two objects she brought were fireworks, which represented the orgasm she desired, and a belt, which represented the restraints used during her sexual abuse as a child.

One benefit of the Wheel is the safety and trust in the very act of holding space and "being there," so it was easy for me to step into a collaborative union with this client—even though her ability to trust had been ruptured at a very young age. As she placed her objects into the ISIS Wheel, she was willing to move effortlessly to the mental and spiritual quadrants, and eventually to the emotional quadrant. However, the physical space was difficult for her. When I urged her to pick up the belt that she had brought to represent the act of being physically restrained by her abuser, she was able to step into the physical quadrant, and here we could begin to investigate the part of herself—and her sexual response—that she had been avoiding. Moving to the physical quadrant brought up the physical memories. She began to articulate the times she had defensively shut down her body to the abusive pain, and made the connection that in the process she had also shut off the physical aspect of herself that had the potential for pleasure. This knowledge occurred very quickly, unlike in a more cognitive therapeutic approach, which might have taken months or even years to discover. Being more aware of her physical needs, this client is now working outside of the therapy room on the exploration of her body and its wonderful, pleasurable sensations.

I learned from this very brave client that the places clients avoid on the Wheel are the places they most need to explore—but in their own time, not my time. The opportunities for movement are present, and it isn't up to me to direct, but rather to allow the process to ebb and flow within the confluence of the clients' own narrative and the sacred space of the Wheel.

More recently, a female client presented with low desire, which may have been associated with some guilt she felt regarding a cult-like religious environment she had experienced as a child. I told her about the ISIS Wheel and described the quadrants to her. When we got to the spiritual quadrant, she was instantly hesitant. I explained to her that, in the language of the ISIS Wheel, "spiritual" refers to connection—with self, a partner, or a "higher power." I asked her to look at the connection as either "vertical" (connection with a deity) or "horizontal" (connection with others)—whatever connection looked like for her. The client tearfully revealed that she had never considered any kind of spirituality other than with a "punitive god."

In the space of the ISIS Wheel, I witnessed her as she stayed in the mental quadrant, noticing the drastic change in what her body was saying when she approached any aspect of emotions and avoiding the emotional quadrant like the plague. I could see tears in her eyes, but she continued to stay in her head, positioned in the mental quadrant, with her arms wrapped tightly around her body. As she began to use language indicative of the emotional quadrant, I gently asked her permission for the two of us to move into that quadrant, and I walked with her to that space. I watched as her body language softened—with tears falling on the memories of the spiritual hurt she had suffered. Following her experience of processing the emotions, she was able to move to the spiritual quadrant, where she processed and considered what spirituality means to her. Finally, she was able to reclaim a spiritual part of herself in an idiosyncratic way, instead of lopping it off like an infected appendage. This discovery of her spiritual voice has renewed passion, a part of herself she had squelched at a very young age.

The very essence of the ISIS Wheel is the freedom to move without rigid boundaries. Clients can weave in and out of the quadrants, finding different aspects of their stories in a way that is expansive and illuminating. As a therapist, I simply act as a witness and a guide, moving with the client in a supportive, empathic way. The Wheel has become an organizing principle for my sessions, with the property of allowing the client to integrate the quadrants in whatever individual way makes sense to that person's narrative. There is no bias, no right or wrong, and no expectations. Neither client nor therapist can predict what will happen or what the path to clarity will be at any given moment.

My practice of sex therapy has changed since Mexico, and my sunglasses sit in a visible place in my office to remind me what can be revealed when you create movement—literally. I am excited about where this will take me, with the hope of many groups and individuals finding themselves and their voices in the depths of each quadrant. The experiential nature of the Wheel is empowering and without judgment. To date, I have used this method with issues such as erectile dysfunction, low desire, affairs, sexual promiscuity, and problems concerning sexual shame. Further, I have been able to work with these issues in a short amount of time while collecting a large amount of information. The client is in control and responsible for his or her own healing. The two objects are catalysts to encourage clients to tell their own story, in their own time, and I get the wonderful opportunity to witness their courage and change.

16

CAVEATS FOR THERAPISTS

The ISIS process is intrinsically collaborative, inviting both clients and therapists to explore the liminal space created by the ISIS Wheel. Entering into this space with our clients means reframing some time-honored therapeutic power roles and boundaries, and this can present both challenges and opportunities for therapists.

The traditional doctor–patient relationship dictates discrepant power roles, which locate ultimate authority with the therapist, not the client. This power discrepancy carries into traditional sex therapy through reliance on the medical model, in which (for instance) therapists diagnose dysfunction and provide treatment and clients follow the therapists' prescriptions. In contrast, ISIS practice involves plasticity in power roles, offering a more give-and-take therapeutic partnership; authority to determine problems and outcomes resides with the client as well as the therapist. The challenge for ISIS therapists is to model within the therapeutic partnership methods of power exchange whose purpose is relational sharing and creative synergy rather than authority and control.

Closely associated with power roles are the therapist–client boundaries dictated by the ethics of psychotherapy. These boundaries establish a rigid wall between therapists and clients. Therapists are permitted no personal sharing and no touching, among other constraints. In contrast, ISIS practice calls for some plasticity in these boundaries, which may include some judicious personal sharing from therapists as well as physical contact connected with the ISIS core dynamics of ritual and movement. A challenge for ISIS therapists is how to create an invitational sense of working in collaboration and also to maintain appropriately client-protective boundaries. Part of the challenge is that, as we expand conventional therapeutic boundaries, our own feelings may well become more actively engaged in our clients' journeys. Such emotional engagement may wave the red flag of countertransference. We must remain mindful that our clients' therapeutic journeys belong to them and not to us.

It is important to note here that, by naming the plasticity of power roles and boundaries, I am not suggesting that ISIS work opens a path to boundary-hopping behaviors such as seduction, sexual touching, or other dual relationships with clients. Rather, I am underscoring that to enter into ISIS work at any transformative level involves shifting the usual imbalance of therapeutic authority in order to create as easy an energy exchange as possible between therapists and clients. The focus always remains on the clients' issues and well-being.

Examples throughout this book illustrate what a collaborative therapy relationship might look like in ISIS sessions. It involves the therapist following the client's lead rather than dictating it or medicalizing it, as in the story of Annette and Chris in chapter 13, or creating and holding space in which clients can perform their own transformational magic rather than just analyzing their dysfunction, as in the story of Curtis and Elsa in chapter 11. In other instances, it might include a level of familiarity and personal sharing that encourages clients to question authority and take initiative for their own growth and change.

All of this said, I offer three specific caveats below, which are variations on the theme of therapeutic power roles and boundaries. These caveats are: allowing our clients to do their own work, not getting caught up in our clients' stories, and taking special care to feed our egos outside of the therapy office so that we are not tempted to feed on the energies of our clients. I invite you to make a list of your own personal caveats and to pay close attention to them.

The bottom line here is that, as therapists, coaches, and healers, we need to assume responsibility for our own thoughts, feelings, and reactions to what is going on in our ISIS sessions. We need to take our work with our clients seriously, without taking our own importance so seriously that we forget to laugh. And we need to find ways to inspire our clients to broaden and deepen their own journeys without offering to carry their loads for them. A crucial way of expanding sex therapy is to allow our clients to explore for themselves those tough lessons they need to learn—body, mind, heart, and spirit.

Caveat #1: Allow Your Clients to Do Their Own Work (And Don't Take Care of Clients' Power Objects)

"Burn baby, burn!" was the chant from the group when Lori stood to reclaim the toxic object she had placed in the circle to be transformed. The object was a badly spelled "Dear Jane" letter from her ex-boyfriend. Throughout the weekend, Lori had related stories of being taken advantage of by one man or another throughout her life. She had punctuated these stories by repeating, "I want to burn this hateful horrible letter." As the group chant ended, she handed the letter toward me with a flourish: "Please burn this for me!"

This was a prime example of what I have come to understand as therapeutic buck-passing. In my early days in practice, I might have considered accepting the charge to burn Lori's letter, imagining that I was helping her. But I quickly learned that doing clients' work for them is not good therapy. It may make the client momentarily happy. It may make the therapist feel momentarily powerful. But doing work that rightfully belongs to the client reaffirms the dis-empowering thoughts and behaviors that bring clients into therapy in the first place. For me to have burned Lori's letter for her would have been enabling behavior on my part and also dis-abling behavior—denying her a prime opportunity to act in her own behalf, however difficult such an action might be for her.

It was important to honor Lori's trust in me, however. So I thanked her for reaching out. Then I declined her invitation, underscoring the golden opportunity she had created to act on her own behalf. I suggested that she take responsibility for burning this letter herself and that she find a way to dispose of the ashes with conscious intent, so that they would not come back to haunt her.

A major caveat of ISIS work is this: If a client tries to give you one of their objects to dispose of, do not accept it. State clearly and kindly that you understand this object represents a significant piece of your client's story. Affirm that both the story and the object belong to your client, not to you. You can also reiterate that a crucial part of the power of a power object is for clients to come to a full appreciation of all that this object may mean in their lives. Such appreciation may develop over time, which is why it is important for clients to consider carefully what to do with each of their power objects beyond the ISIS session.

It is necessary to impart these messages firmly—gently, perhaps, but never lightly, and never defensively. Emphasize that taking responsibility for one's own feelings and actions may be new and risky behavior for clients. Encourage them to notice what happens in their lives, and in their sexuality, as a result of taking the risks.

For Lori, the incident of letter-passing opened her to some deep reflection. Because she seemed so puzzled when I declined to take her object from her, I asked her if she was used to having others take care of her or direct her life. When she again looked puzzled, I rephrased the question: "Do you find yourself going through life as if you're somebody who's blown by the winds of circumstance and not a person who takes charge? Or has there ever been some kind of reward for you in not taking charge—even if the reward seemed to be negative?"

"Oh," she said. "You mean like people feeling sorry for me because I always lose out?"

The invitation for Lori to reflect invoked another level of her story, a crucial one. I invited her to follow her feelings about losing out. She related a scene when she was five years old, being taunted by her much bigger brothers. "I'd have to stay home and help with the laundry, while they got to go out and play—until I got older. Then they'd have their friends over and take me into their bedroom and play with me. They'd stand over me and take their, you know, their *things* out of their pants. And they'd make me suck them. And they'd laugh at me."

As she blurted this story out, Lori's sense of disempowerment and rage at men finally made sense to her, to me, and to the whole group. She suddenly looked as if she were emerging from a long sleep. She blinked her eyes, straightened her spine, took a deep breath, and uttered a string of unprintable words. Members of the group clapped in empathy.

A lesson I took from this exchange with Lori has been helpful in training other clinicians who undertake ISIS practice. The lesson is this: To determine what is holding clients from the power to act on their own behalf may require just a timely question or suggestion, as in Lori's case. Or it may take a thorough investigative process—perhaps a thorough go-round on the Wheel to explore fully the physical, emotional, mental, and spiritual aspects of resistance. Once you and your clients have determined the issues that hold the most energy, you can review together what they may need to do, and together you can create a plan, step by step. This process is, of course, unique to each individual.

What does taking charge of one's own reclaimed object or objects have to do with sexual desire, arousal, and satisfaction? Activating the full responsibility involved in reclaiming and taking charge of a power object enhances the sense of personal coherence and power called self-esteem, which is a huge predictor of sexual desire and satisfaction. This is an "irrational fact" that is finally being acknowledged in clinical research.

"Your Wisdom Please, But Not Your Advice..."

Another way of encouraging clients to do their own work is through judicious disclosure—sharing relevant bits of your own story. Such sharing can be effective as long as it is strongly applicable to your clients' understanding and growth. And, always, this sharing needs to be offered in a spirit of encouragement and collaboration, not of personal seduction or conspiracy. Encouragement and collaboration are empowering to your clients. Personal seduction and conspiracy are Nowhere Streets in terms of effective therapy.

If you are relating to a client in the context of an ISIS group, it may be most valuable to ask group members to do the sharing. When you feel a client might benefit from sharing, ask that client if she or he is willing to hear feedback from the group. Go forward with the request to the group only if you receive a positive response. If the response is negative, respect that as a legitimate boundary and help the client find another path to encourage forward movement.

When you do invite group feedback, make sure you ask group members to share their experience and their wisdom, not their advice. Advice-giving is too often a way of avoiding responsibility—by sticking to the mental quadrant rather than venturing into the realm of feelings. For most of us, it is much easier to tell somebody else what to do than to share at a heart and soul level of our own experience. But advice that is unasked for is seldom empowering for the receiver. By contrast, true sharing can open up a profoundly valuable conversation that is guaranteed to resonate among many members of the group.

In the case of Lori's "Burn baby, burn," the sharing occurred with vitality and good humor. Ultimately, it brought the issue of what to do with the boyfriend's letter around to spiritual meaning and transformation. Talk soon moved into action. One of the women in the group located a fireproof container and the group enacted a ceremonial burning of Lori's letter along with a few items other participants decided they wanted to transform by fire. A tribal consciousness instantly formed. They named themselves the Burning Sisters. They carried the ashes outside and spread them under a tree—to nourish the roots while calling forth the nature spirits to transform the negative energy.

These actions added a richness to the experience that went way beyond the present moment. The group lifted the discussion beyond Lori's badly-behaving boyfriend and directly into the larger issue of women's ways of reclaiming lost power. In the way this particular scene played out, this tribe of Burning Sisters saw themselves as re-enacting an ancient rite that connected them with the transformative power of Goddess energy. This message of transformation and power was one that each woman in that circle said she was able to take home with her.

Letting Go and Letting the Client . . .

When and how does a therapist let go of controlling an ISIS session and allow clients to do the work that rightfully belongs to them? There are no pat answers here. Partly it means understanding what deep lessons the client is ready to learn. And partly it depends on the ability of the therapist to back off being needed, or even being the focus of attention. I am again reminded of Eisler's Partnership model of interaction (described her *Sacred Pleasure*) as distinct from the Dominator model, in which the higher-ranked person in the relationship will call the shots.

In terms of the sexual focus of ISIS work, I think of the dynamic of letting go as the opposite of the patriarchal ethic of *noblesse oblige*, the self-imposed obligation of the lord of the manor to protect and care for his vassals—which is clearly a "dominator" concept. It is no secret that *noblesse oblige* came with sexual perks in days of yore. Caring for the vassals of the manor ensured total control over them, including the license to rape any of the manor's women on her wedding night. This is known as *droit de seigneur*: the lord's right.

Make what parallels you will between a feudal lord exercising his sexual "rights" and a "dominator" sex therapist who may feel endowed with extraordinary sexual powers, feeling the right to exercise responsibility for honing a client's sexual sensibilities. Suffice it to say here that, if we as therapists claim the right to make decisions for our clients' sexual futures, at the very least we take away those clients' opportunity to wrestle with the tough choices that may move them to change their own lives in their own way.

The moral of this story is that, where therapeutic direction is concerned, for many clients, less is more. Knowing when to back off may be hard on the therapist who wants so much to help. But backing off may generate tremendous growth on the part of a client. And it fulfills one of the ISIS principles: The locus of power rightfully belongs with the client.

Caveat #2: Be Wary of Getting Caught Up in Your Client's Story (Let Go of Your Outcome Fantasies, No Matter How Great They Are)

One of the most moving scenes I have witnessed in an ISIS circle involved the freeing of a doll from its Walmart packaging. Joyce arrived at an ISIS weekend, aged 47, unpartnered, and still tied to a childhood where she had had to be Little Miss Perfect—or else. The "or else" had included isolation, starvation, and physical abuse, so Joyce learned early how to travel the survivor road of looking good, never getting her clothes dirty, and never touching herself *down there*—ever. Asking for help was not part of her vocabulary. Asking for fun or pleasure or love was quite literally taboo. Now, nearing menopause, she lived an almost antiseptic life, and she despaired of finding a lover.

Joyce brought to the circle a knee-high box containing a brand new doll which was perfectly dressed in a gray plaid skirt and jacket. She stated that this is what she had looked like as a child. She placed the box on the line between the physical and emotional quadrants. Throughout the weekend, the doll stared at us through a cellophane pane in what looked like a stand-up coffin. Joyce spoke with sarcasm about the doll. She complained about the doll's clothes and hair and all that the doll represented of her own childhood. She remarked that nobody could love such a sterile, ugly doll. Yet Joyce never looked at the doll or moved it from quadrant to quadrant during the many invitations for group members to explore their objects from other quadrants of the Wheel. On Sunday, when it was time to reclaim our objects from the Wheel, she picked up the box without looking at it and started to walk away.

"So Joyce," I asked, "What are you planning to do with the doll when you leave here?"

"Well, it's a brand new doll, and I thought I might drop it off at Good Will or somewhere on my way home."

"Can you think of anything else you might do with the doll?"

Joyce finally took a deep breath and looked at the doll. Then she doubled over in tears and hugged the box.

"What would happen if you took the doll out of its box?" I asked. Joyce nodded, and began to pluck at the corners of the box. Then she began to pluck harder. If you have ever tried to remove a doll—or a screwdriver or a power drill—from its Walmart packaging, you know that it takes the strength of a longshoreman.

"Let me help," said Jaya, who leapt up. "I'm an abuse survivor and I always welcome an opportunity to rip something apart!" Joyce and Jaya banded together in the bioenergetic exercise of releasing the doll. They transformed into Valkyries, littering the floor with metal staples and shards of cardboard, finally bursting the plastic constraints that held the doll captive at neck, waist, wrists, and ankles. They held the doll triumphantly aloft for the group to see.

In the freeing of the doll, each woman in the circle could witness her own struggles to freedom. In the emergence of the doll, each of us could witness our own emergence. It was archetypal dismemberment and liberation all at once. The scene left every one of us sobbing, myself included.

By the time Kleenex had been passed and comments shared, I imagined that the doll would assume a vibrant reality in Joyce's life. I felt the doll might become an alter-ego or maybe a spirit companion to whom Joyce could talk, with whom she could expand and grow, through whom she could wake from her long relational sleep. Others in the group had similar notions. Afterward, at lunch, women spoke of the doll as if she were human, a member of the group: "What will you call her?" "Make sure she wears a seatbelt when you drive her home." "Bye-bye you two—have fun shopping for new outfits!"

So, a couple of months later, it was with excitement and curiosity that I called Joyce to ask her permission to use the story of the doll at a lecture I was to give at a feminist psychology conference because I thought it would be so empowering for other women therapists to hear. "How are you getting along with the doll?" I began, and was unprepared for her response.

"Well, I did what you told me to," she replied. "I went to the store to buy a cuter outfit for her and found that a new jeans outfit would cost $15. But for $20 I could buy a whole new doll . . . ." So now Joyce had two dolls: one in gray plaid, one in blue jeans. I was quite speechless at this turn of events—and miffed. I felt she'd missed the point of the whole exercise. And I was chagrined to hear that her taking any action at all had been because she felt she had had to please me. Mostly, I think I felt cheated of my fantasy outcome for her. My image of the perfect denouement to a classic ISIS Wheel experience was shattered.

While these thoughts were whirling in my head, Joyce's tone shifted. "But a funny thing happened just last week," she said. "I suddenly thought maybe I could write a book. It could be a memoir. And maybe I could even rewrite my whole life!"

OK, my mistake. Something big had happened for Joyce after all. It just wasn't what I had projected for her. In my haste to write my own chapter to Joyce's story, I had committed one of the cardinal sins of effective therapy. I had neglected to trust Joyce to write her own. Now, two years after the freeing of the doll, Joyce has come a long way toward a new life—her own new life. She has not written her memoir, but she is in a new relationship—with a man who has a seven-year-old daughter—just the right age, Joyce points out, to play with her two dolls. Moreover, Joyce has told the story of these dolls to the man in her life. He recently presented her with a third doll—one that represents some of Joyce's new attributes. It is a Divine Warrior doll with a jeweled dagger and "kick-ass stiletto heels."

The moral of this story: Remember (yet again!), this is the client's life, not yours. Projecting a specific outcome is not the job of the therapist. Our job is to create and hold space, initiate movement, incorporate ritual, and concretize abstract concepts as needed. Above all, our job is to listen to our clients. In ISIS work, as in all other therapeutic work, it is also crucial to let go of our clients' stories so that they can follow their own paths to sexual healing and pleasure.

Caveat #3: Check Your Ego at the Door (Never Make Assumptions about What a Particular Sex Toy May Teach)

At a conference recently I found myself speaking with a sex therapist colleague who vigorously maintained that therapy is a product with a measurable result. "Our clients are paying us to deliver a sexier relationship, or the ability to maintain an erection or achieve an orgasm," he maintained. This colleague has a lucrative practice and numerous devotees—clearly signs of skill and success. On the point at issue, I had to disagree with him vigorously, however. In my experience, therapy is not anything like a product. To me, therapy is a process, with outcomes that are often unpredictable and impossible to count and measure. I see both therapy and sex therapy as works in progress, just as sexual development and sexual relationship are works in progress.

Despite our disagreement, I have to thank my colleague for engaging in the conversation about sex as a product. For, during our talk, I had to face some provocative questions, especially about our profession's inability to measure the effects of therapy, let alone sex therapy. What good does therapy really do? We have only hearsay from the handful of clients who return years later to tell us what their experience meant to them. Where are the normative studies of therapy—the really useful ones? Nowhere that I know of. This means that, as therapists, we are all doing this work by the proverbial seat of our pants. In fact, the lack of measurable scientific data could cast doubt on the whole concept of therapy. This includes the DSM, the diagnostic and statistical manual whose contents are predicated on the assumption that sexual problems can be categorized, that therapy actually helps, and that insurance should cover certain therapeutic procedures.

But, instead of going off in that direction, let me instead offer an example of how ISIS work defies the therapist's ego and underscores the argument for therapy as a process, with unpredictable outcomes.

Sex by Remote Control

Samantha brought to an ISIS session a remote control from her TV. "This is what I want to get rid of," she said, and tossed it into the Wheel with disdain. She said she had chosen this object to represent how mechanical sex had become for her, how remote she felt from her partner, and how utterly controlling she felt she was being about their sex life. The dismissive energy she projected moved me to ask her whether or not she was willing to explore her feelings toward this provocative object. After she nodded "Yes," our conversation went as follows.

"What does this object have to teach you?" (I had ideas, but it is always crucial to leave the interpretation to the client.)

"Well, nothing I don't think. It's just an old dead remote control laying there on the floor."

"Would you be willing to pick it up?" (It is sometimes crucial to elicit more than one "yes" response before plunging into therapeutic activity.) Once she had picked it up, I asked, "What do you notice?" (It is always crucial to focus on the client's awareness, not only your own.)

"Oh, nothing. Just, well, maybe it has a bunch of buttons."

"What are some of the buttons you notice?" (It is always crucial to keep the client's focus on what *is* rather than on what is *not*.)

"Well, there's . . . PLAY!"

As Samantha identified the "play" button, she emitted a deep belly laugh. Then she released a torrent of talk about how much of her life as a grief counselor was taken up with caring for others around death and dying, how difficult it was for her to come home and drop back into her body, and how she had forgotten what it felt like to let go and just have fun. By now she was vacillating between laughter and tears.

Taking our directive from her remote control, Samantha agreed to move into the physical quadrant. As she was standing in that place, we played with her

181

breath to bring her back to center and into her body. I asked her to feel her fingers, then her toes. I asked her to be aware of her feet on the ground; of the resilience of her spine; and of the flow of her breath moving in and out of her ribcage. Finally, we returned our attention to her experience of the object she had brought.

"So that's some of what the concept of PLAY brings up for you. What other buttons do you notice on the remote?"

"PAUSE!" In the context of her sexual relationship, this "pause" message turned out to be fully as important to Samantha as PLAY. "It's about slowing down," she said. She proceeded to walk every quadrant of the Wheel, stopping, literally, to reflect how unrelentingly busy she was in her life and how much she needed to stop and take time for herself. She expressed it like this: "Physically, I need to stop rushing around like the White Rabbit—always feeling I'm late everywhere." Instead, she said, she needed to stand barefoot on the grass, to get back to taking evening walks with her partner, to shower together, to spoon their bodies together at night. Emotionally, she said she needed to recharge: "I can do this by singing and playing my guitar if I just give myself permission to take the time." Mentally, she said she needed to leave her work in her office so that home was a clear space for her to be creative. Spiritually, she said she needed to allow more space in her life between clients, between events, between obligations. Within that new space, she said she needed to reach out and touch her partner more.

Once Samantha had told the story of PAUSE from each quadrant, she visibly relaxed and began focusing reverent attention onto the remote—as if it were a Delphic oracle, able to predict all that she needed. She explored more buttons, including FAVORITES (some kinky fantasies) and REPLAY (some delicious memories of sex in her earlier and randier days). All of these pointed to her life as a potentially limitless journey of discovery. And they all pointed to sex as much more than mechanical—an exploration to be savored rather than controlled. She took the lessons of the remote control home to her husband, which became a whole other level of exploration, and which moved the couple into couples therapy and, eventually, much more honest connection with each other.

The moral of this story: When it comes to holding space for clients to explore their own particular sexual mysteries, there is no marketable product involved and no predictable or measurable outcome. It is all about noticing clients and helping them expand their horizons of what is possible in their lives. In this space of exploration there is no place for a therapist's ego to shine or be stroked. In the instance above, the Delphic oracle was the remote control, and the fountain of wisdom was the client herself. The therapist was simply an intelligent, curious creator and holder of space for the transformation to occur.

Contraindications for Using the ISIS Wheel

The ISIS Wheel is an invitation for awareness and transformation. But it is important to state that ISIS is no panacea and that it is not for everyone. Using the Wheel is actually inappropriate in certain instances, and I want to spell out some of these here so that therapists are clear when using the Wheel may be most effective or ineffective.

When a Client Needs Emergency Help and/or Advice About a Life-threatening Situation

Situations such as impending suicide, ongoing domestic violence, or child abuse demand immediate practical intervention, not integrative collaborative exploration. While the ISIS principle of multidimensional assessment and inquiry may hold true even in emergency situations, this is a time for a therapist to be proactive and directive until the client's situation calms down or changes. When the crisis is over, using the ISIS approach may be effective in helping clients put their experience into perspective.

When a Client Has a Degree of Mental Illness that Makes Full Awareness Impossible

ISIS work is not designed for treating personal or relational disturbances that stem from severe cognitive impairment or personality disorders of the kind that move clients to threaten harm to themselves or others. While the awareness offered by the ISIS template might help some of these clients and their partners understand a large picture, specific treatments for severe cognitive impairment and personality disorders are beyond the ISIS scope. Referrals to more cognitive and behavioral modalities are appropriate here, along with medical intervention where necessary.

When a Client Is Drunk or Under the Influence of Drugs, Including Prescribed Medications

Effective explorations in awareness cannot occur while clients are numbing their systems with drugs or alcohol. Again, the ISIS principle of multidimensionality may hold true, but the therapist's early efforts need to be focused clearly on guiding the client to change the substance-abusing behavior that stunts the possibilities of personal and relational growth—perhaps by referring to a Twelve-Step program, a physician, or a hospital. If prescribed medications are a barrier to full awareness, a frank exploration with the client may help determine how much the client actually needs the medication and/or how such medication may be better managed. Once substance use is no longer an active issue, the ISIS process can be invaluable for further insight, emotional growth, and relational awareness, as well as enhanced physical and sexual sensations.

A note about the condition labeled sexual addiction or compulsive sexual behavior, about which there is an ongoing debate in the field of sexology and sex therapy: Suffice it to say here that addictions counselors and therapists have incorporated ISIS as an extremely effective approach for raising awareness in clients who are diagnosed with addictive or compulsive sexual behaviors. However, the effectiveness may be nil when these clients are also actively drinking or under the influence of drugs, including psychotropic medications.

When Clients Cannot Tolerate a Multidimensional Process or a Process That Involves Spiritual Exploration

Meaningful ISIS work presupposes potential openness to exploring all dimensions: physical, emotional, mental, and spiritual. If there is consistent resistance to a multidimensional approach, you and your clients may assess that the most effective treatment may be more limited in scope, even if this means referral to another therapist.

The Good News

The ISIS model offers ways for therapists and clients to reorganize, rethink, and reimagine a complex range of positive and negative sexual information—directly from experience, beyond statistical or medical approaches or hallowed psychological theories. The ISIS template encourages clients and therapists to express the multiple dimensions of sexual experience, connect the effects of memory on present experience, and interrupt repeated story lines that keep clients lodged in unwanted sexual dynamics. The core dynamics of ISIS work present opportunities for growth through creating and holding space, movement, concretizing abstract concepts, and ritualizing ordinary activities. As one ISIS therapist puts it, "The Wheel is a template for planned spontaneity."

All of this is not to suggest that therapists need to disregard or dismiss training that focuses on performance or pharmaceutical interventions. Rather, it is to encourage them to expand on the theories, interventions, and skills they already know, entering into this practice from their own zones of comfort, curiosity, and expertise.

17

EXPLORING ISIS FOR
YOURSELF

When we work with clients, sooner or later we will come face to face with our own issues—those that inhabit our personal living rooms and bedrooms as well as our therapy offices. Sometimes these issues that bubble up from the therapeutic ooze are the ones that disturb us to our core. Almost always, the confrontation is a surprise. We may even feel blindsided, especially when a client's story suddenly opens an old wound we didn't know was still ready to gush with blood.

The formal term for this phenomenon is countertransference—a word coined by Freud in 1910 to signify that the patient's story influences the therapist, and that the influence often lurks beneath the level of conscious awareness. The notion of countertransference figures prominently in psychoanalytic theory and in sex therapy. In fact, it is basic to the understanding of therapeutic boundaries and ethical behaviors. To expand on the definition of countertransference, I also think of it as karma or, simply put, the past coming around yet again to haunt us and remind us that we have not completed our own work on this planet. In real terms, it is often the experience of listening to a client reveal details—often appalling details—of rejection or abuse or betrayal, only to come away with a sense of déjà vu, because in these revelations of our clients we connect with some of the very struggles we have engaged in as well.

As stated in the preceding chapter, the collaborative nature of ISIS work involves such give and take with our clients that we have to remain constantly aware of our own angsts and dramas. We also have to remain constantly aware of the power balances that exist between client and therapist, by whatever names we give these power balances. For therapists to experience a deep level of ISIS work, it is vitally important to understand, or at least to acknowledge, the contents of our own personal issues in a way that allows us to listen openly to our clients. These factors and more lead some of us to work the Wheel for ourselves.

The Gift of Awareness

Seasoned therapists will recognize that the issues that disturb them are their own, not just something that clients need to face up to. The awareness can be humbling. It can trigger a whole raft of feelings, including fear, anger, self-doubt, even shame. The inner voice yammers, "If I'm such a great therapist, how come I haven't already dealt with that abandonment or that hurt or that unspeakable grief?"

In our better moments we may also recognize that there is a gift involved in the recurring awareness of our own issues. Part of the gift is the understanding that our clients offer us daily, on a platter, much of what we need to confront in order for our skills to grow and our souls to flourish. That is to say, in both an earthly and spiritual sense, we may need our clients just as much as they need us, for they truly are our karmic vehicles.

Another part of the gift of awareness is that we get to appreciate the impressive collection of skills we have acquired in all of our training and our client hours. These are skills on which we can draw to become clearer and more aware in our own lives—and ultimately more helpful to our clients. Hopefully, we have also amassed a measure of perspective that lets us know we are not unique, that the issues that plagued us in the past are not going to disappear all by themselves, and that this is our opportunity to integrate them into our lives with increasing curiosity and nuance.

It is not my intent to turn this into a book about how to heal yourself. But I see too many books and articles on how to do therapy that never take into account that the process of practicing therapy inevitably brings up intense emotions, judgments, spiritual quandaries, and even somatic symptoms—such as the client who triggers a very real pain in the neck (or buttocks) that sends us into physical therapy. So it is my intent to acknowledge that all of these awarenesses and pains are hazards of the particular line of work we have chosen. And it is my intent to suggest than any of the ISIS techniques that may work for your clients may also work for you.

I can hear my supervisees saying, "That's fine, but what do we *do?*"

We can begin by thinking, remembering, and imagining for ourselves all that we mean by physical, emotional, mental, and spiritual experience. This process of reflection is not so that we can develop theories or dictate our ideas to our clients. It is to give us a larger and more appreciative context for our own ideas and to hone our sense of curiosity about their process.

Using ISIS in Your Own Life

Let's return to Jorge and Serena from chapter 1. We left Jorge assimilating the fine art of bilocation—that is, the ability to become a conduit of information in two spheres at once. He trained himself to be able to remain fully aware of his own feelings and memories and, at the same time, fully present as a therapist, attentive to his clients. The multidimensional awareness he gained through exploring the ISIS Wheel had helped him reconfigure his early experiences of family violence from a cocoon of terror and powerlessness into images that connected him empathically with his clients' struggles. His ISIS work had also helped him stand solidly in the here and now so that he could focus on his clients' needs. As Jorge grew more and more confident as a therapist, he also became increasingly adept at greeting his early memories as powerful teachers rather than as demons that held power over him.

We left Serena strongly empathizing with clients who were reaching toward more subtlety in their sexual relationships and more spiritual connection in their lives. As a result of ISIS work, she had found herself growing increasingly vulnerable to her clients' issues—actually identifying so intensely with some of them that she feared losing a sense of where those clients ended and she began. When she explored the literature on countertransference she plunged into berating herself for breaching boundaries with her clients. I suggested she look to her ISIS practice to counterbalance the negative interpretations she was finding about therapeutic empathy.

What helped Serena find her own balance was taking her ISIS work to a concrete level—literally. Using one of the core ISIS exercises, she concretized her own issues in various quadrants so that she could locate them in the Wheel instead of attaching them to her clients. Ultimately, she brought into her office a bowl of sand. The countless grains represented to her the multiple abuses both she and her clients had suffered. Sifting through the sand and letting the grains run through her fingers became a conscious reminder of how it had become second nature for her to blend her issues, and her personal boundaries, with those of her clients. This action also reminded her that she needed to exercise her deepest intentions to keep her clients' issues separate from her own, while also keeping her heart open to what they were going through.

The other object Serena brought into her office was a clear quartz crystal that reflected light. She called this her Wisdom Keeper, and she placed it on a window ledge where she could see it while she worked with her clients. This crystal reminded her to "stay in the light," as she put it, so that she could view her clients through a lens of wisdom and clarity.

Working with her two objects helped her become a more effective therapist because these objects continually presented her with a clear choice: blend with clients' pain and feel subsumed or seek the light in herself, and also in each client. It was, as she put it, "a no-brainer." What emerged for Serena's work was an ease and grace in the process of helping clients concretize their own difficult issues so they could find ways to bring wisdom and clarity into their own lives.

187

What we can learn from both Jorge and Serena is this: When our demons of the past re-emerge and threaten to overwhelm us, ISIS is a wonderful place to be. And, here, I want to share that this knowledge is personal for me, not just an insight I experience vicariously through my supervisees. For instance, when I am wracked with self-doubt, I can step into the Wheel to find where the juice is for me—is it physical, emotional, or spiritual, or am I resonating to some message from the culture? Is the problem in the present or in the past? Does it originate with me or with the energy generated by someone else? And so forth.

When trouble brews, I can run the ISIS diagram in my head to assess quickly what's going on. Or I can find more engaging ways to use the Wheel. Often this is in nature. One of my favorites is to draw the Wheel on the beach and let the ocean wash it away, with my doubts and demons in it. When I find myself in relationship hurdles with my partner, we can accompany each other into the ISIS Wheel as a safe place to explore without either of us being tempted to win or come out on top—because there is no top to the Wheel, and no bottom, either. There is only curiosity and awareness, both of which are gracious qualities for an enduring relationship.

The truth is that the ISIS Wheel can be useful even beyond therapeutic quandaries or countertransference issues. The template is always there, however you may choose to have it hold you. The concept of exploring the quadrants is invariably useful, wherever it may take you. So, when you find yourself facing a therapeutic impasse or plunged into a personal instance from hell, I invite you to step into the Wheel yourself. Choose your entry spot. Breathe. Blow your name into the center. Explore, quadrant by quadrant if need be, until you can find the center—your center—where they all converge.

If you feel it would help you to concretize your issues by representing them with tangible objects, allow yourself to know what those objects might be. Or, if your knowing is not instantaneous, search these objects out. Choose one object to represent what you want to expand and nourish and another to represent what you want to release and move beyond. If you want more direction about using the Wheel for yourself, you can review the examples and exercises in earlier chapters of this book—and I invite you to translate these exercises into your own style of assessing and healing. Or you can let go of all my suggestions and tap into your own creativity. Choose only one object or choose eight or ten objects. This is your life, your Wheel. This is your opportunity to expand your practice of sex therapy through your own growth, self-healing, or whatever else you want to name it.

Returning to Basics

Remember that ISIS work is based on clearing energy and on the core dynamics outlined in chapter 9: holding space, ritualizing ordinary experiences, concretizing abstract concepts, and moving through stuck places rather than staying stuck. Just as you can use the template to help your clients change and expand their stories, you can use the same template to change and expand your own story—including your practice of sex therapy.

Above all, ISIS work is based on taking the large, comprehensive view of a situation with its many layers and nuances. What may occur in the expanded view is that a seemingly impassible obstacle may simply transform into something you can go around or jump over. A seemingly threatening adversary may become a potent teacher. Examining a story from every quadrant may reveal a fluid continuum between good and bad or right and wrong rather than a solid wall that keeps you immobilized. What may emerge most clearly is the complexity of the situation itself—and the many options you have for expanding your life.

In the final instance, expanding the practice of sex therapy is about exercising intention. I am reminded of a passage from *A Course in Miracles*—one that has guided me for many years:

> If the situation is used for truth and sanity, the outcome must be peace.

I kept this quote taped to my bathroom mirror throughout my initial training as a sex therapist, a decade-long period in the 1970s and 1980s which included my getting a PhD, writing two books, parenting two teenagers, breaking up a relationship, and entering into my present relationship of more than thirty years' duration. In other words, it was a time filled with chaos, excitement, craziness, laughter, tears, heart-rending decisions, and enormous creative flux. During those years I also entered into many intentional growth experiences, including walking on fire—an adventure I experienced not once, but twice, so that I would believe I really did it the first time.

My learning from all this life experience is that, if we use whatever our particular situation is for the purpose of pursuing truth and sanity for all concerned, then the outcome cannot continue to be the same degree of craziness and unrest. Ultimately, I see the pursuit of truth and sanity as conscious movement toward aligning with the universe—body, mind, heart, and spirit. And, when we are humming along in resonance with the universe, the final result is right relationship—in other words, peace.

A Call to Action

I want to end this book with a call to action. The ISIS approach is about movement and flow rather than only intellectual analysis. If you are intrigued by the stories in this book, or if you are wondering whether ISIS work might help your clients, I encourage you to act on your questions and instincts, not just think about them. First, I ask you please to try ISIS for yourself before trying the process on your clients. ISIS teaching is founded on the principle that you cannot do this work deeply and confidently with your clients until you have experienced it yourself.

There are numerous ways to begin—reading, curiosity, seeking ways to help a client, or just stumbling into it—as outlined throughout this book. Other ways include opting for training and supervision from a variety of ISIS practitioners, including me. You can find us all by surfing my personal website (www. expandingsextherapy.com) and also the ISIS Network (www.ISISNetwork.org). In addition, I invite you to contact me directly at Gina@GinaOgden.com with any questions you may have about expanding your own practice of sex therapy.

APPRECIATIONS

One of the take-home messages of the ISIS approach is to end a session with gratitude. Here, it is my pleasure to express openhearted thanks, beginning with the 3,810 respondents of the ISIS survey, along with the generous colleagues who helped me think through the survey, design it, distribute it, and analyze the results. Particular gratitude to Riane Eisler, Carol Ellison, David Kahn, Joan Duncan Oliver, and Elaine Young, also to the Foundation for the Scientific Study of Sexuality for a research grant, and to the institutions who supported me with visiting scholarships: the Radcliffe Institute for Advanced Study, the Wellesley Centers for Research on Women, and Harvard Divinity School's Center for the Study of World Religions.

Of the many colleagues who have both inspired and supported therapeutic applications of the ISIS approach, I owe special gratitude to Deb Azorsky, Patti Britton, Neil Cannon, Rebecca Chalker, Jim Crabtree, Maril Crabtree, Karen Hicks, Ginger Holczer, Sue Katz, Peggy Kleinplatz, Tammy Nelson, Ruth Neustifter, Tina Nevin, Kamara McAndrews, Tara McAvoy, Esther Perel, Sherri Pominville, Evelyn Resh, Linda Savage, Suzanne Scurlock-Durana, Kenneth Ray Stubbs, Michele Sugg, Chelsea Wakefield, and Beverly Whipple.

To the institutions which have repeatedly supported ISIS retreats and trainings, I am indebted to Esalen Institute, Kripalu Center, the New York Open Center, and Rowe Conference Center. To the organizations which have invited ISIS keynote and pre-conference presentations, I am grateful to Harvard Medical School, the American Association of Sexuality Educators, Counselors, and Therapists (AASECT), the American Association for Marriage and Family Therapy (AAMFT), the Association for Spirituality and Psychotherapy (ASP), the International Society for the Study of Women's Sexual Health (ISSWSH), the Society for Sex Therapy and Research (SSTAR), Psychotherapy Networker, the Society for the Scientific Study of Sexuality (SSSS), the

Theological Opportunities Program (TOP), and the World Association for Sexual Health (WAS). To Judy Norsigian and Wendy Sanford, gratitude for including ISIS in updated editions of *Our Bodies, Ourselves*. To Marta Moldvai, Routledge editor extraordinaire, thank you for your passion for this project.

To Jo Chaffee, my cherished partner, who has lived with ISIS from the beginning, my gratitude for your clinical expertise, your editorial smarts, and your love.

REFERENCES AND
SUGGESTED READINGS

Allione, T. (2008) *Feeding your demons: Ancient wisdom for resolving inner conflict.* Boston: Little, Brown.

American Psychiatric Association (2000) *Diagnostic and statistical manual of mental disorders.* 4th ed., text revision, Washington, DC: American Psychiatric Association.

Anand, M. (1989) *The art of sexual ecstasy: The path of sacred sexuality for western lovers.* Los Angeles: Jeremy Tarcher.

Anapol, D. (1997) *Polyamory: The new love without limits: Secrets of sustainable intimate relationships.* Rev. ed., San Raphael, CA: IntiNet Resource Center.

Bass, E., and Davis, L. (2008) *The courage to heal: A guide for women survivors of child sexual abuse.* 4th ed., New York: William Morrow.

Basson, R. (2001) Female sexual response: The role of drugs in the management of sexual dysfunction, *Journal of Obstetrics and Gynecology*, 98: 350–53.

Bateson, G. (2000) *Steps to an ecology of mind: Collected essays in anthropology, psychiatry, evolution, and epistemology.* Chicago: University of Chicago Press.

Beattie-Jung, P., Hunt, M. E., and Balakrishnan, R. (2001) *Good sex: Feminist perspectives from the world's religions.* New Brunswick, NJ: Rutgers University Press.

Bonheim, J. (1997) *Aphrodite's daughters: Women's sexual stories and the journey of the soul.* New York: Fireside.

Boston Women's Health Book Collective (2011) *Our bodies, ourselves.* 40th anniversary ed., New York: Touchstone.

Britton, P. (2005) *The art of sex coaching: Expanding your practice.* New York: W. W. Norton.

Brotto, L., and Heiman, J. (2007) Mindfulness in sex therapy: Applications for women with sexual difficulties following gynecologic cancer, *Sexual & Relationship Therapy*, 22(1): 3–11.

Chalker, R. (2000) *The clitoral truth: The secret world at our fingertips.* New York: Seven Stories Press.

Conrad, E. (2007) *Life on land: The story of Continuum.* Berkeley, CA: North Atlantic Books.

Csikszentmihalyi, M. (1991) *Flow: The psychology of optimal experience.* New York: Harper.

Daniluk, J. C. (1998) *Women's sexuality across the life span*. Binghamton, NY: Guilford Press.

Davis, K. B. (1929) *Factors in the sex lives of twenty-two hundred women*. New York: Harper & Brothers.

De Beauvoir, S. (1953) *The second sex*. New York: Knopf.

Diamond, L. (2009) *Sexual fluidity: Understanding women's love and desire*. Cambridge, MA: Harvard University Press.

Eisler, R. (1995) *Sacred pleasure: Sex, myth, and the politics of the body*. San Francisco: HarperCollins.

Eliade, M. (1991) *Images and symbols*, trans. P. Mairet. Princeton, NJ: Princeton University Press.

Ellison, C. R. (2000) *Women's sexualities: Generations of women share intimate secrets of sexual self-acceptance*. San Francisco: New Harbinger.

Ensler, E. (2000) *The vagina monologues: The V-day edition*. New York: Villard.

Eriksen, J. A. (1999) *Kiss and tell: Surveying sex in the twentieth century*. Cambridge, MA: Harvard University Press.

Erikson, M. A. (1980) *The nature of hypnosis and suggestion*. New York: Irvington.

Espin, O. M. (1997) *Latina realities: Essays on healing, migration, and sexuality*. Boulder, CO: Westview Press.

Fisher, H. E. (2004) *Why we love: The nature and chemistry of romantic love*. New York: Holt.

Foley, S., Kope, S., and Sugrue, D. (2012) *Sex matters for women: A complete guide to taking care of your sexual self*. Rev. ed., Binghamton, NY: Guilford Press.

Freud, S. (1938) Three contributions to the theory of sex, in *The basic writings of Sigmund Freud*, ed. and trans. A. A. Brill. New York: Random House.

Gottman, J. M. (2011) *The science of trust: Emotional attunement for couples*. New York: W. W. Norton.

Grinder, R., and Bandler, J. (1977) *The structure of magic*. Palo Alto, CA: Science and Behavior Books.

Hall, K., and Graham, K. (eds) (2012) *The cultural context of sexual pleasure and problems: Psychotherapy with diverse clients*. New York: Routledge.

Heyward, C. (1989) *Touching our strength: The erotic as power and the love of God*. New York: HarperCollins.

Hite, S. (1976) *The Hite report: A nationwide study of female sexuality*. New York: Macmillan.

Hunt, V. V. (2000) *The infinite mind: Science of human vibrations of consciousness*. 3rd ed., Los Angeles: Malibu.

Ingerman, S. (2008) *Soul retrieval: Mending the fragmented self*. Rev. ed., New York: Harper.

Irvine, J. (1990) *Disorders of desire: Sex and gender in modern American sexology*. Philadelphia: Temple University Press.

Johnson, H. (2004) *Psyche and synapse: Expanding worlds*. 2nd ed., Deerfield, MA: Deerfield Valley.

Johnson, S. M. (2004) *The practice of emotionally focused couple therapy: Creating connections*. 2nd ed., New York: Routledge.

Judith, A. (2001) *Wheels of life: A user's guide to the chakra system*. Rev. ed., St. Paul, MN: Llewellyn.

Jung, C. G. (1959) *The archetypes and the collective unconscious*, trans. R. F. C. Hall. New York: Pantheon Books.

Jung, C. G. (1970) Civilization in transition, in *The collected works of Carl G. Jung*, Vol. 10. New York: Bollingen.

Kaplan, H. S. (1979) *Disorders of sexual desire*. New York: Brunner/Mazel.

Kaptchuk, T. J. (2002). The placebo effect in alternative medicine: Can the performance of a healing ritual have clinical significance? *Annals of Internal Medicine*, 136(11): 817–25.

Kilbourne, J. (2010) *Killing us softly 4: Advertising's image of women*. Northampton, MA: Media Education Foundation [film].

Kinsey, A. C., Pomeroy, W. B., and Martin, C. E. (1948) *Sexual behavior in the human male*. Philadelphia: W. B. Saunders.

Kinsey, A. C., Pomeroy, W. B., Martin, C. E., and Gebhard, P. H. (1953) *Sexual behavior in the human female*. Philadelphia: W. B. Saunders.

Kleinplatz, P. J. (ed.) (2012) *New directions in sex therapy: Innovations and alternatives*. 2nd ed., New York: Routledge.

Komisaruk, B., Beyer-Flores, C., and Whipple, B. (2006) *The science of orgasm*. Baltimore, MD: Johns Hopkins University Press.

Laumann, E. O., Gagnon, J. H., Michael, R. T., and Michaels, S. (1994) *The social organization of sexuality: Sexual practices in the United States*. Chicago: University of Chicago Press.

Laumann, E. O., Paik, A., and Rosen, R. (1999) Sexual dysfunction in the United States: Prevalence and predictors, *Journal of the American Medical Association*, 281: 537–44.

Leavitt, J. (2012) *The sexual alarm system: Women's unwanted response to sexual intimacy and how to overcome it*. Northvale, NJ: Jason Aronson.

Linn, D. (2005) *Sacred space: Enhancing the energy of your home and office*. New York: Random House.

Loe, M. (2004) *The rise of Viagra: How the little blue pill changed sex in America*. New York: New York University Press.

Maltz, W. (2012) *The sexual healing journey: A guide for survivors of sexual abuse*. 3rd ed., New York: William Morrow.

Maltz, W., and Maltz, L. (2009) *The porn trap: The essential guide to overcoming problems caused by pornography*. New York: William Morrow.

Maslow, A. (1998) *Toward a psychology of being*. 3rd ed., New York: Wiley.

Masters, W. H., and Johnson, V. E. (1966) *Human sexual response*. Boston: Little, Brown.

McGoldrick, M. (2008) *Genograms: Assessment and intervention*. 3rd ed., New York: W. W. Norton.

Michaels, M. A., and Johnson, P. (2012) *Great sex made simple: Tantric tips to deepen intimacy & heighten pleasure*. St. Paul, MN: Llewellyn.

Mosher, C. D. (1980) *The Mosher survey: Sexual attitudes of 45 Victorian women*, ed. J. MaHood and K. Wenburg. New York: Arno Press.

Nelson, T. (2008) *Getting the sex you want: Shed your inhibitions and reach new heights of passion together*. Gloucester, MA: Quiver.

Nelson, T. (2013) *The new monogamy: Redefining your relationship after infidelity*. Oakland, CA: New Harbinger.

Northrup, C. (2010) *Women's bodies, women's wisdom: Creating physical and emotional health and healing*. Rev. ed., New York: Bantam.

Ogden, G. (2001) Integrating sexuality and spirituality: A group therapy approach to women's sexual dilemmas, in P. J. Kleinplatz (ed.), *New directions in sex therapy: Innovations and alternatives* (pp. 322–46). New York: Brunner-Routledge.

Ogden, G. (2001) The taming of the screw: Reflections on "A new view of women's sexual problems," *Women and Therapy*, 24(1&2): 17–21.

Ogden, G. (2002) *Sexuality and spirituality in women's relationships: Preliminary results of an exploratory survey*, Working Paper 405. Wellesley, MA: Wellesley College Centers for Research on Women.

Ogden, G. (2006) *The heart and soul of sex: Making the ISIS connection*. Boston: Shambhala/Trumpeter.

Ogden, G. (2006) The spiritual dimensions of sexual health: Broadening clinical perspectives of women's sexual desire, in M. Tepper and A. Owens (eds), *Sexual Health* (Vol. 4, pp. 131–52). Englewood Cliffs, NJ: Praeger.

Ogden, G. (2007) *Women who love sex: Ordinary women describe their paths to pleasure, intimacy, and ecstasy*. 3rd ed., Boston: Shambhala/Trumpeter.

Ogden, G. (2008) *The return of desire: A guide to rediscovering your sexual passion*. Boston: Shambhala/Trumpeter.

Ogden, G. (2009) It's not just a headache dear: Why some women say no to connecting sex and spirit, in A. Mahoney and O. Espin (eds), *Sin or salvation: Implications for psychotherapy* (pp. 105–25). New York: Routledge.

Ogden, G. (2012) Keys to the sexual mysteries: An integrative model for exploring clients' stories, in P. J. Kleinplatz (ed.), *New directions in sex therapy: Innovations and alternatives* (pp. 337–53). 2nd ed., New York: Routledge.

Ogden, P., Minton, K., and Pain, C. (2006) *Trauma and the body: A sensorimotor approach to psychotherapy*. New York: W. W. Norton.

Perel, E. (2007) *Mating in captivity: Unlocking erotic intelligence*. New York: Harper.

Perls, F. (1992) *Gestalt therapy verbatim*. Rev. ed., Gouldsboro, ME: Gestalt Journal Press.

Reich, W. (1973 [1942]) *The function of the orgasm*, trans. V. Carfagno. New York: Farrar, Straus & Giroux.

Resnick, S. (2012) *The heart of desire: Keys to the pleasure of love*. New York: Wiley.

Rosenbaum, T. Y. (2009) Physical therapy evaluation of dyspareunia, in A. Goldstein, C. Pukall, and I. Goldstein (eds), *Female sexual pain disorders: Evaluation and management*. Oxford: Wiley-Blackwell.

Satir, V. (1983) *Conjoint family therapy*. 3rd ed., Palo Alto, CA: Science and Behavior Books.

Savage, L. E. (1999) *Reclaiming goddess sexuality: The power of the feminine way*. Carlsbad, CA: Hay House.

Scurlock-Durana, S. (2010) *Full body presence: Learning to listen to your body's wisdom*. Novato, CA: New World Library.

Shapiro, F. (2012) *Getting past your past: Take control of your life with self-help techniques from EMDR*. Emmaus, PA: Rodale Press.

Siegel, D. J. (2010) *The mindful therapist: A clinician's guide to mindsight and neural integration*. New York: W. W. Norton.

Sprinkle, A. (2005) *Dr. Sprinkle's spectacular sex: Make over your love life with one of the world's great sex experts*. New York: Tarcher.

Stubbs, K. R. (1999) *The essential Tantra: A modern guide to sacred sexuality*. New York: Tarcher.

Tiefer, L., and Kaschak, E. (eds) (2001) *A new view of women's sexual problems*. Binghamton, NY: Haworth Press.

Tolman, D. L. (2003) *Dilemmas of desire: Teenage girls talk about sexuality*. Cambridge, MA: Harvard University Press.

Villoldo, A. (2007) *The four insights: Wisdom, power, and grace of the earthkeepers*. Carlsbad, CA: Hay House.

Wade, J. (2004) *Transcendent sex: When lovemaking opens the veil*. New York: Paraview Pocket Books.

Wakefield, C. (2012) *Negotiating the inner peace treaty*. Carlsbad, CA: Balboa Press.

Whipple, B., Ogden, G., and Komisaruk, B. (1992) Physiological correlates of imagery-induced orgasm in women, *Archives of Sexual Behavior*, 21(2): 121–33.

Wilber, K. (2001) *Sex, ecology, spirituality: The spirit of evolution*. 2nd ed., Boston: Shambhala.

Yeats, W. B. (1996) *Collected poems of W. B. Yeats*. Rev. ed., New York: Scribner.

Zolbrod, A. (1998) *Sex smart: How your childhood shaped your sexual life and what to do about it*. Oakland, CA: New Harbinger.

INDEX

THE READER'S THEATRE OF
HOLIDAY PLAYS

ADAPTED BY HENRY GILFOND

S0-ADS-266

TABLE OF CONTENTS

ISBN 0-89187-477-1
Curriculum Associates, Inc.
North Billerica, MA 01862

Reprinted by arrangement with Walker and Company

No part of this book may be reproduced by any means without
permission from the publishers.
All Rights Reserved.
Printed in USA.
15   14   13   12   11   10

THREE DAYS MORE

a play for Columbus Day

Columbus Day is celebrated in most of the United States, in Puerto Rico, in a number of Latin American countries, and in a number of cities in Spain and Italy. It is a day given to honor the Italian-born Christopher Columbus, who sailed under the Spanish flag and discovered America on October 12th, 1492.

This play takes place aboard the Santa Maria, one of the three small sailing vessels under the command of Columbus. It should give you some understanding of the difficulties the explorer encountered and the strong will and faith with which he overcame the fear of his sailors, and their threat of mutiny. The story of Columbus is indeed a story of courage.

THE CAST   Columbus   1st Crewman
             Martin Alonso Pinzon   2nd Crewman
             Vicente Yanez Pinzon   3rd Crewman
             Officer   Announcer
             Sailor (the lookout)   Voice

THE SET   Aboard the Santa Maria

Text Copyright   ©1967 Henry Gilfond
Illustrations Copyright   ©1967 by George Blevins

3

Announcer	We are on board the *Santa Maria*. For thirty days the boat has moved westward in the Atlantic, in search of the East Indies. For thirty days the crew of the *Santa Maria* has seen nothing but water. The men are restless, afraid. Columbus said that the world was round; not many believed him. It seemed there must be an end to the ocean somewhere, and that boundary must mean death.
	The men have been grumbling. They want to turn back to Palos, where they started from. Columbus, walking the deck, knows that he cannot keep his westward course much longer, that at any moment the crew will rise in mutiny, murder him, and turn the sails for the winds to carry them home.
	He speaks to one of his officers.
Columbus	It can't be long now.
Officer	There is nothing. No sign of land. Nothing.
Columbus	We saw birds. Where there are birds, there must be land.
Officer	That's true, when we are near home. It may not be true out here, thirty days from home.
Columbus	Have you become afraid too, Pedro?
Officer	I am not afraid! I wasn't forced to sign on your ship! I'm not one of those prisoners they released from the jails to make up your crew!
Columbus	You are angry, Pedro.
Officer	I am angry!

4 *Three Days More*

Columbus	And you're also. . . afraid.
Officer	I'm not afraid of dying, if that's what you think, Captain. If I fear anything at all, it's for you. You are up on the deck. You don't hear the talk that goes on below. There's mutiny brewing below, Captain. Fear and mutiny! We are sailing on a powder keg!
Columbus	And where will you stand, Pedro, when this powder keg blows up? Will you stand at my side?
Officer	Of course! But they are so many and we are so few. If they rise in mutiny, we are lost! And if we do not find land soon, Captain, nothing will keep these men from turning the ships home.
Columbus	The Lord has taken us this distance, Pedro. He will see us all the way to our goal. We will still plant the flag of Spain in the East Indies.
Sailor	(From the watch) Land ho! Land ho! Land ho!
Officer	(As members of the crew rush to the deck) A miracle, Captain! A miracle!
Columbus	(Looking through his glass) Pray to the Lord!
1st Crewman	Where? Where is it? Where's this land?
2nd Crewman	I can't see a thing!
3rd Crewman	Land! There's nothing but water! And more water!
1st Crewman	Hey! Lookout! Where do you see this land?
Columbus	He sees nothing.
Officer	Nothing?

6 *Three Days More*

Columbus	He sees what he wants to find. A mirage.
2nd Crewman	What did you see, Lookout? Did you see land, or didn't you?
Sailor	*(From the watch)* It's gone.
3rd Crewman	What's gone? Say what you see there, Lookout. Land?
Sailor	*(From the watch)* Nothing but water—I thought it was land.
1st Crewman	We'll never see land.
2nd Crewman	Nothing but water.
3rd Crewman	*(To Columbus)* Where are these Indies you promised us?
2nd Crewman	We were fools to believe you.
1st Crewman	Turn the ship back!
3rd Crewman	Turn the ship back, before we all die on it!
Officer	Go back to your quarters! Go back to your posts!
2nd Crewman	We'll hear from the captain first!
1st Crewman	We'll hear from Columbus!
Officer	You'll hear from him when he's ready for you! Go back to your quarters!
3rd Crewman	We'll go back when we've heard from the captain! How long do we sail? When do you turn the ship back home?
Officer	Do you disobey an officer?

1st Crewman	Put us in irons, Officer.
Officer	I'll arrest every last man of you!
Columbus	Not now, Pedro.
2nd Crewman	You tell him, Captain. He'll have to put the whole crew into irons.
1st Crewman	And let the wind take the sails wherever it pleases.
3rd Crewman	Tell us, Captain. When do you turn the ship around and sail home to Spain?
Columbus	After we have planted the flag of the King and the Queen on the East Indies.
2nd Crewman	We'll never reach the Indies!
Columbus	We will reach them, and land. We will bring back to Spain their gold and their spices. You will share in the honor and glory, and be rich with the profits you will make on this journey.
3rd Crewman	That's what you promised us in Palos!
Columbus	I will keep my promise.
1st Crewman	If we ever find the islands.
Columbus	We will find them. I promised you that. Is there any promise that I have made to you and not kept?
2nd Crewman	We have been sailing for thirty days.
Columbus	And we have not fallen off the edge of the earth! I said the world is round. *(Pointing)* It is not flat like that plank of wood. We do not go to its end, then drop off into space. We sail west to reach the east.

3rd Crewman	Twenty-four hours more in this westward course and we may all be done for!
Columbus	We sail west till we land in the Orient. There is no edge to this earth, I promise you!
1st Crewman	Ay, you promise!
Officer	Back to your quarters now!
Columbus	No, Pedro. Not yet.
3rd Crewman	We'll go when we're ready to go.
2nd Crewman	And we're not ready to go, yet.
Columbus	You'll go back to your quarters. You'll go back to your posts. You will keep the *Santa Maria*, for God and the King and the Queen, in its course. I am your captain, and you will have faith in your captain. He will lead you safely across these waters to the rich Indies, and he will lead you home safely, with all the riches the Indies hold in wait for you.
1st Crewman	We will go back to our posts. But we had better sight land soon!
2nd Crewman	Do you think it was a sea monster that the lookout spotted, and thought was land?
Columbus	You still believe there are sea monsters?
2nd Crewman	How would I know what the lookout saw?
Columbus	But we have sailed for thirty days, with nothing but the ocean around us, and has anyone yet seen one of these monsters you worried about? I told you there are no sea monsters, and you will see none on this journey.

10 *Three Days More*

3rd Crewman	We haven't finished the journey yet.
Voice	*(Offstage)* God give us a good night and good sailing; may our ship make a good passage.
Columbus	They have begun the evening prayers. Have faith, my good men, and join them.
Announcer	The *Santa Maria* sailed on. So did the *Nina* and the *Pinta*. The three small ships which Columbus led out of Spain in search of a western route to the East Indies kept to their course. Every once in a while, there was the cry of "Land ho!" to bring the crew rushing to the decks, only to discover that the cry was false. The sighting of birds raised hopes of land in the hearts of the crewmen, but it seemed that those hopes would never be realized. The men's fears grew larger, and their tempers grew short and their patience shorter. Mutiny, it seemed, was inevitable.
	On October 9th, Columbus made a fateful promise. He met with the captains of the *Nina* and the *Pinta*.
Martin	How much longer, Columbus? Give us a date, a time. We can't sail forever with nothing but water around us. Our food is beginning to give out. Our water is already bad. When do we call a halt to this mission?
Columbus	I do not call a halt to this mission, Martin.
Martin	Be reasonable, Columbus. We have made an error. It is human to err. I say, let us turn back.

Vicente	I must agree with Martin, Columbus. If we don't turn back, the men will take over the ships. They have had enough. We can't hold them.
Columbus	Is it the men you are afraid of? Or have you lost courage?
Vicente	We haven't lost courage! But where are the Indies?
Columbus	They wait for us. Another day, two days, three. Perhaps we have erred in our calculations, but in three days, I promise you—
Martin	*(Interrupting)* Land!
Columbus	The Indies, gentlemen! The Indies! By my Lord, Martin! Vicente!
Vicente	There is no need to swear it, Columbus. I have sworn it a dozen times to the men who man my ship. Two days more! Three days more! All right! I believe you! But how will I convince my men?
Martin	And how will I convince my men, Columbus? Vicente is right. We must turn back.
Vicente	They are waiting for the word, Columbus. They know why we are meeting.
Martin	They'll cut our throats and turn the ship back themselves, if we don't bring the order with us. Let us turn back, Columbus.
Vicente	Give us the word. We are here to follow your orders. We will not act without your command. Order us to return to Spain.

12 *Three Days More*

Martin	We made the effort. No one can say we did not try.
Vicente	There is no dishonor in this failure.
Martin	Send us home, Columbus!
Vicente	We wait for the command. Speak, Columbus!
Columbus	My command is to sail forward. Keep the ships west. We move west, gentlemen, till we reach the Indies.
Martin	Impossible!
Columbus	Then we do the impossible.
Vicente	Be reasonable, Columbus. If you do not give the order, then we will give the order ourselves. You cannot sail on alone with the *Santa Maria*.
Columbus	You make yourselves clear, at last. You will obey my orders only if they meet with your demands. And you demand that we turn back.
Martin	We have no choice. We sail with our crew, or they sail without us.
Vicente	Give us the order Columbus.
Columbus	Give me three more days.
Martin	You have had three times three days!
Columbus	Three days more. That's all I ask for.
Vicente	And if, after three more days, there are no Indies, you will give the command to return to Spain?
Columbus	You give me no choice.

Martin	Then three days, and no more! This is the message we will take back to our men. The Lord grant that they agree to it!
Announcer	The crews of the three ships weren't happy with the results of the conference. They grumbled. They made threats. When the captains swore they would turn the boats back to Spain after three days, the crews finally agreed to the bargain with Columbus. The first twenty-four hours went by, and there was no sight of land. When the second day dawned, the crew saw nothing but water around them.
3rd Crewman	I should have listened to my wife. A fool's journey, she called it.
2nd Crewman	Patience. One more day.
3rd Crewman	We'll crawl back to Palos. They'll laugh us out of the town!
1st Crewman	Let them laugh. All I want to do is to get my feet back on dry land again.
3rd Crewman	I'm for turning the boat around right now! What do you say? Why give him another day? There's nothing out there but more water! And maybe worse!
2nd Crewman	We said three days. We agreed to it. One more day. . . .
Announcer	All through that second day, the crewmen cursed under their breaths. They followed orders, but they followed them slowly, unwillingly. A harsh

14   *Three Days More*

word, an irritated command, and they should have been quick to murder their captains, and take charge of the boats themselves.

But. . . on the third day. . . at two o'clock in the morning. . . .

Sailor	*(From the lookout)* Land ho! Land ho!
1st Crewman	*(As crew rushes to the deck)* Another mirage!
Sailor	Land ho!
2nd Crewman	He's seeing things again!
Sailor	Land ho! Land ho!
3rd Crewman	It's land! Land! Land! Land!
2nd Crewman	Land! The Lord preserve us! Where is the captain?
Crewman	Land, Captain! Land!
Columbus	*(Looks through his glass)* Land. Land. Let us go down on our knees. Let us give thanks to the Lord.
All	Our Father, Who art in Heaven. . . .
Voice	*(Offstage, chanting)* Blessed be the light of day. And the Holy Cross.
Announcer	And on October 12, 1492, Columbus and his men landed on the shores of what would one day be called America. He had not discovered a new route to the Indies. He had done something far greater; he had discovered a New World.

THE GHOSTS OF HALLOWEEN

a play for Halloween

Halloween has a long history. The Druids of old England had an autumn festival which they celebrated much as we celebrate the holiday today. Rin-Tan-Tan, on the 28th of October, was another English festival, celebrated with parades and masks and lots of noise. The Romans had a similar holiday in honor of Pomona, the goddess of fruits and gardens. Actually the original name for Halloween was All Hallow Even, the holy eve of All Saints Day. Today, of course, children all over the United States celebrate it by dressing up in strange costumes, playing pranks, trick-or-treating, or by collecting money for some worthwhile organization. But perhaps we think most often of Halloween as the night when witches ride their brooms, and ghosts and evil spirits roam the land.

This play is about some boys and girls, some Halloween ghosts, and a Halloween prank that is played.

THE CAST   Harold   Bill
                     Tom   Helen
                     Connie   Three White-Sheeted Figures
                     Fred   Announcer

THE SET   The living room of an old deserted house

17

18 *The Ghosts of Halloween*

Announcer	It is the night of Halloween. We are in the living room of a deserted old house. A number of young boys and girls enter.
Harold	I've been here before. So what? It's just an old house, like any other old house.
Tom	But you've never been here at night, have you?
Connie	You've never been here on Halloween, have you?
Harold	We ought to be out trick-or-treating. We're just wasting time here.
Helen	Look at the way the moon comes through that window!
Harold	It's the same moon we saw out in the street.
Connie	But it's eerie, isn't it?
Harold	What are you trying to do, scare me? I don't scare so easily. It's an old house, and that's all it is. No ghosts, no evil spirits, nothing. Why don't we go out and have some fun?
Fred	We just got here. Do you want to run?
Harold	I'm not running. I'll stay here as long as the rest of you. *(He sits on a chair, and the chair collapses.)*
Connie	*(Screams)* Oh!
Harold	*(Picking himself up)* What's the noise about? Just an old chair!
Connie	I'm sorry.
Tom	Funny! The last time I sat on it, it was solid.

The Ghosts of Halloween **19**

Harold	How often do you come here?
Tom	Not often.
Harold	Well, it's an old chair and it fell apart.
Bill	You're awfully cool, for a Halloween night, Harold.
Harold	Halloween or any other night, there are no ghosts, and no evil spirits.
Helen	Shh!
Harold	Now what?
Helen	Can't you hear it?
Harold	That's nothing but the wind.
Helen	No. It sounded like someone crying. They say Old Man Brady beat his wife before he murdered her. I'm scared.
Harold	Scared? What's there to be afraid of?
Connie	Old Man Brady did murder his wife, didn't he? Right in this room.
Harold	That's just a story you tell kids to keep them from wandering in here.
Bill	They say there are still blood stains on the floor.
Harold	Did you ever find any?
Bill	It's too dark to look.
Harold	You wouldn't find them—How long ago did Brady live here, anyway? Two hundred years ago?

Tom	Ghosts live forever. Or until they find some peace, they say.
Fred	There's that noise again.
Helen	I'm scared.
Connie	*(As they hear a hammering against the walls)* What's that?
Bill	Someone's here!
Harold	I guess somebody else wants to find out whether this old house is haunted. He'll be in for a surprise when he finds us in here.
Fred	That's no one who has walked into the house. That's someone who lives in the house. It's banging inside the walls!
Helen	I'm scared! Let's get out of here!
Bill	Don't move! You don't want to get the spirits angry, do you?
Harold	Spirits! Nonsense! Mice, maybe?
Connie	*(Scared)* Mice!?
Fred	That's not mice. That's Old Man Brady looking for his wife.
Harold	*(As they hear a scamper of feet)* That's mice, all right.
Tom	That's Old Lady Brady, running away from her husband.
Bill	It didn't do her any good, did it?

The Ghosts of Halloween **21**

22 *The Ghosts of Halloween*

Fred	No. He got her, all right. Killed her.
	(There is a sudden scream.)
Fred	Wow!
Connie	Let's get out of here!
Bill	He got her, didn't he?
Tom	*(As white-sheeted figure enters)* Poor woman!
Harold	*(Pointing to white-sheeted figure)* Is that supposed to be Old Lady Brady?
Tom	*(As if the white-sheeted figure is invisible)* That was her last scream, I guess. Until the next time.
Harold	I mean that thing in the white sheet!
Bill	What thing?
Harold	You can see it as well as I can! Who is it?
Tom	What are you talking about, Harold?
Harold	That white sheet!
Connie	What white sheet?
Harold	*(As another white-sheeted figure enters)* There! There's another one!
Fred	You're seeing things, Harold.
Helen	He's trying to scare us!
Harold	No I'm not! There are two sheets in the room! Can't you see them? There! *(As one leaves)* One's going out!
Fred	Stop kidding us, Harold! This isn't funny!

The Ghosts of Halloween **23**

Harold	It isn't funny at all! *(As second sheeted figure enters again)* There! It's back! The two of them!
Helen	I'm scared! I'm scared!
Bill	Cut it, Harold! You're frightening the girls!
Harold	They're here! There! There! *(As the figures get near him)* Get away from me!
Connie	Oh, I'm frightened!
Fred	Get hold of yourself, Harold! There are no ghosts!
Harold	Whatever they are, they're here! Leave me alone! *(As another white-sheeted figure enters)* There's another one!
Bill	*(Grabbing Harold by the arms)* Harold!
Harold	*(Really frightened)* Leave me alone, will you?
Bill	Come one, Harold. It's all in your mind.
Harold	Oh, no, it isn't. They're right here. *(As wind howls in through the windows)* And there are more of them coming!
Connie	Where? Where?
Fred	Quiet, girls!
Harold	*(As the figures begin to leave)* What are we going to do, Bill? They're going now. They're gone.
Bill	Are you all right now, Harold?
Harold	I'm all right.
Fred	What was the matter with you?

Harold	You didn't see anything?
Tom	See what?
Harold	You're not kidding me, are you?
Bill	There's something wrong with you, Harold. There are just the six of us here.
Harold	I'm sure I saw spooks. Two, three of them, I think. They were all around the room.
Fred	It's the stories you've been listening to, all about Old Man Brady and his wife.
Harold	One of them looked like Old Man Brady.
Tom	How would you know how Old Man Brady looked? Did you ever see his picture?
Harold	No, but I'm sure it looked like Old Man Brady. Let's get out of here.
Fred	Why? I thought you didn't believe in ghosts.
Harold	I don't but—
Bill	But you want to get out of here.
Harold	Well, it is Halloween, and—
Fred	You're scared.
Harold	I'm not scared! I'll stay as long as you do. Maybe I was seeing things. I said before that there are no ghosts and evil spirits. Well, I'll say it again.
Tom	That's the boy! Stick to your guns! No spirits! No ghosts! Do you believe there are ghosts, Connie?

The Ghosts of Halloween **25**

Connie	I didn't see any tonight, but I believe they get around.
Harold	You didn't see any, eh?
Connie	No. But I'm sure we'll see them, if we wait long enough.
Harold	Well, take it from me, you'll never see them. *(As white-sheeted figure enters again)* There it is again!
Connie	Where?
Bill	Don't start that again, Harold!
Harold	*(Another white-sheeted figure enters)* There's another! *(He begins to run to the open door, away from the figures)*
Fred	Where are you going, Harold? There's nothing here, Harold!
Harold	They're all over the house! I'm getting out of here! *(He exits on the run)*
	(There is a moment of silence, then everyone laughs.)
Bill	It sure got him, didn't it?
Fred	Did you see him run?
Tom	You can take those sheets off now, kids. I haven't had so much fun on a Halloween in all my life. Take off that sheet, Jerry!
1st Sheeted Figure	Whooooo! Whooooo!
Fred	Come on, Jerry! Take off that bedspread!

1st Sheeted Figure	*(Moving away)* Whooooooo! Whooooooo!
Bill	Very funny, Jerry. *(To 2nd sheeted figure)* Take that thing off, will you, Cynthia? Harold is still running.
2nd Sheeted Figure	*(Moving about)* Whooooo! Whoooooo!
Connie	What's going on?
Helen	*(As 3rd sheeted figure enters)* There were only Cynthia and Jerry. Who is this one?
Tom	Hey! Whoever you are! Take those sheets off!
Sheeted Figures	Whoooooo! Whoooooo!
Connie	Let's get out of here!
Fred	Why don't you pull that sheet off him, Bill?
Bill	Why don't you do it yourself?
Helen	*(Beginning to cry)* Let's get out of here! We didn't mean you any harm, Old Man Brady. Let's get out of here!
Bill	Jerry! Cynthia!
Sheeted Figures	Whooooooo! Whooooooo!
Fred	Let's go, Tom!
Tom	Yeah! Let's go!
Connie	*(Screams)* I've got to get out of here! *(She runs.)*
Bill	Let's go! *(They all run out.)*
Sheeted Figures	Whooooo! Whooooo! Whooooo!

The Ghosts of Halloween **27**

Announcer   What do you think? Was it Cynthia and Jerry and someone else dressed up to look like ghosts? Or were they the real thing, haunting an old deserted house on Halloween night?

A CRISIS IN THE NEWSPAPER OFFICE

a play for Election Day

Election day comes on the first Tuesday in November. Some years there is more excitement about the campaigning and balloting than others, but for most boys and girls Election Day is just one more welcome day off from school. Most young people leave arguments about who should be elected to the grown-ups. However, as people grow older and closer to the voting age, their interest in the candidates, parties, and platforms begins to develop. There has been much talk about lowering the voting age from twenty-one to eighteen. That brings the right to vote a little closer to young people; it makes Election Day mean something more to them than just that day off from school.

This play is about some young people who are beginning to get interested in the right to vote and the proper use of the ballot.

Walter, editor of his school newspaper wants to endorse a candidate for mayor. He runs into some tough opposition. Even if he can beat down the opposition, there is the faculty adviser to contend with. How does Walter tackle the problem? Does he succeed?

THE CAST	*Walter*	*Bob*
	Sybil	*Mr. Fields*
	Jane	*Announcer*
	Ed	
THE SET	*School newspaper office*	

30 *A Crisis in the Newspaper Office*

Announcer	We are in the office of the school newspaper. Election Day is just a week or two away, and Walter, one of the newspaper's editors, is busily writing at his desk. Sybil, another of the newspaper's editors, enters with a sheaf of papers.
Sybil	Here's the story on the drama club. Pretty good, I think. Ed is bringing in the story on the football team.
Walter	*(Still writing)* Good. Good.
Sybil	*(Looking over some papers on her own desk)* We've got the article on the parents association. Here's the glee club story. Here's the story on the astronauts. Where's the chess club story? We couldn't leave that out, could we?
Walter	What?
Sybil	I said we couldn't leave the chess club story out! What are you doing there, anyway?
Walter	I'm finishing the editorial.
Sybil	That wraps it up. Another issue of *The School Examiner* ready for the printers.
Walter	Not quite. We've got to talk about this editorial. I've called a meeting.
Sybil	Nobody told me about it.
Walter	Well, I'm telling you now.
Sybil	You sound serious.
Jane	*(Entering)* Where is everybody?

A Crisis in the Newspaper Office **31**

Walter	They'll be here.
Sybil	What is this all about?
Jane	Ask Walter. *(To Walter)* When are you going to let us in on it?
Walter	As soon as everybody gets here.
Jane	*(As Bob and Ed enter)* We're all here now.
Bob	What's the story, Walter? Trouble with Mr. Fields?
Walter	I don't know. *(Picking up the papers from his desk)* He hasn't read this editorial yet.
Ed	You don't think he'll like it, eh?
Walter	It really won't matter. We're the elected editors of this school paper. We print what we like.
Jane	With the approval of the faculty.
Walter	Or without it.
Sybil	That isn't the way we were told. You've got to have the faculty approval, Walter.
Bob	What are you pushing for, Walter? A school swimming pool?
Jane	Mr. Fields can't object to that. What's on your mind, Walter?
Walter	The elections.
Ed	We don't have elections until some time in May. Why do you want an editorial on that?
Jane	He's talking about the November elections, not student elections.

32   A Crisis in the Newspaper Office

Walter	That's right!
Ed	That's just as bad. What have we got to do with the elections anyway?
Walter	That's just the point! I've got it all down here in this editorial.
Bob	Aw, come off it, Walter! Election Day is just a day off from school.
Jane	What are you going to write, Walter? The ballot is the precious possession of the citizen? The right to vote is sacred in a democracy?
Ed	We get all that in our history classes, and we can't even vote. There's an editorial!
Walter	I'm serious about this. I'm printing this editorial.
Sybil	Not before we approve it, Walter. We're on the editorial staff, too.
Jane	And don't forget Mr. Fields.
Walter	I'm not forgetting anybody. If you'll just simmer down, maybe we can get to this editorial.
Bob	What's it about, Walter?
Walter	Well, the long and short of it is that we endorse Mr. Gregory for mayor of our city.
Bob	Because he's a Republican?
Walter	He happens to be a Democrat, Bob. But that isn't why we should endorse him.
Ed	I can't think of any better reason.

A Crisis in the Newspaper Office **33**

34 *A Crisis in the Newspaper Office*

Sybil	Hold on a minute. My father is a Republican.
Ed	Too bad!
Sybil	Too bad for whom?
Walter	All right! All right! Let's not get into that kind of fight!
Jane	But you're asking for it. What do you expect?
Walter	I expect that we're smart enough to look at this thing objectively.
Sybil	Well, I've looked at it objectively, and I think we ought to endorse Mr. Sanders for mayor of this city.
Ed	Because he's a Republican!
Sybil	Because he's a Republican!
Walter	Examine the issues! The men! Look at their platforms!
Jane	They're both kind of wobbly, to me.
Sybil	And if you're going to look at faces, I'll look at Mr. Sanders's face any time!
Jane	He's cute, isn't he?
Sybil	You can say that again.
Walter	Are you people going to be serious about this, or aren't you?
Ed	How are you going to be serious about it, Walter? What do you know about Gregory or Sanders?
Walter	I've read their speeches and studied their records.

A Crisis in the Newspaper Office **35**

Bob	So what?
Walter	So Gregory has come out for an increase in the budget for education.
Ed	And higher taxes.
Walter	What do I care about higher taxes?
Sybil	My father cares.
Bob	It affects us all. That's what we learn in economics.
Walter	I know all that, but our first interest is education!
Ed	Sanders isn't against education, is he?
Walter	No, but he's for cutting the budget. That means the schools!
Jane	How would you know that?
Bob	We can't vote anyway, so what difference does it make?
Walter	You're missing the whole point.
Jane	Don't give up, Walter. Tell us. What point are we missing?
Walter	It's important that the better man be elected.
Sybil	That's Sanders!
Bob	Come on, Sybil. We know the better man is Gregory, but let Walter talk.
Walter	I'm beginning to think I'm wasting my time.
Jane	I could have told you that in the beginning, Walter, but you insisted.

36 *A Crisis in the Newspaper Office*

Walter	Insisted on trying to get you people to take a stand, let everybody know the election is important to us, too, even if we're too young to vote. But it's all a big joke.
Bob	Suppose we took it seriously, Walter. There are five of us here. And five opinions. You'd have to run two editorials. One for Gregory and one for Sanders.
Walter	Then let's run two of them!
Mr. Fields	(Entering) Two of what?
Jane	You tell him, Walter. It's your idea.
Walter	Mr. Fields, we're going to run two editorials. I'm writing an editorial endorsing Mr. Gregory for mayor. Someone else is going to write one for Sanders.
Mr. Fields	It sounds like a good idea.
Walter	You don't object?
Mr. Fields	Why should I?
Walter	There! I told you!
Bob	But what do we know about these candidates?
Walter	We know as much as anybody else knows. We can read the facts and figures like anyone else.
Ed	There is more than facts and figures. There's the question of party, the influence on state politics and national politics.
Walter	We're only going to print our opinions.

A Crisis in the Newspaper Office **37**

Jane	What are our opinions worth?
Walter	I don't know. I just feel we ought to say something about the elections. I think it's our responsibility.
Mr. Fields	I think Walter has a good point.
Jane	But you've got some doubts!
Mr. Fields	Well, I think Ed has a good point, too. And Bob had a good point.
Sybil	I think we'd sound awfully foolish, writing as if we had any real knowledge of politics. Sure, everyone is going to say smart young kids, writing about the election—but who is going to take us seriously? And maybe some people will think we're acting too smart. I suppose there is something we can do about the election; but tell people which candidate to vote for? I don't see it.
Mr. Fields	Sybil has a point, too, hasn't she?
Bob	You're playing both sides, Mr. Fields. Where are you heading us?
Mr. Fields	It's your paper. You make the decisions.
Walter	It looks like I'm a minority of one here.
Mr. Fields	Don't give up that easily, Walter.
Walter	I don't give up easily, Mr. Fields, but if I can't write an editorial for Gregory, I'd just as soon we said nothing.
Sybil	How about urging all the parents to go out and vote?

38 *A Crisis in the Newspaper Office*

Walter	They get that in their ears all day long, from radio and TV. Half the people don't vote anyway.
Sybil	There's a lady who lives in my apartment house. I baby-sit for her so that she can go out and vote.
Jane	That's a good idea.
Sybil	It's my mother's idea. She works with the you-know-what party. It helps get out the vote.
Bob	There's an idea, Walter!
Walter	What? Baby-sit?
Bob	Why not? Why not get the whole school involved? Organize volunteer squads. Baby-sit, help old ladies, anything to help get out the vote. That's really constructive!
Walter	We're running a paper, not a political club.
Ed	This could be nonpartisan, and we don't need to organize these squads. We write an editorial. Announce the organization of election squads. Start them going, maybe. There's a way we can do something real for this election. What do you say, Walter?
Walter	I'm only one of the editors.
All	It's a good idea! Great!
Ed	(Sitting down) Here. I'll write the editorial.
Walter	(To the others) What are you standing around for? How about the layout? Are we running a newspaper or are we running a newspaper?
All	Yes, sir! Yes, sir!

THE SOUND OF THE GUNS

a play for Veterans' Day

It was on November 11th, 1918, at precisely eleven o'clock in the morning, that the shooting came to an end in World War I. It was a day to be remembered and almost all over the world November 11th was declared a legal holiday. In the United States we called it Armistice Day, for on this day, in 1918, an armistice, ending hostilities between the Allies and the so-called Central Powers, was signed. It was a day given to celebrating peace and to honoring the veterans of our armed services.

Since 1918, however, we have been involved in a second World War, the Korean War, and the struggle in Vietnam. We still maintain November 11th as a national holiday, but we have changed its name. We now call it Veterans' Day and honor, on this day, the veterans of all our armed conflicts. It is to celebrate this day and to honor these veterans that this play was written.

The scene for the play is a field hospital, just behind the lines of battle. The battle might have taken place in World War I, World War II, or any other major engagement in which American forces have taken part. Although the characters might just as well have been marines, sailors, or airmen, in this play they are soldiers and nurses and doctors. It is a story of the courage of those who risk their lives for their country.

THE CAST	1st Nurse	Doctor	Frank Ellis
	2nd Nurse	Tom Gordon	Announcer
	3rd Nurse		

THE SETS	Office in a field hospital
	Room in the field hospital

Announcer	We are in a field hospital, just behind the battlefield. We can hear the occasional thunder of the big guns and, every now and then, the sharp bark of the smaller firearms. Several doctors, very busy, walk in and out, making inquiries at the desk, filing papers, talking to each other, all very quickly. One nurse sits at the desk; another, standing at the desk, fumbles with some papers, apparently very nervous.
1st Nurse	*(Standing)* Do you want these papers, or shall I file them?
2nd Nurse	*(Seated)* If they're charts, file them. If they're special requests or doctors' orders.... Here! Let me help you with them.
1st Nurse	Thank you. *(Giving her the papers)* I'm sorry, but I'm new here.
2nd Nurse	I know that.
1st Nurse	This is my first day here.
2nd Nurse	*(Sorting the papers)* You'll catch on. It won't take you long.
1st Nurse	*(Listening to the thunder of the big guns)* Is it always so noisy?
2nd Nurse	*(Looks up at 1st Nurse, smiles)* You'll get used to it. Where do you come from?
1st Nurse	Ohio. Oh! That sounded awfully close!
2nd Nurse	It is close!
1st Nurse	*(Worried)* How close?

42   *The Sound of the Guns*

2nd Nurse	Don't worry. They don't reach us too often.
1st Nurse	What do you mean? *(Slowly)* You mean that we can actually be hit by one of those big shells?
2nd Nurse	It happens. *(Looks at the papers)* These are all for me. You don't have to file them.
1st Nurse	Have you ever been hit by a shell? I mean, one of those big ones?
2nd Nurse	No. I wouldn't be here to tell you, if I had been in the way of one of those. But it does happen. It has happened.
1st Nurse	Oh!
Doctor	*(Stopping at the desk)* Did that plasma come in yet?
2nd Nurse	Not yet, sir.
Doctor	How about the beds? Any word on that yet?
2nd Nurse	Nothing, sir.
Doctor	Well, I suppose we'll have to do with what we've got. Let me know as soon as the shipment of plasma gets here. *(He exits.)*
1st Nurse	There aren't enough beds?
2nd Nurse	They'll be here.
1st Nurse	I should think they'd rush the blood plasma. That's so important.
2nd Nurse	Everything is important here. It's important, too, miss, that you get back to your job, don't you think?

1st Nurse	I'm sorry. It's just that everything here is so new to me. *(After a particularly heavy burst of firing)* That was very close, wasn't it?
2nd Nurse	Yes, that was very close. You've got to expect it if you're working in a field hospital. After a while, you get so you don't hear it at all. It gets to be like the street noises outside your apartment.
1st Nurse	I never lived in an apartment. Out where I come from there are just a lot of little houses. We never hear any noise like this, where I come from.
2nd Nurse	You can always get a transfer, if you want one badly enough. Not everybody can take a field hospital.
Tom Gordon	*(Entering, his arm in a sling)* Hi!
1st Nurse	Hi!
Tom	*(To 2nd Nurse)* Hi!
2nd Nurse	Can I help you, soldier?
Tom	I was just looking around.
2nd Nurse	Do you have the doctor's permission?
Tom	Nothing wrong with me. *(Indicating)* Just this arm.
2nd Nurse	It's all right with me, just as long as the doctor gave you the OK. Did you ask him?
Tom	No. I didn't ask him.
2nd Nurse	Then you ought to be back in your bed.
Tom	Sure. I was just looking for a buddy—Frank Ellis. That's his name. We came in together. He was shot up pretty badly. You couldn't tell me what room he's in, could you?

44 *The Sound of the Guns*

2nd Nurse	I could, if he's still here, but . . . .
Tom	He's got to be here. They couldn't have moved him. He was hit too badly. He was my buddy, miss. All I want to do is say "hello" to him.
2nd Nurse	You ought to be back in your room, soldier.
Tom	I'm not asking too much of you, am I? All you've got to do is look in your files there.
Doctor	*(Entering)* What are you doing out here, soldier?
Tom	I was just taking a walk, sir.
Doctor	You ought to be back in your bed, fellow. We'll let you know when you can walk around.
Tom	It's just the arm. Nothing the matter with my legs, is there, Doc? I was just looking for my buddy, Frank Ellis. A big guy, Doc. Two hundred fifty pounds. Used to play professional football. You couldn't tell me where he is, could you, Doc?
Doctor	There are so many rooms here—and so many buddies. I'll let you know, as soon as you can walk around.
Tom	Ellis, Doc. A big fellow. Used to play football.
Doctor	He's in the left wing, I think. Get back to your bed, soldier. That's an order now.
Tom	Sure. Thanks, Doc. *(He exits.)*
Doctor	That boy lost a lot of blood. You had better call me if he comes out here again. Pretty nearly lost his arm. He needs all his strength to bring it back to normal. How about the plasma, Nurse?

46 *The Sound of the Guns*

Announcer	Let us leave the doctor and the nurses for a moment, and follow Tom Gordon. He has wandered into the left wing of the field hospital, forgetting the doctor's orders. He has searched among the rows and rows of wounded soldiers, looking for Frank Ellis, his buddy. Suddenly a voice calls out his name.
Frank Ellis	Tom! Tom Gordon!
Tom	*(Seeing his buddy, and moving quickly to his bed)* Frank!
Frank	*(As they attempt to shake hands)* Hey! You've got only one arm!
Tom	Two of them! They've got this one tied up so that I don't hit you one! You old dog! Lazying around, as if you've got nothing else to do!
Frank	This is the life, isn't it?
Tom	It's good to see you again, Frank! The way they were pulling you in, I had you figured for a goner.
Frank	I don't go that easily. Who stepped on that land mine, anyway? I couldn't have done anything as stupid as that, could I?
Tom	I guess you did. But, say Frank, I'm glad you're all in one piece. This arm is going to be all right after a while, I guess. You look as if nothing happened to you at all. What have you got, a headache?
Frank	*(Laughs)* You can call it that, if you want to.
Tom	I think you're just goofing off. Had enough fighting. Want to take it easy. I can't blame you.

The Sound of the Guns 47

Frank	You paint the picture, Tom. I won't be doing much fighting anymore. How about you? I guess they'll send you back as soon as your arm gets mended.
Tom	I guess so. But I'm not rushing it. But what's the matter with you? Don't you expect to be sent back?
Frank	I'm afraid not, Tom.
Tom	What's the formula? Maybe I can use a little bit of it?
Frank	I don't think you'd want to use it, Tom.
Tom	Why don't you try me!
Frank	(Quietly) I lost a leg, Tom.
Tom	(Shocked) What!?
Frank	They had to amputate my right leg. Just above the knee.
Tom	(Horrified) It was your kicking leg! How are you going to kick a football without that right leg?
Frank	It had to be done. The whole thing was just shattered.
Tom	They couldn't save it?
Frank	No.
Tom	And all I got was a broken arm . . . . What are you going to do, Frank? I mean, when you get back home? You can't play football anymore. What are you going to do?
Frank	Oh, I'll do all right, Tom. I'll do something. They'll fit me with one of those fancy artificial things, and I'll do all right.

Tom	And I was kidding you about going back to the front!
Frank	*(Laughs)* That would be fun, wouldn't it? Hopping around on one leg!
Tom	I've got two legs.
Frank	And a bad arm.
Tom	Nothing wrong with this arm. It's mended. They're just keeping me in this hospital to fill a bed.
Frank	They won't keep you any longer than they have to. There's a shortage of beds, I hear. The fighting must be pretty heavy in this sector.
Tom	There's a lot of fighting. You can hear those guns going all day long. Those doctors are kind of stupid, keeping me in here.
Frank	They know what they're doing.
Tom	They're not stepping on land mines. They're not getting their legs cut off.
Frank	Those medics are all over the place, Tom, getting shot up like the rest of us. They're right up there in the front lines.
Tom	And that's where I belong. *(Abruptly)* Take care of yourself, Frank! Get back on your feet! I mean ....
Frank	I know what you mean.
Tom	I'll be seeing you, Frank!
Frank	Sure. But what's your hurry? You're not going anywhere, are you?

The Sound of the Guns **49**

50 *The Sound of the Guns*

Tom	Where would I be going?
Frank	I don't know. I thought you might be having some ideas.
Tom	I won't be long, Frank. (He exits.)
Announcer	The fighting continues. It is early in the evening. The 2nd Nurse is at her desk. The 3rd Nurse enters with a tray in her hands.
2nd Nurse	Carrying your dinner?
3rd Nurse	Some soldier isn't in his bed. It's his dinner. (She exits.)
1st Nurse	(Entering with a tray of pills) That soldier isn't in his bed. He just isn't anywhere.
2nd Nurse	He'll turn up after a while. He'll get his pill.
1st Nurse	It's that soldier who was in here this morning. The one with his arm in the sling, the one asking to find his buddy. His name is Gordon.
2nd Nurse	He got you worried, eh? The soldiers will worry you a lot, if you let them. (As the Doctor enters) She can't find her soldier.
Doctor	(Laughs) You're new here, too, aren't you?
1st Nurse	It was that soldier who was in here this morning, the one you were sending back to bed. Well, he isn't in his bed. I haven't seen him all day.
Doctor	Oh, you'll find him. He got restless, probably. Maybe he found his buddy. Look for him there.
1st Nurse	I did, sir. His buddy's an amputee.

Doctor	Oh! He probably got all fired up. Couldn't wait to get back into the lines. Had to make somebody pay for his buddy's leg. These soldiers! *(He exits.)*
1st Nurse	Aren't they going to try to find him?
2nd Nurse	Sure. But they'll have to go up to the front lines to get him . . . if he's still alive.
	(There is the thunder of heavy cannon.)
2nd Nurse	That one was really close!
1st Nurse	Close?
2nd Nurse	The guns! That's what you call heavy bombardment, Nurse.
1st Nurse	Heavy bombardment? Funny! I didn't even hear it.

THANKSGIVING FOR SIX

a play for Thanksgiving

We all know the story of the Pilgrims and the first Thanksgiving. We know, too, that Thanksgiving is a day of family reunions and big dinners. There are some people, however, who are separated from their families by many, many miles; there are people, too, who are kept by their duties from attending these festive occasions. The policeman, the fireman, the nurse, the waitress, and so many others cannot take time off from their jobs and their obligations. There are others, too many to mention, who find themselves alone, when the rest of the city, the town, the countryside, is celebrating this very warm holiday.

This story is dedicated to these people. It is a simple play about the lonely ones and how they find a way to make Thanksgiving their holiday, too.

THE CAST	*Joe* (a night watchman)	*Agnes* (a waitress)
	Bill (a policeman)	*Rose* (Joe's wife)
	Debbie (a nurse)	*Announcer*
	Young Man	

THE SET	*The street, outside a building under construction*

Text Copyright ©1967 Henry Gilfond
Illustrations Copyright ©1967 by George Blevins

Announcer	It is the afternoon of Thanksgiving Day. We are on a street where a new building is going up. Joe, the night watchman, is seated on a box in front of the building, reading a newspaper. He looks up and sees someone.
Joe	(Standing up and shouting) Hey, you! You! Where do you think you're going?
Bill	(Entering) What's the trouble, Joe?
Joe	Someone has been sneaking around this building!
Bill	Which way did he go?
Joe	He just turned the corner!
Bill	You scared him off, Joe.
Joe	Maybe! Do you want to take a look, Bill?
Bill	What for? He's probably still running.
Joe	I don't like it. I don't like these fellows sneaking around here, especially on a day like today. Everything is too quiet.
Bill	Afraid they'll steal the building, Joe?
Joe	No. But it's getting dark. There aren't too many people on the streets on Thanksgiving.
Bill	I guess not. Just people like you and me, who have to work.
Joe	Someone has to watch the building.
Bill	Sure. And someone has to patrol the streets. Oh, I could have had the day off. I just let some other cop have it. Besides, there's nobody home. They all flew the coop.

Joe	No trouble, Bill?
Bill	No! No trouble. The wife and the kids are just visiting the wife's mother. She makes a big thing of Thanksgiving. The whole family gets together. It's upstate. I couldn't have made it if I wanted to. How about you, Joe? No turkey for you either?
Joe	Oh, I guess there'll be some turkey when Rose brings me my supper. We haven't got much of a family now that the kids are all grown up, and moved all over the country. You know how it is.
Bill	Yeah. I know how it is. Still you could have been having your Thanksgiving dinner with one of them.
Joe	Sure. But they all have big families. They ask me. I'm better off here. I've got a job. I'm independent. Let them have a good time. Rose and I are comfortable here. *(Suddenly pointing)* There he is again!
Bill	Who?
Joe	That fellow prowling around the building!
Bill	You're seeing things, Joe.
Joe	There! He's coming right at us!
Bill	That's no he. That's a she, Joe. That's Debbie, coming from the hospital. Don't you frighten her, now, with your story about prowlers.
Joe	She shouldn't be walking the streets alone at this time of the day.
Bill	How is she going to get home, by helicopter? She is walking kind of slowly.

Joe	She must be tired.
Bill	*(As Debbie enters)* Big day at the hospital, Debbie?
Debbie	It always is, Thanksgiving.
Joe	*(Offering his seat)* Here. Sit down, Debbie.
Debbie	*(Sitting)* Thank you. I've been on my feet all day. *(To Bill)* How come you're working today, Bill? No Thanksgiving dinner?
Bill	Not this year. How about you?
Debbie	Me? Thanksgiving? That's for everyone else and his cousins and his aunts. Not Debbie. I'll be glad just to get home and take these shoes off.
Joe	No family, Debbie?
Debbie	Not here. Oh, I suppose I could have taken the weekend off. It's only a couple of hours by plane, and I'm home.
Bill	You should have done it, Debbie. It's only a couple of times a year that a family gets together.
Debbie	Are you kidding? Haven't you heard? There's a shortage of nurses. How could I take off? It just wouldn't be right. *(To Joe as she sees him move away)* Where are you going, Joe?
Joe	*(Turning back)* Nowhere! I thought I heard something.
Bill	Joe's hearing things tonight.
Joe	Never mind! There's someone around this building somewhere!

56 *Thanksgiving for Six*

Debbie	Going to steal it, Joe?
Joe	I'm not worried about the building, Debbie. I'm worried about you! You shouldn't be walking these streets at night, all alone.
Debbie	*(Laughs)* Bill will walk me home.
Joe	You're laughing at me! You think it's a big joke!
Debbie	I'm not laughing at you, Joe. *(To Bill)* Walk me home, Bill. I'll whip up a dinner for the two of us, if you haven't already had your dinner. It won't be turkey, but I can open up a can of hash quick enough.
Bill	You can't frighten me with hash. I'll take it, if you wait till I get off my beat.
Debbie	What's the matter, Bill. Did your family desert you?
Bill	Just for the weekend. We're the lonely ones in town tonight, Debbie.
Debbie	How about you, Joe? Waiting for Rose? She brings you a nice dinner every night, doesn't she? Turkey tonight, eh?
Joe	I guess it'll be turkey tonight. We have some things to be thankful for.
Debbie	I'm sure you have. I might even have a few things to be thankful for myself, if I think hard enough. You too, eh, Bill?
Bill	If I think hard enough.

58 *Thanksgiving for Six*

Debbie	Well, do your little thinking, Bill. I'll amble on home. That's what I call my one room and kitchenette. Home.
Joe	*(Suddenly darting out)* I've got him! I've got him! *(As he returns, holding fast to a young man)* Here he is! What do you think you're doing around here anyway?
Bill	Take it easy, Joe. Take it easy.
Joe	He's been prowling around here all night!
Young Man	Tell him to take his hands off me, Officer.
Joe	I'll take my hands off you!
Bill	All right, Joe. Let him go.
Joe	I won't let him go! Ask him why he's been hanging around the building all night!
Young Man	*(Yanking himself free)* I'll tell you why I've been hanging around all night!
Joe	Go ahead! Talk!
Bill	Easy, Joe. Easy. He'll talk. *(To Young Man)* Go ahead; you want to talk? Talk.
Young Man	I don't have to, do I?
Joe	Yeah! You have to talk! Talk!
Young Man	To you? I don't feel like talking to you!
Joe	*(To Bill)* There! What did I tell you? Run him in, Bill! Run him in! He's a bum! What's that sticking out of his pocket?

Young Man	*(Pulling an apple out of his pocket)* It's a gun!
Joe	Hey! *(Then seeing the apple)* It's an apple. What are you going to do with the apple?
Young Man	*(Taking a bite)* Eat it!
Bill	All right, that's enough. If you're walking, keep walking.
Joe	You're not going to arrest him?
Bill	What for?
Joe	He has been poking all around this building!
Bill	He didn't walk into it. He didn't steal anything.
Young Man	You tell him, Officer.
Bill	You keep quiet, young fellow.
Young Man	I was only walking, just the way you said it, Officer. It's kind of quiet tonight. I like to walk around new buildings, watch the way they go up. *(To Joe)* Nothing wrong in that, is there?
Bill	Nothing wrong in that, is there, Joe?
Joe	Better stay away from them in the nighttime. I'm still not sure you're telling the truth.
Young Man	*(Pulling an identification card out of his pocket)* Here's my I.D. card, Officer. I'm at the college. First year.
Bill	*(Examining the card, returning it)* Don't they have Thanksgiving dinner at the school?

Young Man	Big. They spread it out. I just didn't feel like it. *(To Joe)* Sorry I caused you all this trouble.
Joe	No trouble. Maybe I'm a little too jumpy.
Young Man	It's that kind of night, I guess.
Bill	A little lonely, eh?
Young Man	*(Grins)* I guess so. Thanksgiving is big back home, with the whole family fighting for the drumsticks. It's my first year away from home.
Debbie	You'll get used to it.
Young Man	I suppose so.
Debbie	But you don't need to be alone, you know. You could find someone to have dinner with. I'd ask you myself, except . . . .
Young Man	Oh no, thanks. Thank you.
Bill	What's the matter with you? Debbie doesn't invite everybody to a home-cooked meal.
Debbie	Now, now, boys. *(To Young Man)* Go find yourself a nice girl and have yourself a nice Thanksgiving dinner. This overworked nurse is going home.
Agnes	*(Entering with a package)* What is this, a street meeting?
Bill	Agnes! You haven't closed up the restaurant, have you?
Agnes	Closed! Shut! Boy, did I serve turkey today! You wouldn't believe it! Where's Rose, Joe? I brought you something for Thanksgiving. Don't ask me

what it is! Turkey! I could have brought more, if I knew I was going to meet a crowd. Who is this young fellow?

Debbie   He's up at the college.

Young Man   And I think I had better be getting back there.

Agnes   One of the homesick ones! Give him some of that drumstick, Joe. He looks hungry, too.

Joe   Sure. Sure.

Young Man   No, thank you.

Joe   *(Shoving the package into the Young Man's hands)* Here. Hold it. There'll be more, when my Rose comes.

Agnes   Not enough for all of us. One, two, three, four, five, and Rose; that's six. I've got an idea. *(To Young Man, as she takes the package from his hand and gives it to Debbie).* Come with me, young man. *(To all, as they exit)* We'll be right back!

Rose   *(Entering with a large lunch-pail)* Oh! So much company. How nice to see you.

Joe   *(Pointing to the pail)* And that's all you bring for the company? This is Thanksgiving.

Rose   I brought a little extra. I thought maybe Bill would be around.

Joe   How about Debbie?

Rose   So we'll eat a little less.

Joe   And Agnes, and that young college man?

Rose	Which college man? Where's Agnes? I don't see Agnes.
Agnes	*(Entering with Young Man, carrying a huge pot of food, a tablecloth and silverware)* Here's Agnes! How are you, Rosie? Go find a big board, Joe! *(To Young Man, as they set down the pot of food)* Go help him bring out a couple of boxes! We need something to sit down on, don't we?
Bill	*(As all men exit)* I'll give them a hand.
Rose	What are you doing, Agnes?
Agnes	This is Thanksgiving, isn't it? *(As Joe returns with a large board)* Here! Give me a hand with this table.
Rose	*(As men bring out boxes for seats, and the table is spread)* It's nice! It's nice to have Thanksgiving dinner with a lot of people.
Debbie	Even if it isn't your own family.
Rose	So we make another family. This is a nice family, isn't it?
Debbie	It's a nice family, Rose.
Agnes	*(Viewing the set table)* There! It couldn't be prettier at the Waldorf-Astoria! Sit down, everybody!
	(Everybody sits.)
Agnes	Well, what are we waiting for? Let's eat!
Rose	Somebody will have to say grace.
Agnes	Sure. You say it, Joe.

Joe	Let the college boy do it. He must know some good words.
Young Man	All words are good at times like these.
Joe	There! Didn't I tell you! These college boys can talk. *(To Young Man)* All right now. Say grace. We're hungry.

MERRY CHRISTMAS, ALL!

a play for Christmas

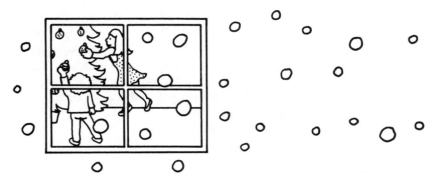

Christmas (originally "Christ's mass") celebrates the birth of Jesus. It is both a holy day and a children's holiday. Of course, everybody, young and old, exchanges cards and gifts during the Christmas season, but it still is really a holiday for the younger people. The hero of this play is not a child. He is an older man, who has played the part of Santa Claus during the holiday season for many years; and who is dearer to children than the white-bearded, red-suited man who climbs down the chimney with a sack full of Christmas presents?

But how does such a man feel when he is finally all alone, after playing Santa Claus in a department store for more than a month? And how does he feel when, for the first Christmas in many years, he has not been asked to play Santa for the poor children who come to the Firehouse to collect their Christmas gifts?

THE CAST	Mr. Busby	Two Boys
	Mr. Cooper	Carol Singers
	Mrs. Cummings	Mr. Williams (a fireman)
THE SET	Mr. Busby's one-room apartment	

Busby	(*Dressed in a Santa Claus costume, he looks like Santa Claus as he enters his one-room apartment. He puts on the lights. He opens a window and the sound of a group of young people, singing Christmas carols, comes up from the street.*)
Singers	(*Singing offstage*) The first Nowell the angels did say, Was to certain poor shepherds in fields as they lay; In fields where they lay keeping their sheep, On a cold winter's night that was so deep, Nowell, Nowell, Nowell, Nowell, Born is the King of Israel.
	(*Shouting*) Merry Christmas! Merry Christmas!
Busby	(*Shouts back to the singers*) Merry Christmas! Merry Christmas! (*He closes the window. He makes an effort to take off his Santa Claus costume, but he is too tired. He sits down in a chair.*)
	(*The doorbell rings*)
Cooper	(*Outside the door*) Mr. Busby! Mr. Busby!
Busby	The door is open!
Cooper	(*Enters. He looks at Mr. Busby and is amused by the costume.*) Well, if it isn't Santa Claus, himself! Ho! Ho! Ho! And a merry Christmas!
Busby	And a merry Christmas to you, Mr. Cooper! Come in!
Cooper	Tell me, Mr. Busby—it must be fun, playing Santa Claus for all those kids who come romping into the department store.

Busby	It's fun. I enjoy it.
Cooper	I'll bet you do! But right now you look worn out.
Busby	Oh, I am a bit tired. It's been a long day.
Cooper	More like a long month! What did you have, a million kids!?
Busby	I didn't count them. There were plenty of them.
Cooper	Well, I've got to be running. I thought you might have some extra tree lights. *(As he looks around quickly)* But you have no tree.
Busby	No. Every year I sort of promise myself a tree, just a little tree. That's all I need. There's no one here but me. But . . . .
Cooper	It's a bother. The house gets crowded, and you've got to throw the thing out in a couple of days anyway.
Busby	Still, it would be nice. A Christmas tree livens up a house, I think. It gives it that extra festive touch— the Christmas touch. But I'm just a little too tired. I'm not as young as I used to be, you know.
Cooper	We all keep getting older, Mr. Busby.
Busby	And the youngsters keep getting heavier.
Cooper	I'll bet they do.
Busby	Oh, I'm not complaining. I enjoy every minute of it.
Cooper	Aren't they ever a little bit frightened of that get-up you're wearing? I mean the very little ones.

Merry Christmas, All! 69

70 *Merry Christmas, All!*

Busby	(Smiling, as he remembers) Some of them. But they loosen up, once they climb up on my knees and I tell them what I'm going to bring them for Christmas. (Getting up from his chair, and moving to the window) I can just hear their little hearts beat, and they're so full of joy.
Singers	(Offstage, as Busby opens his window again, singing) Joy to the world! the Lord is come; Let earth receive her King, Let ev'ry heart prepare Him room, And heav'n and nature sing, And heav'n and nature sing, And heav'n—and heav'n and nature sing. (Shouting) Merry Christmas!
Busby	(Shouts to street) Merry Christmas! (As he shuts his windows, speaking to Cooper) It makes me want to get up and get that tree. (Sitting in his chair again) But I'm just too tired.
Cooper	Well, Mr. Busby, maybe a nice, big spruce tree will just pick itself up and walk right into your room here. It could happen, couldn't it, Busby?
Busby	It could. But it won't. The age of miracles, Mr. Cooper, is no longer with us.
Cooper	You say that, Busby? You play Santa Claus for all those youngsters, and then tell me you don't believe in miracles?
Busby	I didn't say that I don't believe in miracles, Mr. Cooper, but no Christmas tree is going to walk into my house tonight. (The doorbell rings.)

Busby	Now who can that be? Come in! The door is open!
Boys	*(Opening the door)* Mr. Busby?
Busby	What can I do for you?
Two Boys	*(Bringing in a Christmas tree)* Where do you want this?
Busby	There must be some mistake. I didn't order a Christmas tree.
Two Boys	The name is Busby, isn't it?
Busby	That's the name, all right, but I didn't . . . .
Two Boys	*(Finding a spot for the tree)* Is it all right to put the tree up here?
Busby	There must be some mistake.
Cooper	No mistake, Busby. That's your tree, and it walked right in here.
Busby	*(To boys, who are putting up the tree)* Can I help?
Two Boys	We can manage it.
Cooper	*(To the boys)* Good work. Very pretty. *(To Busby)* I better go buy the lights for my tree. They'll be thinking I got lost. Merry Christmas, Busby! *(He exists.)*
Busby	*(In a bit of a daze)* Merry Christmas.
Mrs. Cummings	*(Entering as Cooper leaves)* My! Isn't that a beautiful tree!
Busby	I don't know where it came from.

Mrs. Cummings	And I just came by to invite you to look at our tree. *(To the boys)* That's lovely!
Two Boys	Is that all right, Mr. Busby?
Busby	Fine! Fine! *(Reaching into his pocket)* Here, let me give you something for your trouble.
Two Boys	No, thank you, Mr. Busby. It's all paid for.
Busby	Yes, but something for yourselves.
Two Boys	That's all right, Mr. Busby. Everything has been paid for. Everything! Merry Christmas! *(They exit.)*
Busby	Merry Christmas. *(To Mrs. Cummings)* Now who could have done that, sending me this beautiful Christmas tree?
Mrs. Cummings	Oh, I could think of a lot of people who might have done it. You've been Santa Claus around here for a long time, haven't you, Mr. Busby?
Busby	I guess so.
Mrs. Cummings	I remember when I was a little girl, you used to come home in that Santa Claus outfit. You used to be the Santa Claus down at the Firehouse, giving out toys to all the poor children in the neighborhood.
Busby	I still do. I guess they've got somebody a little younger to do it this year. I *am* getting on in years, Mrs. Cummings.
Mrs. Cummings	Come on, now, Mr. Busby! You know what they say. You're as young as you feel.

Merry Christmas, All! **73**

Busby	Well, to tell you the truth, I'm not feeling very young at this moment.
Mrs. Cummings	Now don't you say that, Mr. Busby. Have you had your dinner yet?
Busby	Oh, I had something before I came home from the store.
Mrs. Cummings	You haven't had any dinner, though, have you?
Busby	I'm not hungry, thank you, Mrs. Cummings.
Mrs. Cummings	I'm not asking you whether you're hungry. I've got a big bowl of hot soup for you, and a beautiful roast.
Busby	You're very kind, Mrs. Cummings, but I think I'd rather just rest a while, then go to bed.
Mrs. Cummings	And disappoint my children? You wouldn't disappoint my children, Mr. Busby, would you?
Busby	Well, maybe I'll come in and just say "hello."
Mrs. Cummings	The children will love to see you in the red suit and that big white beard. And we'll have dinner together.
Busby	Mrs. Cummings . . . .
Mrs. Cummings	I won't hear of anything else. Mr. Busby.
	(The doorbell rings.)
Busby	Who can that be now?
Mrs. Cummings	My children, probably. Hurrying me home to dinner.
Busby	The door is open! Come in!

74 *Merry Christmas, All!*

Mrs. Cummings	My children, probably. Hurrying me home to dinner.
Busby	The door is open! Come in!
Singers	*(Enter, carrying ornaments for the tree and singing)* On the first day of Christmas My true love sent to me A partridge in a pear tree
Busby	Where are you going? Who sent you?
Singers	*(Decorating the tree)* On the second day of Christmas My true love sent to me Two turtledoves And a partridge in a pear tree.
Busby	What are you doing?
A Singer	We're decorating your tree, Mr. Busby.
Singers	*(Singing)* On the third day of Christmas My true love sent to me . . . .
Busby	But I didn't order the tree! I never asked for these decorations!
Mrs. Cummings	Why don't you just let them do what they're doing? They're certainly making the tree look even prettier than it was.
Busby	But I don't know where it all comes from.
Singers	*(Singing)* Three French hens, two turtledoves And a partridge in a pear tree.
Busby	*(To singers)* Where do you come from? Who sent you?
Mrs. Cummings	Why don't you just come along with me and have a nice dinner with my family?

Merry Christmas, All! **75**

76 *Merry Christmas, All!*

Singers	(As other singers with gift packages in all sizes and shapes enter and begin to put their packages under the tree)
	On the fourth day of Christmas My true love sent to me Four calling birds, three French hens, two turtledoves And a partridge in a pear tree.
Busby	I don't know who sent you, but this must be some wild mistake. Are you sure you have the right apartment?
A Singer	The name is Busby, isn't it?
Busby	That's the name.
A Singer	Then this is the right place.
Singers	(Singing) On the fifth day of Christmas My true love sent to me Five gold rings, Four calling birds, three French hens, two turtledoves And a partridge in a pear tree.
A Singer	It looks like it's all done. We can bring the rest tomorrow.
Busby	The rest of what? I don't understand.
A Singer	The rest of the Christmas packages. Unless it's all right for us to come back later, after dinner.
Busby	Won't someone tell me what is happening?

Cooper	*(Entering, the tree lights in his hand)* Say! This is even more of a miracle than I thought! Merry Christmas!
Everybody	Merry Christmas!
Busby	I can't explain it at all.
Cooper	Who tries to explain a miracle? Look! I got my Christmas lights. That was a bit of a miracle, too, with all the stores closing up early. I better go fix them before Santa Claus comes. Merry Christmas! *(He exits.)*
Williams	*(Enters)* Looks good, doesn't it, Mr. Busby?
Busby	It looks fine, but I must say that I'm a bit bewildered by it all.
Williams	You're a good sport, Mr. Busby. We thought we would give you a bit of a surprise.
Busby	Surprise?
Williams	Well, you've been Santa Claus for the poor kids down at the Firehouse now for almost twenty years. We thought you might like being Santa in your own house for once.
Busby	You mean . . . ?
Williams	Instead of the kids going to the firehouse, they'd go to Santa's house. You are Santa Claus in this neighborhood, Mr. Busby, and if you don't know it, all the kids do know it!
Busby	Why didn't you tell me about it, instead of springing it on me like this?

Williams	It's our way of saying "thank you." We wanted to give you some sort of gift, and some of the boys thought that bringing all the kids to your own house was the kind of gift you would like.
Busby	I certainly do like it! *(To singers)* Thank you, boys and girls!
Singers	Thank *you*, Mr. Busby! Thank *you*, Mr. Santa Claus! *(Singing, as all except Mrs. Cummings and Busby exit.)* We wish you a merry Christmas. We wish you a merry Christmas. We wish you a merry Christmas and a happy New Year.
Busby	A merry Christmas, Mrs. Cummings.
Mrs. Cummings	A merry Christmas, Mr. Busby. Are you joining us for dinner?
Busby	Thank you, Mrs. Cummings—I will. Merry Christmas! Merry Christmas, all!

ABRAHAM LINCOLN AND THE LADY

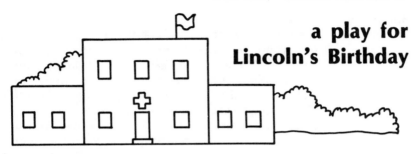

a play for Lincoln's Birthday

Next to George Washington, Abraham Lincoln is perhaps the most beloved figure in American history. Born in a rude log cabin, he rose to the Presidency of the United States and led his country through a bitter civil war, only to die a martyr in his country's cause.

There are many well-known stories about Abraham Lincoln— about his boyhood, his honesty, his humor, his wit, his wisdom, his strength. We are proud of Abraham Lincoln, and we love him. But the story you are about to read is one that few people know. It is a true story. In it you will see Lincoln tired and sometimes irritable and angry. But you will see Lincoln's greatness, too.

Mrs. Harvey wants a hospital in the North to which soldiers wounded in the South may be sent and where, she is sure, they will have a better chance for recovery. Mr. Lincoln is not sure that this is a valid request; his desk is crowded with special requests and petitions. Will Mrs. Harvey be able to convince the President? And what will the President reveal of his own thinking and feelings in his interviews with Mrs. Harvey?

THE CAST   Abraham Lincoln
                      Mrs. Harvey
                      Messenger
                      Announcer

THE SET   Lincoln's office

Announcer	Abraham Lincoln, President of the United States, sits at his desk. The desk is cluttered with papers—important papers. There are reports from his generals. There are requests for additional troops and supplies. The Union Army is on the march to victory and Abraham Lincoln, as Commander-in-Chief, must read these reports, make decisions and act on them. There is a letter here, too, from a lady. He is reading it a second time as a messenger enters his office.
Lincoln	*(Continues to read for a moment, then looks up)* Does the Secretary of War want to see me?
Messenger	No, sir. It's a lady.
Lincoln	*(Looks at the letter)* Mrs. Harvey? Mrs. Louis Powell Harvey?
Messenger	Yes, sir. Mrs. Harvey. She said you were expecting her.
Lincoln	Yes. I've been expecting her.
Messenger	Shall I ask her to wait, sir?
Lincoln	No, no. Send her in, please.
Messenger	Yes, sir. *(He exits.)*
Lincoln	*(Reading the letter)* Hospital. Hospital. How many more hospitals are we going to need?
	(As Mrs. Harvey enters) This war must end soon.
Mrs. Harvey	I pray for that, constantly.
Lincoln	*(Looking up)* You are Mrs. Harvey?

Mrs. Harvey	Mrs. Louis Powell Harvey, sir. From Wisconsin.
Lincoln	(*Motioning Mrs. Harvey to a chair*) Please sit down. I hope you have been well, Mrs. Harvey.
Mrs. Harvey	I've been quite well, thank you, Mr. President. I hope you have been well, too. I pray for that, too, sir, that you keep well. You are under such a constant strain.
Lincoln	Your husband was a brave man.
Mrs. Harvey	Thank you, Mr. President.
Lincoln	I must thank you, Mrs. Harvey. But how does that bring comfort to a woman who has lost her husband?
Mrs. Harvey	I did not come to be comforted, Mr. President. He was a soldier in the war. He gave his life to his country. He could not have done less.
Lincoln	He was the Governor of the State of Wisconsin. He didn't need to move the supplies. It should have been enough for him to issue the orders.
Mrs. Harvey	Many were wounded at the Battle of Shiloh, Mr. President. It was for the wounded that my husband gave his life.
Lincoln	Yes. And you would give your life to the wounded too, Mrs. Harvey?
Mrs. Harvey	I am only asking for a hospital.
Lincoln	(*Pointing to the letter*) But you have wandered up and down the Mississippi, according to your letter, visiting the wounded, visiting the hospitals. There are enough hospitals, aren't there?

Abraham Lincoln and the Lady 83

Mrs. Harvey	We need hospitals in the North, sir. There are enough hospitals in the South, but our boys just die there. They are not used to the climate, the heat. There are thousands of graves along the Mississippi and the Yazoo rivers. Northern boys who might have lived, if they had been shipped to hospitals in the North. Sir, if you send these wounded Northern men to Northern hospitals, you will have ten able-bodied soldiers where you now have only one. We need those hospitals in the North.
Lincoln	You speak with considerable passion.
Mrs. Harvey	With reason, too, sir.
Lincoln	Reason? I don't see how sending one sick soldier North is going to give us ten well ones.
Mrs. Harvey	You have a reputation for humor, sir. I think this is hardly the time for it. (Realizing she has been a little too bold with the President of the United States) I beg your pardon, sir.
Lincoln	No, no, no. You are perfectly right.
Mrs. Harvey	I am sure you understand me, Mr. President.
Lincoln	I understand you. What you don't understand is, send the men North and they'll desert. Where's the difference, then?
Mrs. Harvey	Dead men can't fight, sir. And they will not desert.
Lincoln	We would never get a man back. Not one of them.
Mrs. Harvey	Pardon me, sir, but I believe you are mistaken. You do not understand our people. They are as true and as loyal as yourself.

Lincoln	This is your opinion! Have you seen the Secretary of War?
Mrs. Harvey	No, sir.
Lincoln	*(Writing as he speaks)* Admit this lady at once. A. Lincoln. *(Handing the note to Mrs. Harvey)* You are a lady of intelligence. You talk sense. See the Secretary of War.
Mrs. Harvey	May I come back to see you, Mr. Lincoln?
Lincoln	Certainly! Certainly!
Announcer	Mrs. Harvey saw the Secretary of War, but he could not help her. Mrs. Harvey passed the President's office, saw that he was alone, and walked right in.
Lincoln	*(Motioning Mrs. Harvey to a chair)* You saw the Secretary of War?
Mrs. Harvey	He can't help us. He sent me back to you. It is up to you, Mr. Lincoln, to make the decision. Please.
Lincoln	I will see the Secretary of War myself. Tonight. You may come back tomorrow morning. You are a gentle lady. I will see what I can do.
Announcer	Had Abraham Lincoln come to a decision right then? In all his talk with Mrs. Harvey, he seemed to be arguing against himself. He had been gruff with Mrs. Harvey, then most kind. The pressures on the President, the demands he had to meet, were indeed great. He needed great strength and great courage to meet them all.

The next morning, Mrs. Harvey waited to be ushered into the President's office. |

Abraham Lincoln and the Lady **85**

86 *Abraham Lincoln and the Lady*

Messenger	*(To Lincoln, seated again at his desk)* The lady, sir. Mrs. Harvey. She says she has an appointment with you.
Lincoln	Send her in, please.
Messenger	Yes, sir.
	(Lincoln looks through his papers, as Mrs. Harvey enters. She stands, waiting for him to ask her in. Lincoln looks up from his papers.)
Lincoln	Well?
Mrs. Harvey	Well?
Lincoln	Don't you have anything to say?
Mrs. Harvey	Nothing. Nothing until I hear what you have decided to do about the hospital. You asked me to come this morning. Have you decided?
Lincoln	No, I've not decided. I think all this business about Northern hospitals is just humbug. I'm tired of hearing about it.
Mrs. Harvey	I'm sorry to add to your cares and responsibilities, Mr. President. I know how much you have to carry these dreadful days. I would rather have stayed at home.
Lincoln	*(Smiling weakly)* I wish you had.
Mrs. Harvey	You smile, Mr. President. But it is true. I don't care to add to your burdens and it is only a sense of duty to the men who are fighting for our government, and respect and regard for you, which brought me here. I still think you will be glad I came.

Lincoln	To torment me?
Mrs. Harvey	No, sir. To plead for those young men who volunteered to endanger their lives for their country. Send them to a Northern hospital. Build a Northern hospital, so these young men may recover from their wounds, and live. Let them fight again for their country. That is what they want to do, and you must help them, Mr. President. They die in the Southern hospitals. They need to be sent North.
Lincoln	You seem to know more about these matters than I do, Mrs. Harvey.
Mrs. Harvey	I mean no disrespect, sir. If you knew what I know, I should not have needed to come to you, Mr. Lincoln. You would have ordered the hospitals in the North, if you had seen what I have seen. We believe in you, Mr. Lincoln. We trust you, Mr. Lincoln. I wish you could believe what I say.
Lincoln	I do get reports from the hospitals, Mrs. Harvey. Do you presume to know more than our doctors?
Mrs. Harvey	No, sir. I could not cut off an arm or a leg as well as they do. But these past eight months I have visited hospitals from Quincy to Vicksburg, all up and down the Mississippi River, from early in the morning till late at night, and I have come from the cots of men who have died, and who might have lived, if they had been sent North. If you believe me, Mr. Lincoln, you will give us these hospitals in the North. If not . . . .

88 *Abraham Lincoln and the Lady*

Lincoln	How many from Wisconsin are fighting in the Union Army?
Mrs. Harvey	About 50,000.
Lincoln	That means that there are about 20,000 in the field. You don't need to look so sober. The other 30,000 are not all dead.
Mrs. Harvey	*(Quietly)* Mr. Lincoln . . . .
Lincoln	I've a good mind to send them all home, and have no more trouble with them.
Mrs. Harvey	You are jesting again. They have all been faithful to the government. They have all been faithful to you. They will still be faithful, however you decide on the hospitals. But, Mr. Lincoln, grant my request, and you will be glad as long as you live.
Lincoln	*(Quietly, sadly)* I shall never be glad anymore.
Mrs. Harvey	Oh, do not say that, Mr. Lincoln. You will have many reasons to be glad. When the war is over, you will have many reasons to be glad.
Lincoln	Perhaps. Perhaps. But the springs of life are wearing away. I shall not last.
Mrs. Harvey	You are in good health, Mr. President?
Lincoln	At the last report, I am.
Mrs. Harvey	Do you sleep well, Mr. President?
Lincoln	I never was a good sleeper. Of course, I sleep less now.

Abraham Lincoln and the Lady **89**

90 *Abraham Lincoln and the Lady*

Mrs. Harvey	*(After a short pause)* I have taken too much of your time. Have you decided your answer for me, Mr. President?
Lincoln	No. Come tomorrow morning. I'll tell you then.
Announcer	There was no doubt that Abraham Lincoln wanted to give that hospital to Mrs. Harvey, and she knew he wanted to give it to her. But could he? Mrs. Harvey was at the President's office the next morning. She had to wait. He was in a Cabinet meeting. But, finally, he appeared.
Lincoln	I'm sorry I kept you waiting. We just finished with our meeting.
Mrs. Harvey	I didn't mind the wait, but you must be tired. Shall I come back tonight? Or tomorrow?
Lincoln	No, no. Please sit down.
Mrs. Harvey	Thank you. *(She sits.)*
Lincoln	*(Sitting down beside her)* Mrs. Harvey, you will have your hospital. The orders have already gone out. As a matter of fact, the order for the hospital was sent out yesterday, right after you left.
Mrs. Harvey	God bless you. God bless you, Mr. President.
Lincoln	I suppose you would have been angry, if I had said "no."
Mrs. Harvey	No, Mr. President. But I should have been back here in your office the first thing tomorrow morning.
Lincoln	Don't you ever get angry?

Abraham Lincoln and the Lady **91**

Mrs. Harvey	Not when I have something important to do.
Lincoln	Well, Madam, you acted very wisely.
Mrs. Harvey	*(Standing)* Well, I suppose you don't want to see me again.
Lincoln	I didn't say that, and I shall not say it. You have been very kind to me, and I am grateful for it. *(After a pause)* You almost think I am handsome, don't you?
Mrs. Harvey	You are perfectly lovely to me now.
Lincoln	*(Laughs. Reaches out his hand to say good-bye)* Lovely, you say? Lovely?
Mrs. Harvey	*(Taking Mr. Lincoln's hand)* We love you, Abraham Lincoln. God bless you, Abraham Lincoln. God bless you. *(She turns and exits.)*

THE DIFFERENCE A VALENTINE MAKES

a play for Valentine's Day

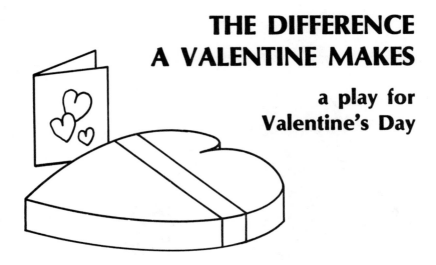

A Roman priest, some 1,700 years ago, was imprisoned and then martyred. While he was in prison, the story goes, he wrote letters of love to all his friends. The priest was St. Valentine and each year, on February 14th, his works of love are celebrated.

With time, however, St. Valentine has become for most people just Valentine; and this name is now given to all messages of love, especially those sent on the saint's day. It is also said that the February 14th celebration goes back much earlier to pagan practices. Whichever is true, and they may both be true, February 14th is a day for greetings of love.

This play is written to help celebrate Valentine's Day. You will find love sentiment in it. You will also find some humor in it. And maybe you'll find in it someone you know.

THE CAST   *Mrs. Mary Burton*
Mr. John Burton
Billie (their ten-year-old son)
Sara (their sixteen-year-old daughter)
Mr. Todd
Announcer

THE SET   *The Burton home*

Text Copyright ©1967 Henry Gilfond
Illustrations Copyright ©1967 by George Blevins

94 *The Difference a Valentine Makes*

Announcer	It is February 14th, Valentine's Day—a day when friends and sweethearts exchange greetings of love.
	We are in the Burton home. Mrs. Burton looks at a huge card, smiles, puts the card on the table in the center of the room, and begins to exit as Billie Burton enters. He is carrying his schoolbooks.
Billie	*(Entering)* Hi, Mom!
Mrs. Burton	You're home early, Billie. *(As Billie throws his books down on the sofa)* Don't leave things around, now. I want this place clean.
Billie	*(As Mrs. Burton exits)* Sure, Mom. *(He tosses his coat on the sofa, then sees the huge card on the table. He picks it up. He examines it. He reads the message on the card.)* "A Valentine Message to My Darling Wife," *(He looks for his mother, but she is gone)* Humph! *(He continues to read.)* "Today and always, As you've been told, My heart is yours To have and hold." Mush! *(Reading again)* "Your loving John." *(Repeating)* Your loving John? Wow!
Sara	*(Entering with schoolbooks)* Are you reading my mail?
Billie	*(Holding Sara off)* Who's reading your mail? This is Mom's!
Sara	Let me see it!

The Difference a Valentine Makes **95**

Billie	I told you, it's Mom's!
Mrs. Burton	*(Entering)* What's all the fighting about? Put that card down, Billie! Put it down!
Billie	OK.
Mrs. Burton	Now what's the matter with you, Sara?
Sara	There was no reason he couldn't let me see the card, was there? I just wanted to look at it, that's all.
Billie	Yeah? She always says I'm reading her mail. *(To Sara)* What's so important about your mail, anyway?
Sara	It's private! And you keep your nose out of it!
Mrs. Burton	All right! That's enough battling for today. The card was for me.
Sara	Didn't I get any mail, Mom?
Mrs. Burton	No, Sara. You didn't get any mail.
Sara	That's funny. Not even one card?
Mrs. Burton	Not even one card. *(Going to the chest of drawers)* There's a letter for you, though, Billie.
Billie	Me!?
Mrs. Burton	*(Smelling the envelope)* And it smells awfully, sweet.
Billie	For me? Who's writing to me?
Sara	*(As Billie opens his letter)* There should have been something, Mom. I should have gotten something from Larry.

96 *The Difference a Valentine Makes*

Billie	*(Looking at the card he has pulled from the envelope)* Listen to this: "How did you ever get so ugly?" What kind of letter is that? And look at this picture, will you? It sure is ugly, isn't it?
Mrs. Burton	*(To Sara, who is rummaging through the mail on the chest of drawers)* You won't find anything there, Sara. There's nothing for you.
Billie	Who sent me this letter, Mom?
Mrs. Burton	Look and see who signed it.
Billie	It just says, "Your Valentine." Who's my valentine?
Mrs. Burton	Maybe it's Alice.
Billie	Alice? Who's Alice?
Mrs. Burton	That pretty little girl with the big blue eyes.
Billie	That ugly thing!? *(To Sara)* How come you didn't get any valentines, Sara?
Mrs. Burton	Why don't you go on to your room and start doing your homework?
Billie	I was just asking. Boy, you sure got a mushy one from Dad! *(Going for his father's valentine)* Did you read it, Sara?
Mrs. Burton	Now you leave that alone! It's a lovely card. And your father never forgets.
Sara	Not like some people I know.
Billie	Larry, for instance?
Mrs. Burton	Go to your room, Billie!

The Difference a Valentine Makes 97

Billie	Sure, sure. (*As he exits, looking at his valentine*) This sure is a stupid card!
Sara	It's all foolish, isn't it, Mother? It's all right for kids, but after all, I'm sixteen. I'm not a kid anymore. It's all right, when you're married, or going steady. I mean really steady, and going to get married . . . That's when it has real meaning, isn't that right, Mother? I mean, it would have been silly if I sent a valentine to Larry, for instance. Do you know what I mean, Mother?
Mrs. Burton	I know what you mean, Sara.
Sara	Do you agree with me, Mother?
Mrs. Burton	Did you send Larry a valentine, Sara?
Sara	It burns me up. I feel so ashamed. What will he think of me now? Sending valentine cards, like a kid! But is was a nice card, Mother. A pretty card. Not one of those funny ones. I hate those funny ones! Don't you?
Mrs. Burton	Oh, I think they're all right, if they're sent in the proper spirit. They're all love messages of one kind or another.
Sara	I suppose so. Except, if you really love someone, you don't just have to send him a message on Valentine's Day. That's acting like sheep, doing what everyone else is doing. Larry is different. He doesn't like to follow the crowd. He's not a loner, but he won't do something just because everyone else in the crowd is doing it. And he's right!

Mr. Burton	*(Entering)* Are you talking about me again?
Sara	Oh, Dad!
Mr. Burton	Well, I always am right! You know that. Ask your mother. She'll tell you.
Mrs. Burton	That's a lovely card you sent me, John.
Mr. Burton	What card?
Mrs. Burton	You know very well what card!
Mr. Burton	Oh, that? That's nothing at all. How many cards did you get today, Sara?
Sara	We don't send cards, Dad. Didn't you know that? Valentines are all right for little kids, and maybe for people who are married as long as you and Mother.
Mr. Burton	Maybe?
Sara	Well, all right! They're fine, when you're married as long as you and Mother are. But it's not for us. Larry didn't send me a valentine. He'd never think of sending me a valentine.
Mr. Burton	No. Of course not.
Sara	I'd have been disappointed in him if he had sent me a valentine. I'd have been embarrassed.
Billie	*(Entering)* Hi, Dad!
Mr. Burton	Hi, Billie!
Billie	Do you want to see a funny valentine I got? She didn't sign it, but it must have been Alice. You know. The pretty girl with the big blue eyes.

The Difference a Valentine Makes **99**

Mr. Burton	*(Looking at the card)* That's funny, all right.
Sara	You see what I mean! It's all just plain silly! Kid stuff!
Billie	Just because you didn't get any! What do you know? Larry didn't send her a valentine, so it's kid stuff! Sour grapes!—That's what I call it!
Mrs. Burton	That's enough, Billie!
Sara	Let him rave, Mother. After all, he's only ten years old.
Billie	Going on eleven!
Mr. Burton	OK, Billie. OK.
Billie	Just because Larry didn't send her a valentine!
Mrs. Burton	Do I have to send you back to your room, Billie?
Sara	Don't bother to send him anywhere, Mother. I was just about to leave you people to your lovely valentines.
Billie	Sour grapes!
Mr. Burton	Billie!
	(The doorbell rings.)
Mrs. Burton	Who can that be, at this time in the afternoon?
Billie	I'll answer it.
Sara	You stay where you are!
	(The bell rings again.)
Mr. Burton	Well, somebody answer it!

100   *The Difference a Valentine Makes*

Mrs. Burton	Mother will do it! Mother will do everything!
Mr. Burton	I don't know why one of you couldn't have opened the door!
Billie	She wouldn't let me!
Mrs. Burton	*(At the door, as she opens it)* Yes? Oh! Mr. Todd! Come on in, won't you?
Mr. Todd	*(Entering)* Thanks. I've got this package for you. Special Delivery.
Mrs. Burton	For me? But I don't think I ordered anything.
Mr. Todd	*(Examining the package)* It's Miss Burton, I think. Miss Sara Burton. Yes, that's it. Sara Burton.
Sara	*(Running to the door)* Me? Me? What is it, Mother?
Mr. Todd	Package for you, Sara. Nice and big, too.
Sara	Oh, thank you, Mr. Todd.
Mr. Todd	*(Handing Sara the receipt to be signed)* You'll have to sign right here, Sara.
Sara	Where? Where?
Mr. Todd	Right here.
Sara	Sure. Where's a pen, or a pencil?
Mr. Todd	*(Offering a pencil)* Here. You can use this.
Sara	Oh, thank you! *(She signs.)* Is that all right?
Mr. Todd	Fine! Thank you.
Sara	Thank you!

The Difference a Valentine Makes 101

102 *The Difference a Valentine Makes*

Mr. Todd	Good night, all.
All	Good night.
Sara	*(As Mrs. Burton closes the door)* I wonder what it can be? Who could have sent it?
Billie	I give you three guesses.
Mr. Burton	Billie.
Billie	Well? Isn't she going to open it?
Sara	Not while you're around here!
Billie	Aw, come on. Sara. Open it.
Sara	If you're quiet, I will.
Billie	I'll be quiet. Just open it.
Sara	*(Unwrapping the package)* It's so tightly packed. *(As she pulls out a huge heart-shaped box)* Oh! Isn't it beautiful, Mother?
Billie	Candy!
Sara	I thought you were going to be quiet!
Billie	I only said "candy."
Mr. Burton	Quiet, Billie.
Mrs. Burton	There's a card, too, isn't there?
Sara	*(Taking out the card)* It's a beautiful card! It's almost as big as the one Dad sent you. Beautiful, isn't it, Dad?
Mr. Burton	Quite nice.

The Difference a Valentine Makes **103**

Billie	What does it say on the card?
Mrs. Burton	Hush, Billie!
Sara	*(Reading the card)* "A Valentine to My Sweetheart." Isn't that lovely?
Billie	Wow! *(As his mother looks at him)* I didn't say anything.
Sara	*(Who hasn't heard anything, still reading from the card)* "As the snow is white And the sea is blue, My thoughts, my dear Are ever with you," *(She sighs)* Ah!
Billie	*(Quietly)* Mush!
Sara	*(Continuing as if uninterrupted)* Signed "Your own Larry." *(She smiles at her mother, but she is far, far away.)*
Billie	Aren't you going to open the box of candy?
Sara	*(Still far away)* I knew he wouldn't forget me.
Billie	Sure. Valentines are only for kids like me.
Sara	*(Beginning to walk off the stage, with her valentine and her box of candy)* Valentine's Day is a beautiful day, isn't it, Mother? Isn't it, Dad? *(She exits.)*
Billie	Say! Is she going to eat all that candy by herself?
Mrs. Burton	Don't you worry. She'll be back, and she'll offer you some.

104 *The Difference a Valentine Makes*

Billie	Wow! She sure has a thing for that Larry! What does she see in him, Dad?
Mr. Burton	Oh, you'll find out soon enough. As soon as you're old enough to appreciate Valentine's Day.
Billie	I appreciate it, all right. I appreciate it. Didn't I get a valentine from Alice? The prettiest girl in my class?
Mrs. Burton	That's right, Billie, Now you had better go off and finish your homework.
Billie	Yeah. I'll go finish my homework. *(He moves to exit. Stops.)* How come you sent Mom such a mushy card, Dad? *(He exits.)*
Mr. Burton	I guess it is sort of a mushy card, Mary.
Mrs. Burton	It was just fine, John. Just fine. And I'd have been awfully mad, if you hadn't sent it.

The Difference a Valentine Makes **105**

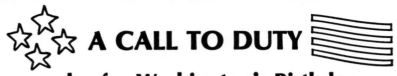

A CALL TO DUTY
a play for Washington's Birthday

The war was over. The battle had been won. With George Washington as their commander-in-chief, the armies of the American colonies had defeated the British and their hired Hessian troops. America was free and, after more than ten years of fighting, George Washington retired to his home in Mount Vernon, Virginia, to begin again the life of a gentleman farmer.

But his retirement was a brief one. America was free, but it had yet to establish itself as a united country, a country to be respected and honored among the other nations of the world. It needed a President who could inspire confidence among the people and keep them united. There were many men of the American Revolution who could inspire this kind of confidence, but there was only one man who could claim the confidence of all the American people, and lead them, united. That man was George Washington.

The nation called on George Washington to become its first President. But Washington was not certain that the nation's choice was the wisest one it could make. Besides, there were other reasons—personal reasons—which made the great soldier reluctant to accept the bid of the people.

This is the critical moment, the moment when George Washington must make a decision that will affect the whole history of the United States.

THE CAST	George Washington	Young Lady
	Martha Washington	Messenger
	Benjamin Lincoln	James Madison
	Alexander Hamilton	Charles Thomson
	Henry Lee	Announcer
	Marquis de Lafayette	

THE SET   A room in the Mount Vernon home of George Washington

Announcer	We are at the home of George Washington. There is a small party in progress. We are in one of the sitting rooms and we can hear the music of the minuet in the next room. People are dancing. George Washington enters, followed closely by Benjamin Lincoln.
Washington	Don't you find it pleasant here?
Lincoln	A lovely party, General Washington, but I must have your answer.
Washington	I haven't seen you dancing yet, Benjamin Lincoln. Don't you find our Virginia ladies attractive?
Lincoln	Most attractive, General, but you are changing the subject. I take some courage in that. You haven't made up your mind yet. Ah, how can I convince you? You cannot deny a whole country. The country called on you to lead it in war. You did. Brilliantly. The country calls you to lead it in peace. You can't refuse.
Washington	Mount Vernon is peaceful.
Lincoln	You can't separate yourself from the rest of the states.
Washington	I looked forward to it. For so many years I've dreamed of returning to my own home. I'm not a young man anymore, Lincoln.
Martha	*(Entering)* There you are! What are you two gentlemen doing here? Don't tell me that you're hidding from all the pretty young ladies!
Lincoln	My fault, Mrs. Washington. I wanted a word with the General.

Martha	It can wait, can't it? We spend so much time with serious talk. This is a moment to relax, Mr. Lincoln. Come. Join the others now.
Lincoln	How can I refuse you, Mrs. Washington? *(To George Washington)* We will speak of this again. A general in peace, George Washington, is sometimes more important than a general in war. *(He exits.)*
Martha	Why must they bring their politics into every house and every party? Haven't you done enough for your country?
Washington	They argue well, Martha.
Martha	And they will convince you. You will leave Mount Vernon again.
Washington	I don't want to, Martha. No one knows that better than you. But it would be a poor argument, if my country called on me. There are other and better arguments, Martha. I'm afraid I'm *not* the best choice the people can make.
Martha	You would make an excellent President, George. I don't like to hear you belittle yourself. And if the country needs you, you will go. I suppose I was wrong, saying what I did about doing enough for one's country.
Hamilton	*(Entering)* Oh, excuse me.
Martha	Not at all. You wish to speak privately with the General.
Henry Lee	*(Who has entered behind Hamilton)* We can wait.

A Call to Duty **109**

Martha	No, no. Speak with the General, but don't be too long. The General and I have still to dance our minuet, and you know how much the General loves to dance. *(She exits.)*
Hamilton	Have you heard the news?
Lee	Massachusetts has cast its ballot.
Washington	For John Adams, I hope.
Hamilton	For George Washington! Every state in New England will cast its vote for you. You cannot refuse such a unanimous election.
Washington	There are other states to be heard from. The vote is far from unanimous.
Lee	Unanimous, General! That's what the vote will be!
Washington	They don't know what they're doing. I can't accept this election.
Hamilton	But you must, General. It is your duty to accept the will of the nation.
Washington	Duty? Yes, duty! But I am a soldier. What do I know about the office of the President? Put me in a uniform. Direct me to my troops. Show me a battle to be fought—this is my business. What will I do in a chair behind a desk? Call on Benjamin Franklin, or some younger man—John Adams, Thomas Jefferson, Patrick Henry. They'll know what to do with this office of President.
Hamilton	These younger men have made their selection, General. They have already cast their votes, all except Patrick Henry; and they have voted for you, General.

110 *A Call to Duty*

Washington	Very good! Very good! Are they afraid to take on the responsibilities of the office?
Lee	Are you, General Washington? Are you afraid to take on the responsibilities of the Presidency? I think not.
Washington	No. I should not be afraid. Nor would the others, I'm sure. I spoke angrily about them. But there are other considerations, gentlemen.
Lafayette	*(Entering with Young Lady)* Excuse me, gentlemen, but we have been sent as a delegation of two to return you to the party.
Young Lady	We are beginning to feel neglected, General. You haven't danced with any of us this evening.
Washington	I will. I will. *(To Hamilton and Lee)* This is an immediate obligation. I beg your pardon.
Lafayette	We have accomplished our mission.
Young Lady	And I will have the first dance with the General, as my reward. If it pleases the General.
Washington	Nothing should please me more.
Messenger	*(Entering)* I was told I would find you here, sir!
Lafayette	You're rather rude, bursting into the room, young man.
Messenger	I'm sorry. The message is for the General. *(To Washington)* It's for you sir. I came as fast as I could.
Washington	*(Taking the message)* You rode hard.
Messenger	The message is important, sir.

112 *A Call to Duty*

Washington	You know what is in this letter?
Messenger	I think so, sir. I didn't open the letter. But I think it carries good news, sir.
Young Lady	Open it! Open it! What does it say, General?
Washington	I'll open it. Presently. *(To Lee—indicating the Messenger)* Take this young man. See that he has a change of clothes and something to eat and drink.
Messenger	Thank you, sir!
Lee	I'd like to hear the contents of that message.
Washington	You shall. But this young man is tired. Please attend to him.
James Madison	*(Entering, as Lee and Messenger exit)* You have it! I've already heard!
Washington	You, too, Madison?
Madison	The whole country, sir! Doesn't it please you?
Washington	I should be pleased with a little peace.
Young Lady	Excuse me. I think you gentlemen must have something serious to consider. I shall wait for my dance with you, General Washington.
Washington	I'm not asking you to leave.
Young Lady	Of course not. You are much too gentle for that. *(To Lafayette)* Come. The music is playing and my feet want to dance.
Lafayette	*(To Washington)* You will accept the invitation your people are sending you? My country, France, expects no less. And you must accept this young lady's invitation to dance. That is important, too, General Washington. Is it not?

Washington	*(As Lafayette and Young Lady exit)* I wish it were as easy to accept this invitation *(indicating message)*, as it will be to accept the lady's.
Hamilton	You haven't opened the letter, sir.
Washington	*(Opening the letter and giving it to Madison)* Here. You read it. You know its contents already.
Madison	*(Perusing the letter)* Patrick Henry, sir, has cast his ballot for the President of the United States: George Washington!
Hamilton	Unanimous! How will you be able to refuse?
Washington	I will be sixty years old soon.
Madison	You are not yet fifty-seven! You are a young man to this young country! You were the man of the hour when we needed a soldier to lead it in its fight for freedom. You are the man of the hour now, when our country needs a man to lead it in peace!
Washington	A fine speech, Mr. Madison.
Madison	And every word of it true.
Hamilton	The country worships you, General Washington.
Washington	Today. It worships me today. It may look at me with different eyes, with different hearts, if I should become President.
Hamilton	I will not believe, sir, that you are afraid of losing your position in the hearts of the American people. I do not wish to be rude, sir. I should not have said what I did, except that you spoke of it yourself.

Washington	Don't apologize, Hamilton. I have indeed thought of my reputation. What man doesn't? And what man doesn't want to keep his reputation, if it is good?
Hamilton	Nevertheless, I beg your pardon, sir.
Washington	There's no need for me to pardon you. I have thought of my reputation, but it would mean nothing if I could serve my country.
Madison	Then you will accept the voice of the people? You will become President of the United States?
Washington	Won't this seem ambitious? I am retired in my home in Mount Vernon. I come out of my retirement to assume the highest position in the government of the country. They will say that I would become a king! King of the United States!
Madison	There is no danger of that, sir. The people of this country love their freedom. When they choose you, they know they choose a man who loves freedom no less than they do. They want a man they respect, a man they love, a man who will guard their freedom.
Washington	And I am that man?
Lee	*(Returning and entering quickly)* The boy is washed and fed, and we gave him a fresh horse for his journey home. He brought good news, sir. He deserved the best, and we gave it to him.
Washington	Thank you. And now, gentlemen . . . .
Lee	And have you come to a decision, General Washington?

116 *A Call to Duty*

Washington	I am thinking about it.
Lee	Then your answer is not "no"?
Washington	Lee! You are as determined as the rest.
Lee	Oh, there are so many with me, General. A whole country of people.
Washington	I wish I were as sure as they are.
Martha	(*Entering*) Isn't it about time you released the General, gentlemen? This is a party, if you remember.
Washington	We are coming now, Martha. We'll test our feet with the minuet.
Madison	You'll decide soon, General?
Hamilton	The country waits on your decision, sir.
Washington	It shall not wait long. I hope, gentlemen, whatever decision I make will be in the best interests of my country.
Announcer	George Washington made his decision. On April 14, 1789, the General opened his door to Charles Thomson, Secretary of Congress. Mr. Thomson delivered his message immediately.
Thomson	Sir, you have proved your patriotism and your readiness to sacrifice all you possess—your life too—to promote the liberty and happiness of your country. There is not a single doubt in either house of Congress: the House of Representatives or the Senate. There is no voice among the people of America which does not call on you to become the

first President of our republic. You have been requested by a unanimous vote of the people to take this great office. We trust that this request will be accepted as a mark of confidence and a pledge of affection from a free and enlightened people.

Washington   Mr. Thomson . . .

Thomson   It is a call to duty, General.

Washington   So it would seem.

Thomson   You have always answered the people when they called on you, General.

Washington   I had hoped to spend the rest of my years here in Mount Vernon, quietly.

Thomson   But your country calls.

Washington   I am grateful to my countrymen. They do me honor. How can I show them my gratitude?

Thomson   They ask you to lead them once more, in peace.

Washington   I hope they never regret their choice. All I can promise them is that I will do what I can, all that can be done with honesty and zeal.

Thomson   Then you will accept this call to duty, General Washington.

Washington   I am at my country's service, Mr. Thomson. I will accept their charge. My answer is: I will undertake my country's call to duty.

Announcer   And George Washington, to the greater glory of the United States of America, became its first President. First in war, first in peace, first in the hearts of his countrymen: George Washington of Mount Vernon, Virginia.

NO SNAKES IN IRELAND

a play for St. Patrick's Day

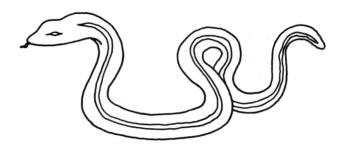

On March 17th Irishmen all over the world celebrate the birthday of their patron saint, St. Patrick. They say that St. Patrick was born somewhere in England about the year 385. It is known that, as a boy, he was taken by some Irish marauders and brought to Ireland as a slave. He escaped, became a priest, then a bishop, and returned to Ireland to convert its people to Christianity. They say that he was a handsome man, a man with much charm, and that the Irish, who had been Druids and sun-worshippers, were quickly won to the faith of St. Patrick.

There are many legends about St. Patrick, and this play is concerned with one of them.

As the play opens, St. Patrick has been successful in converting many of the Irish, but he feels that he will never be able to complete his mission—to convert the entire population of Ireland to his faith. Yet, he will do it. This story tells the legend of how he had the inspiration to speed up the pace of conversion in Ireland.

THE CAST	St. Patrick	Sichu
	Father Finn	Irishman
	Kathleen	Announcer

THE SET   An open field, somewhere in Ireland, sometime in the middle of the fifth century.

Announcer	We are in an open field. A man in priests' clothing *(St. Patrick)* enters, looks around, sits down on a rock. Another priest *(Finn)* enters. He looks at St. Patrick.
Finn	*(Afraid to be interrupting)* You're not praying, Bishop?
St. Patrick	Now do I look like I'm praying, Father Finn.
Finn	It is generally on your knees that you pray, Bishop.
St. Patrick	Then I'm not praying. Ah, you worry too much about me, Father Finn. I'm fine. I'm just sitting here and thinking.
Finn	Couldn't you sit somewhere else, Bishop?
St. Patrick	Is it that you want to be sitting here?
Finn	Faith, no! I'm thinking there are better places to be sitting, Bishop, than resting yourself on a cold stone.
St. Patrick	Is it the cold stone that worries you, Father Finn?
Finn	It's you that worries me. There is never a moment you take for yourself. You work too hard. And, to my way of thinking, you've not been too happy about it.
St. Patrick	Ah, Father Finn. There isn't too much to make a man happy in this old land.
Finn	On the contrary, Bishop, begging your pardon. I see more of the heathens turning to the Lord every time that you speak with them. You'll have them all walking in the ways of the Lord before you're done, Bishop.

St. Patrick	You speak kindly, Father Finn, but you play a bit with the truth.
Finn	And didn't you convert that old Druid, Milchu, who used to be your master? Didn't you take him from his pagan worship and convert him to the true faith?
St. Patrick	Yes, Milchu, and a lot of others, but Ireland swarms with heathens, and I don't know that I shall ever have the years to bring them all into the church.
Finn	You'll do that, Bishop. You'll live to be 120 years. You're doing the Lord's work. He'll see that it's done.
St. Patrick	Pray for it, Father Finn. Pray for it.
Finn	(Getting down on his knees) Our Father . . . . The grass is a bit cold, Bishop, and wet with the morning dew.
St. Patrick	(Thinking aloud) I must be patient. But if the Lord would show me a way, some way I could reach these people quickly, bring them into the Lord's fold quickly.
Finn	(Getting up from his knees) It was quickly enough you got to the Chief Dichu and his people, Bishop. And Laoghate, the King of Tara, came into the fold quickly. The rest will be coming, Bishop, as sure as it is yourself, sitting on that rock in the fields.
St. Patrick	Are you done with your prayers already, Father Finn?

No Snakes in Ireland 121

122 *No Snakes in Ireland*

Finn	No, Bishop. My knees were getting wet with this Irish dew. I think I'll be praying for the Lord to look kindly on our work with the heathen, where it is warmer, and drier.
St. Patrick	Of course, Father Finn.
Finn	I say my prayers better when my body has more comfort to it; and, faith, the roof of the house won't be keeping my prayers from reaching the ears of the Lord. Could I warm up some broth for you, Bishop? It'll help take the chill out of you. I'll have it for you when you come in. You're not hearing me, are you, Bishop?
St. Patrick	*(Who has not been listening to Father Finn)* If there were some sign of the Lord, some miracle I could show these people.
Finn	Ah, you're away from me, Bishop. But you'll be coming into the house soon, and I'll have the hot broth steaming for you.
St. Patrick	Yes, do that, Father Finn. And thank you.
Finn	*(Moving out)* Ah, Lord, give the Bishop strength. He is a true servant. It shouldn't be too much for you, Lord, to give him that one sign. Just a little miracle, Lord. A very little miracle will do, Lord. *(He exits.)*
Kathleen	*(Enters. Looks at St. Patrick. Waits for him to look back at her.)* A lovely morning to you.
St. Patrick	And a very lovely morning to you.
Kathleen	You're a strange one here.

No Snakes in Ireland **123**

St. Patrick	I've been here before.
Kathleen	It's your ways I'm talking about. They say that you don't pray to the sun in the sky, the way we do.
St. Patrick	No. I pray to God.
Kathleen	But the sun *is* god.
St. Patrick	No, young lady. It was God who put the sun where it is, high in the sky.
Kathleen	It's an odd speech you have. My father doesn't like it. He told me not to speak with you.
St. Patrick	And you are disobeying your father. Not a nice thing for a young lady to do.
Kathleen	You're not my father to tell me that. Whose father are you? I hear them call you father, and they can't all be your children. They've their own fathers and mothers. What is your name?
St. Patrick	They called me Succat, when I was born. Now it is Father Patrick, or Bishop Patrick.
Kathleen	I like Succat. My name is Kathleen.
St. Patrick	A pretty name for a pretty young lady.
Kathleen	You're very handsome, Succat. They tell me you were a slave in Ireland, once.
St. Patrick	When I was about your age. Sixteen.
Kathleen	And you escaped. That was a very brave thing to do. Why did you come back?
St. Patrick	To take Ireland out of the ways of darkness. To bring Ireland to the ways of the Lord.

124   *No Snakes in Ireland*

Kathleen	*(Alarmed)* Look out! Sit still!
St. Patrick	What is it, child?
Kathleen	Hush! Ah! Now it's gone.
St. Patrick	What's gone? What was here? I see nothing, child.
Kathleen	I am not a child. And what you did not see was a snake.
St. Patrick	Does a snake bother you?
Kathleen	Of course a snake bothers me. All snakes bother me. And Ireland is just full of snakes. Everywhere you turn, everywhere you look, there's a snake! If we could only get rid of them!
St. Patrick	*(Thinking)* Snakes. I hadn't noticed.
Kathleen	Hadn't noticed! They're the bane of our existence here. Ireland would be a lovely land, the loveliest land, if we could get rid of these snakes.
St. Patrick	They turn the soil, and that's good for what grows in the soil. They eat the field mice. And that's good.
Kathleen	I don't know what good they do. They do more harm. I know my father—not you, Succat—my father would give anything to rid the fields he plows of the ugly snakes.
St. Patrick	*(Thinking aloud)* It's a sign, I'm beginning to think.
Kathleen	Sign?
St. Patrick	Yes, it is *the* sign. *(Suddenly very happy)* God sent you child. God sent you to me with the sign.

No Snakes in Ireland **125**

126   *No Snakes in Ireland*

Kathleen	I don't know what you're talking about. Nobody sent me to you. And that's for certain. *(Suddenly looking offstage, and spotting her father)* But it's going I am now. And that's for certain. Because here is my father on the road, and I don't choose that he see me here, talking with you in the bright light of the day. Good-bye to you now, Succat. Good-bye. *(She exits.)*
Sichu	*(Entering)* Was that my daughter here and gone this instant?
St. Patrick	If your daughter is young and pretty, and moves as gracefully as the wind, it was your daughter here and gone.
Sichu	I ordered her not to speak with you!
St. Patrick	Pray to the Lord, and thank Him that she did stop to speak with me.
Sichu	Your Lord! Don't fill my ears with prattling about your Lord! If my daughter spoke about your Lord, I shall . . . .
St. Patrick	*(Spotting a snake)* Stop! Don't move!
Sichu	And is it orders you are giving me now!?
St. Patrick	Still! On your life!
Sichu	My life! Why I'll . . . .
St. Patrick	A snake!
Sichu	Snake!?
St. Patrick	Ah, it's gone now. You can move, if you want to.

No Snakes in Ireland 127

Sichu	A snake, was it? Ah, they are everywhere. If we could only be rid of them!
St. Patrick	That's what your daughter was saying.
Sichu	*(Doubtful)* It was snakes she was speaking of?
St. Patrick	And how you'd like to clear them from your fields.
Sichu	Ah, what a land Ireland would be without a snake in it! Why did she speak with you about it? You couldn't do anything about the snakes, could you?
St. Patrick	With God's help, I might.
Sichu	Ah, the sun shines down on them, as it does on us. No! That won't do. God, did you say?
St. Patrick	The Lord. My Lord.
Sichu	Your Lord could drive the snakes out of Ireland?
St. Patrick	He might help.
Sichu	But your Lord is all peace and love. He wouldn't lift a stick to a snake now, would he?
St. Patrick	The ways of the Lord are many, and mysterious. A man may only look on them and wonder and worship.
Sichu	I'm not praying to your Lord, if that's what you're asking.
St. Patrick	Pray to the Lord. Show Him your love. You might be rid of your snakes.
Sichu	Let him drive the snakes out first. Let him drive the snakes out of Ireland. Then I think I could love him. Surely, I'd be grateful. I might even pray to him.

St. Patrick	Don't bargain with the Lord. He doesn't bargain.
Sichu	I'm not bargaining with your Lord! I was just saying that I'd pray to him, if he drove the snakes out of Ireland.
St. Patrick	Do you think you might pray to Him, *asking* Him to drive the snakes out of Ireland?
Sichu	*(After a pause to think)* I might. But how about Chief Dichu, and the King of Tara? They're Christians along with you, aren't they?
St. Patrick	They are.
Sichu	And aren't they praying?
St. Patrick	They say their prayers.
Sichu	There are still snakes in Ireland!
St. Patrick	Perhaps there isn't enough praying in Ireland, yet.
Sichu	You mean, we don't make a big enough noise!
St. Patrick	You've yet to make a noise that will please the Lord.
Sichu	I'd make a noise loud enough to deafen both his ears, if it would get him to move the snakes out of this land. So would every man, woman and child in Ireland. Try us. Where is this place you pray to your Lord? I'll have a hundred men and women with you, down on their knees, the way you do it, praying to your Lord, quicker than I can shake this shillelagh! Just promise us your Lord will scurry the snakes out of Ireland! Now where is that daughter of mine? *(Begins to exit.)*

St. Patrick	Wait on a moment!
Sichu	I'll be back! I'll be wanting your answer, too! But I have to fetch my daughter, first! *(He exits.)*
St. Patrick	Thank you, Lord. Thank you.
Finn	I've been waiting for you, Bishop. The broth is still hot.
St. Patrick	I've had a sign, Father Finn.
Finn	*(On his knees quickly)* A sign, Bishop. *(He crosses himself.)*
St. Patrick	A sign from the Lord.
Finn	You're not going to leave us, Bishop? You're not going to leave us?
St. Patrick	No, no. Not before the Lord drives the snakes out of Ireland.
Finn	He's going to do that?
St. Patrick	And all Ireland will flock to His Church.
Finn	Because he drives out the snakes?
St. Patrick	You don't understand, Father Finn. The Lord will drive the snakes out of Ireland, and the people will know that He loves them, that He is there, that He *is* the Lord; and they will love Him and worship Him.
Finn	That's all very good, Bishop, but are you sure He is going to do that, drive the snakes out of Ireland?
St. Patrick	We'll pray for it.
Finn	And He'll answer our prayers.

130 *No Snakes in Ireland*

St. Patrick	I'm sure of it.
Finn	God bless you, Bishop.
St. Patrick	*(Thinking)* Of course we might help.
Finn	Help the Lord?
St. Patrick	Yes, Help the Lord. *(Suddenly, brightly)* I've got it!
Finn	What, Bishop? What?
St. Patrick	The shillelagh! Every man prays and every man carries a shillelagh! The prayers and the shillelaghs, and with God's help, we'll do it!
Finn	The Lord be praised!
Announcer	The snakes were driven out of Ireland. St. Patrick did it. Ask any Irishman, and he'll tell you . . . .
Irishman	Sure and it was St. Patrick drove the snakes from Ireland's green and lovely land!
Announcer	And if you know what's healthy for you, you won't contradict him.

No Snakes in Ireland **131**

HOW WISE THE FOOL!

a play for April Fools' Day

Sometimes called *All Fools' Day*, and sometimes *April Fools' Day*, the origin of this holiday has never really been established. It is said that April 1st was the day Noah sent the dove from the Ark. We know that the day was celebrated as far back as 1713 in England, and as long ago as 1564 in France. Today, it is celebrated even in India, on March 31st, and is called the Feast of Huli.

This play is based on one of the theories about the origins of this day. It is set many, many years ago, in a town somewhere in eastern Europe at a time when armies of men marched ruthlessly from east to west, destroying everything in their paths.

Such an army is about to enter the small town of Belden, a village much too weak to resist the conquerors. Certainly the townspeople could not defend themselves with arms, however brave they might be. But perhaps there was another defense for Belden. You'll soon discover how Belden met its peril.

THE CAST	John	Deborah	4th Soldier
	Luke	1st Soldier	5th Soldier
	Harrah	2nd Soldier	Crowd of Men
	(the Commander)	Mark	and Women
	Mary	3rd Soldier	Announcer

THE SET   *The Town Square*

Text Copyright   ©1967 by Henry Gilfond
Illustrations Copyright   ©1967 by George Blevins

Announcer	The whole town has gathered in the town square. Everyone is nervous. There is a good deal of fear. One of the younger men is speaking to the crowd.
John	I say let every man arm himself and fight!
Crowd	Fight! Fight! Let every man arm himself and fight!
John	A man dies only once!
Crowd	Only once! A man dies only once!
John	Let the enemy come with its huge armies! We will battle to the last man! To the last drop of our blood!
Crowd	We will fight to the last drop of our blood!
John	To arms, men of Belden! To arms!
Crowd	To arms! Death to the invader!
John	Death to the invader!
Some of Crowd	*(As they begin to band together)* Death to the invader!
Others of Crowd	To arms! To arms!
Others of Crowd	To the last drop of our blood!
Luke	*(Shouting)* You don't know what you're doing!
Crowd	We fight! We destroy the invader!
Luke	Listen to me! Listen for one moment! I am one of the elders among you! Listen to me!
Crowd	Speak, then!
Others in Crowd	One moment! No more!

John	Listen to Luke! But be ready to move fast! The enemy is almost on us! Speak, Luke!
Luke	You are brave men.
Crowd	We will die for our city!
Luke	There will be no need to die.
Crowd	And let the enemy make slaves of us!?
Luke	If you would only listen to me!
Crowd	We listen! Speak!
Luke	The enemy outnumbers us. For every man, woman, and child in Belden, they have fifty soldiers.
Crowd	Let them have one hundred to each of us! We are not afraid!
Luke	No, you are not afraid to fight.
Crowd	No!
Luke	Are you afraid not to fight?
Some of Crowd	What are you saying?
Others of Crowd	What kind of talk is that?
Luke	I say, if we meet them with arms, we are defeated and our town will be destroyed.
Some of Crowd	Not before they have paid for it!
Others of Crowd	With their blood!
Luke	But there is no need for blood to be spilled. Not your blood, and not theirs.

How Wise the Fool **135**

136 *How Wise the Fool*

Women of Crowd	How not? Tell us how, Luke!
Luke	We will fight them!
Men of Crowd	Fight! Fight! Fight!
Luke	But without arms.
Women of Crowd	How, Luke? How?
Luke	We will fight them with our minds.
Men of Crowd	You can't wound with the mind! You can't kill!
Women of Crowd	Hush! Let Luke speak. How, Luke? Tell us how?
Luke	We will outwit them. We will let them march into our square, in triumph.
Men of Crowd	Never! Never!
Luke	And we will watch them run from us, as if we had the plague!
Women of Crowd	How do we do this, Luke? How?
Luke	We will become a strange people. They will not understand us. They will run from us.
Men of Crowd	They will kill us first!
Luke	They might. And they might not. We have no other choice. Fight them with arms and we all die. Fight with our wits, and we may all live to celebrate our freedom.
Men of Crowd	Rubbish! Fight! Fight! To arms!
John	Let us hear Luke's plan first!
Men of Crowd	Death to the invader! To arms! To arms!

John	Listen to Luke! Let us hear what he proposes!
Women of Crowd	Listen to him!
Men of Crowd	We are listening! Speak quickly, Luke!
Announcer	Luke spoke and the crowd grew quiet. At first, the crowd laughed at his ideas.
Some of Crowd	He's mad!
Others of Crowd	They'll think we're stupid! Fools!
Others of Crowd	That's the idea. Let them think we're fools.
Announcer	Soon, everyone realized the wisdom of Luke's plan. They could not be sure it would work, but it would give them their one chance against the invader.
John	Luke is right. There is glory in dying for your city. There is greater glory in a victory over an invader. Do what Luke has asked you to do. Go about your business quickly. There is little time. I see the dust of the invading armies and they cannot be too far away. Do Luke's bidding, and we may yet emerge victorious!
Crowd	*(Moving away)* Victorious! Victorious!
Announcer	The invading armies soon marched into the city. No one had blocked their way. Now the commander of the invading forces stands in the square, surrounded by his soldiers.
Commander	What kind of people are these? They made no effort to resist us.
1st Soldier	Perhaps they have fled farther west.

2nd Soldier	*(Bringing in John)* Here is a man you might ask. I questioned him, but he answers in a curious manner. I can't make head or tail of what he says.
Commander	Let me speak with him. *(To John)* What do they call you?
John	My mother calls me brilliant. My sweetheart calls me love. My father . . .
Commander	What is your name? How were you born?
John	I was born, sir . . . I could not say. There are many stories they tell about how children are . . . .
Commander	My name is Harrah! Do you know that name?
John	In my language, sir, it is "hurrah!"
Commander	I do not care about your language! I am the Scourge of the East. I have laid waste to every city and town I have entered.
John	Indeed, a waste, sir!
Commander	Are you a fool!?
John	That is what my father has called me.
Commander	Take him away! Find me someone I can talk with!
3rd Soldier	*(Entering with Mark)* Here, sir! He looks strong enough to bear arms!
Mark	Indeed, I do, sir!
Commander	Where are your arms?
Mark	*(Lifting his arms)* Why, here, sir. That's plain enough to see.

140 *How Wise the Fool*

Commander	Your weapons! Where do the men of this town keep their arms?
Mark	I know nothing of weapons, sir. But their arms? Why each man carries his own.
Commander	Are there nothing but fools in this town?
Mark	I would be a wise man, if I knew that, sir.
Commander	And you certainly are not a wise man! Take him away!
4th Soldier	(*Bringing in Mary*) This one was running all around the town, shouting "Fire, fire," I would have killed her myself, except that she might have some knowledge of where their soldiers are hidden.
Commander	Speak, woman!
Mary	Fire! Fire!
Commander	(*After the soldiers and Commander have moved as if to meet with an enemy*) Where are they?
Mary	They?
Commander	Your soldiers!
Mary	What soldiers?
Commander	You ordered them to fire! Where are they?
Mary	There are no soldiers. But there is a fire in my house, unless someone has put it out.
Commander	I see no houses burning. I smell no smoke.
Mary	The fire was in my kitchen. I was cooking. I was running home, when that soldier of yours stopped me. I shouted, "Fire! Fire!" but he wouldn't believe me.

How Wise the Fool **141**

Commander	*(Weakly)* Take her away.
1st Soldier	*(As Mary is taken out, enters with Deborah)* Here is another!
Commander	As foolish as the others, I suppose.
1st Soldier	They're all fools here, sir. I ordered her to collect the purses in the town. *(Presenting the Commander with a number of purses)* She brought me these.
Commander	*(Opening the purses)* They're empty. Ah! Here's one! *(He opens it and takes out nothing but paper)* Is this what you carry in your purses!? Where is your gold? Where are your jewels?
Deborah	Gold is in the sun at sunrise, and sometimes at sunset. You can't carry the sun in a purse. *(She pulls a torn wreath of flowers from behind her back)* And these are jewels enough for us. Your soldier tore them from my head.
2nd Soldier	*(Entering with empty sacks)* I asked for the sacks from their grain storages. *(Showing the sacks)* This is what they gave me.
Deborah	He wanted to take these jewels from me. I wouldn't let him!
2nd Soldier	They're all mad here! Or fools!
3rd Soldier	*(Entering all wet)* I walk into a door and a barrel of water falls on me!
5th Soldier	*(Holding his head, as he enters)* They told me something stunning could be found, if I walked into their barn, and I swear it was a mule that kicked me!

142   *How Wise the Fool*

1st Soldier	They have nothing in this town, sir. They are all fools.
Commander	I am not certain. Either they are fools, or we are the fools. You found nothing.
Soldiers	Nothing.
Commander	No gold? No treasure?
Soldiers	Nothing. No gold, no treasure.
Commander	No wheat? No corn?
Soldiers	Nothing. We found nothing.
Commander	Then let us move on!
1st Soldier	Don't we kill anybody, sir?
2nd Soldier	To rid the world of fools?
Soldiers	Let us burn down their houses!
3rd Soldier	And their fields!
Soldiers	Let them remember that we were here!
Commander	Kill them and burn their houses? Then who will be here to remember that we were here? Order the troops to form their ranks! We move forward!
	(The Soldiers exit)
	The more I think about it, the more I become convinced—a clever people live in this town, and it is my soldiers who are the fools.
Announcer	And so the invading army departs, leaving the town of Belden untouched. After the soldiers have left, the townspeople move slowly back into the square.

Luke	They're all gone now. You can dig up your little gold and silver, wherever you buried it. You can carry the grain back into the storage houses.
John	This will be a day to remember.
Crowd	Victory!
Luke	(Softly) Quiet.
Deborah	But we did make fools of them.
Crowd	We did!
Mary	Let us mark the date. Let us never forget it.
Luke	By my reckoning, today is the first day of April.
Crowd	We won't forget the first April day! We won't forget.

A FLOWER FOR JOHNNY REB

a play for Memorial Day

This is a play for Memorial Day, or Decoration Day as it is called in certain sections of the United States — a day set aside each year to honor the men and women who have given their lives in the service of our country. In the North, Memorial Day is May 30th; in the South, it is celebrated on April 26th, or May 10th, or June 3rd.

The first official Memorial Day was celebrated in 1868, although it was unofficially celebrated before that year. The bitterness between the North and the South had been severe, but the wounds each had caused the other could not last too long. After all, in a civil war it is brother against brother and, no matter how sharp the difference, family quarrels have a way of disappearing before long.

This play deals with this family quarrel, the wounds it inflicted and the pain it left. It also deals with the feelings which must ultimately bring people together again.

THE CAST   *Mr. Anderson*
Mrs. Anderson
Margaret (their daughter-in-law)
Peggy (their nine-year-old grandchild)
Young Lady (Mrs. John Somers)

THE SETS   *The Anderson home*
The cemetery

146 *A Flower for Johnny Reb*

Announcer	We are in a small town in Pennsylvania not far from Gettysburg, where Abraham Lincoln dedicated the great battlefield. The war is over now. But all the wounds are not yet healed. We are in the Anderson house with Mr. and Mrs. Anderson, their daughter-in-law, Margaret, and their grandchild, Peggy. It is early, but some talk has already disturbed the morning.
Mr. Anderson	You keep forgetting, Margaret. The war is over.
Mrs. Anderson	Thank God.
Mr. Anderson	No more Confederacy. No more Johnny Rebs. You have to forget it, Margaret.
Margaret	How can I forget it? Come here, Peggy. Let me fix your hair.
Peggy	You've been crying, Mamma. Don't cry.
Margaret	(*Combing her daughter's hair*) I'm not crying.
Peggy	Your eyes are all red, Mamma.
Margaret	I must have a little cold.
Peggy	Then maybe we shouldn't go out today?
Margaret	Don't you want to visit your father? Don't you want to put some flowers on his grave?
Peggy	Of course I do, Mamma. But maybe we can do it tomorrow, when your cold is all better.
Margaret	It won't ever get better. Just you go outside now, and wait for us. We won't be long.
Peggy	I can wait here, Mamma.

A Flower for Johnny Reb **147**

Margaret	No, you go on outside. Do what your mother asks.
Peggy	If that's what you want, Mamma. *(Peggy exits.)*
Mrs. Anderson	For the child's sake, Margaret. You should learn to control yourself.
Margaret	He was my husband, Mother Anderson. We loved each other so much. There was so much we had to live for.
Mrs. Anderson	He was my son, Margaret.
Margaret	Oh, I hate them! I hate them! Oh, my God. I can't forget a minute of it. I can see the man in the doorway, with the letter in his hand. I didn't want to read it.
Mr. Anderson	That was three years ago, Margaret.
Margaret	It was yesterday. Why do men have to kill each other? There was peace here before the Johnny Rebs came marching through our cornfields and our gardens. Why did they have to march through here? Why didn't they stay in the South, where they belonged? Why didn't they do their killing down there?
Mrs. Anderson	There's no more killing now, Margaret. The men are all home — in their cornfields, in their cotton, in their wheat.
Margaret	Not my John! He's not in the cornfields, Mother Anderson. He's in that little cemetery. He's covered over. He's dead.

Mr. Anderson	He's lying with his comrades, Margaret. There's Frank Dugan and Samuel Weatherby and Turner Bright. They fought with him, by his side. They fell together. He is not alone.
Margaret	No, Father Anderson. He's not alone. I'm alone.
Mrs. Anderson	I'm sorry you said that, Margaret.
Margaret	Oh, you've been good to me, Mother Anderson, and Father Anderson. And good to Peggy.
Mrs. Anderson	I wasn't thinking of that, Margaret.
Margaret	You think I'm sorry for myself. Yes, I'm sorry for myself. Shall I be sorry for Johnny? He's dead. *(She begins to sob)* My Johnny.
Mrs. Anderson	*(Dabbing the tears from her eyes)* That's enough now, Margaret. He was my Johnny, too.
Margaret	Yes, you nursed him. You watched him grow. You were so proud of him. Then they killed him! How can you forgive them, Mother Anderson? How can you forgive them? And some of them lying in the cemetery, and near John, too! There should be more of them! More of them!
Mrs. Anderson	Margaret!
Margaret	Yes, Mother Anderson?
Mrs. Anderson	Dry your eyes. Peggy is waiting. We'll still have to pick the flowers on the way.
Margaret	Aren't you coming, too, Father Anderson?
Mr. Anderson	I'll join you there. I've got some things to do before I go.

A Flower for Johnny Reb **149**

Announcer	The cemetery is only a short walk from the Anderson house. It isn't a large cemetery and it isn't a rich one, but it is well kept. Almost all the stones marking the places of those who have died are small, modest stones, but almost all are decorated with an abundance of flowers. This is a cemetery of young people — the men who have died in the fighting. There is one section for those who fought for the North, another for those who died for the South. Only a step or two divides the soldiers who have fallen under different flags. Margaret, Mrs. Anderson and Peggy stand at the grave of John Anderson.
Margaret	This is your father's grave, **Peggy**.
Peggy	I know, Mamma.
Margaret	*(Indicating the graves of the Confederate soldiers)* And there are the men who killed him!
Mrs. Anderson	Margaret!
Margaret	*(To the grave)* Forgive me, John. I should speak only kind words when I come to visit you. You were so kind. *(Silence of memory and sorrow)*
Peggy	Mamma.
Mrs. Anderson	Hush, Peggy.
Peggy	She's crying again.
Mrs. Anderson	She's thinking of your daddy. You remember your daddy, don't you, Peggy?
Peggy	Not too well, Grandma. *(Quickly)* But I do remember him. He was so tall and . . . he was much taller than Mamma.

Margaret	*(Who has heard the last words)* Yes, Peggy, he was much taller than Mamma.
Peggy	And strong! Strong as Grandpa. Wasn't he, Mamma?
Margaret	Yes, he was strong. *(Giving Peggy the bouquet of flowers)* Here. Would you like to put these on Daddy's grave?
Peggy	If you'd like me to, Mamma.
Margaret	I'd like you to. Put them against the headstone.
Peggy	There are flowers around all the stones, aren't there, Mamma?
Margaret	*(Absently)* Yes. Flowers around them all.
Peggy	*(Spotting an undecorated headstone)* Except that one!
Margaret	*(After a quick look)* Put the flowers down on Papa's headstone, Peggy.
Peggy	Why doesn't that grave have any flowers, Mamma?
Margaret	He was a Johnny Reb. Peggy! The flowers.
Peggy	*(Putting down the flowers)* He was a soldier, wasn't he, Mamma?
Margaret	Your papa was a soldier, Peggy. He died fighting for his country.
Peggy	Didn't Johnny Reb fight for his country, Mamma?
Margaret	Peggy, please. Just leave the flowers there, and take a little walk. Leave Mamma alone here for a minute.

JOHN
SOMERS
BORN
JUNE 2, 1839
DIED
JULY 3, 1863

152 *A Flower for Johnny Reb*

Mrs. Anderson	Mamma will be all right, Peggy. I'll stay close by.
Peggy	*(Rises. She has kept one flower in her hand)* I won't go too far. You watch Mamma, Grandma.
Mrs. Anderson	I'll watch her.
Announcer	Peggy doesn't walk very far at all. She walks only to the undecorated grave. A young lady enters, as Peggy examines the graves. The young lady is carrying, as you might expect, a bouquet of flowers.
Peggy	I've only got one flower, Johnny Reb. I'm sorry. But one flower is better than none. *(She places the flower at the headstone)* There. That's better, isn't it.
Young Lady	Thank you.
Peggy	Oh! I'm sorry. Is this your grave?
Young Lady	No. Not my grave. But thank you. That was very kind of you.
Peggy	It looked so empty, and all the other graves have flowers. My father had so many, I thought . . . he wouldn't miss just one.
Young Lady	Your father . . . is buried here?
Peggy	Yes. Over there. He was killed by the Johnny Rebs. *(Pointing to the grave)* He was a Johnny Reb, wasn't he?
Young Lady	He was a Johnny Reb.
Peggy	But he's dead now. And the war is over. And Grandpa says we must forget.

A Flower for Johnny Reb **153**

Young Lady	It's hard to forget.
Peggy	That's what Mamma says. It's hard to forget, but Grandpa says that the war is over and we have to.
Margaret	*(Entering, and antagonistic)* Excuse me, Madam! What are you doing here, Peggy?
Peggy	*(As Mrs. Anderson enters)* I was putting a flower on this grave. It didn't have any flowers at all.
Margaret	It'll have flowers now! He's a Johnny Reb! You don't put flowers on the graves of Johnny Rebs! Come on, now!
Young Lady	You forgot your flower, Madam.
Peggy	*(As Margaret is about to snatch it up)* Leave it there, Mamma.
Margaret	Leave it there? He killed your father, Peggy! *(To Young Lady)* He killed my husband!
Young Lady	Perhaps it was your husband who killed mine. Mine fell here. My husband lies here, Madam.
Margaret	*(Suddenly sobered)* I'm sorry.
Young Lady	I'm sorry too. He was only twenty-four when he died.
Margaret	Do you have any children?
Young Lady	A boy. He is too young to travel this distance. It's a long way here from Atlanta.
Margaret	It is a long way. *(Thoughtfully)* My John fought for his country.
Young Lady	My John fought for Georgia, and for his country.

154 *A Flower for Johnny Reb*

Margaret	I'm sorry about the flower.
Young Lady	I understand how you feel. I suppose we both feel alike. Full of hatred.
Mr. Anderson	*(Enters)* Ah, here you are. *(To Young Lady)* Excuse me, Madam.
Margaret	*(By way of introduction)* This is . . . .
Young Lady	Mrs. John Somers.
Margaret	Her husband is buried here.
Mr. Anderson	Pleased to meet you, Mrs. Somers. You're from Virginia?
Young Lady	Georgia.
Mr. Anderson	Ah, yes. Our boys gave you a pretty rough time in Georgia.
Young Lady	We battled them as best we could.
Mr. Anderson	But they were no match for us Yankees!
Mrs. Anderson	I thought the war was over.
Mr. Anderson	So it is, so it is. Forgive me. I . . . . Your husband is buried here?
Young Lady	And your son?
Mr. Anderson	Here.
Young Lady	I must beg your pardon. I have a long journey.
Margaret	Mrs. Somers . . . . We have a common grief. I'm sorry I was so rude to you.

Young Lady	I must have been as rude to you.
Margaret	Could you stop for some tea before you go, before you start your journey home?
Young Lady	Why, I'd be glad to.
Margaret	We live quite nearby.
Young Lady	Let me give John my flowers first, and stay with him just a little while.
Margaret	Of course. And this little flower, the one Peggy put on his stone — may she leave it there?
Announcer	And in this way did old wounds begin to heal. Everywhere in the United States, where soldiers of the North and South lay buried, men and women, children too, began to forget who fought against whom; they put flowers on the graves of both, in memory and honor of their dead.
	Then in 1868, only three years after the end of the war, the United States set aside a day for such ceremonies. The day is called Decoration Day, or Memorial Day. Once flowers were laid only on the graves of those who had fallen in the Civil War; today flowers are laid on the graves of all who have given their lives in defense of their country.